A PA STEAMING BATS

Life in the Royal Navy

By

Rocky O'Rourke

While all the stories in this book are true, some names and identifying details have been changed to protect the privacy of the people involved. The author shall have no liability or responsibility to any person or entity regarding any loss or damage incurred, or alleged to have incurred, directly or indirectly, by the information contained in this book.

This book is dedicated to the men and women of the Royal Navy.

CONTENTS

ACKNOWLEDGEMENTS

Adrian Clode (over a few beers in Devon)

Larry Lamb (Facebook)

Scouse McCann (Facebook)

Bob Cowley (over a few beers watching Luton Town in Cardiff and Bristol)

Nick Wilkin (Facebook)

1. SQUARE-BASHING

"O'Rourke, you march like a fucking giraffe." And so it had begun, my Royal Naval career, being shouted at by a loudmouth with a stick on a wet, windswept slab of Cornish concrete. Now I for one had never seen a marching giraffe but the Petty Officer with the stick didn't look like he wanted to engage in debate and in any case it might have been a compliment – maybe giraffes were good at marching?

A few days before, having hit the tender age of 17 a few weeks earlier, my mum had waved me off at Peterborough railway station for the long trip down to Plymouth, via London, to start the adventure of a lifetime (and if truth be told to get away from the hassles of living with bickering divorced parents and an attempt to forget the girl of my dreams who dreamt about lots of things no doubt but certainly not me). I'd had my hair cut and visited the dentist for a clean bill of health so I was ready for whatever the Senior Service could throw at me (yeah, right).

On arrival at Plymouth station there were a bunch of other confused-looking, spotty, skinny teenagers so I guessed I had bumped into other wannabe Horatios. We were whisked off in a smelly Royal Navy bus across the River Tamar into the land of the Celts and then up to HMS Raleigh on the outskirts of a Godforsaken place called Torpoint, the Royal Navy's square-bashing centre of excellence. The bus reminded me of those buses you'd see carting prisoners around in the sitcom 'Porridge'; more similarities with Slade Prison would become apparent over the ensuing weeks. HMS Raleigh seemed to go on forever – over 200 acres of training facilities awaited us.

I was in a mess (bedroom to you civvies) of just over 30 young lads and everyone paired off with the guy next to them, left or right, they had a choice. Except me. I was stuck in the corner next to the window and the only empty bed in the whole mess was the one next to me. Unfortunately it was claimed a few hours later by a very miserable Scotsman; unbeknown to me it was his birthday and he'd had rather a messy send-off the night before in Alloa (a town I would later become very familiar with and almost as Godforsaken as Torpoint). He didn't want to talk and to be honest, looking at his miserable face, I wasn't too keen on talking to him. Matelots have a nickname for Scotsmen, other than the obvious 'Jock', and that is 'FRISP', which stands for 'Fucking Repulsive Ignorant Scottish Pig' (in the case of this particular Scotsman it took me 30+ years to fully understand the meaning of this rather discourteous if sometimes appropriate nickname).

Day One involved a visit to the barber and a visit to the dentist. The barber told me that my short hair wasn't short enough so he cut it all off and the dentist told me that I needed four fillings. Funny that, as my civilian dentist a week earlier had told me that my teeth were "perfect" and I'd never had a filling in my life. When I informed my Naval dentist of this he replied, "You'll need them soon enough," followed by, "fucking civvies," and proceeded with some gusto in filling my mouth with whatever constituted fillings in September 1982. So with a lot less hair than I'd woken up with and a mouth full of foreign matter, I was now ready to face the mad men on the parade ground.

The giraffe comment was confusing in itself and so too was the remark, "O'Rourke, the best part of you ran down your father's leg." OK, I should have known what that meant but Google and Wikipedia weren't around then and neither was PornHub. The parade ground was run by a group of narcissists known as 'GIs', not that any gunnery was being taught (good job as I later discovered that guns and I weren't a match made in heaven). Chief among the narcissists was the king of narcissists, old 'Shovel Face' himself, Lieutenant Andrews. Shovel Face had been in the Royal Navy for several decades and, legend had it, owed his distinctive features to a fire extinguisher that a young matelot introduced him to whilst at sea. Whether or not his obvious hatred for young matelots started before or after this incident never became clear but the hatred was genuine and practised with a significant degree of expertise. His constant shouts of "Schtand Schtill!!" will forever ring in my ears and the ears of all others who had the pleasure of his company. I guessed that his odd way of speaking, shouting rather, could have been a consequence of his altercation with the fire extinguisher but who knows?

One particularly pleasant feature of basic training in the Royal Navy is the kit muster. Essentially you have to fold every item of kit to the same size of the Royal Naval Seamanship Manual, a manual I never read, display said items on your bed in a very particular order and then a Senior Rating (known in the lesser services as a SNCO) would come around and fling your belongings all over the place whilst shouting and calling you all the names under the sun. The Scotsman in the next bed to me, Jock to his friends and foes, didn't exactly excel in this department and only his reactions to his constant failures made this particular Naval tradition worthwhile (and often entertaining). All of this kit is issued to young matelots on Day One in a place known as 'Slops', or Naval Stores ('slops' being the name given to the ready-made clothing sold to young matelots prior to 1857). These wonderful places, features of all Naval ships and establishments, are operated by Stores Accountants, referred to as Jack Dusties by one and all.

The key elements of Naval kit comprised of Number 1s, Number 2s and Number 8s; other items included overalls (ovies), physical training kit, boots known as 'steaming bats' and many other oddities including a gas mask. Number 1 kit is worn on formal occasions and the various badges are gold in colour; Number 2s with red badges are for day-to-day wear, dependent upon duties, and Number 8s are more workmanlike consisting of fairly rough blue shirts, blue trousers, a blue pullover ('woolly pully') and a blue beret with a metal badge. Number 1s and 2s consisted of jacket, white front, white cap (with a 'cap tally' containing the name of one's ship or shore establishment), trousers, lanyard and blue collar – the 'suit' most people associate with sailors. The white fronts are ironed so that there is a crease in the middle on the front, running from top to bottom; the blue collar is ironed so that it has three creases – the crease in the middle faces inwards and the two creases on either side face outwards. The lanyard is a white piece of rope and, in conjunction with a black ribbon, is worn with the jacket.

So with very short hair, a mouth full of fillings, a locker packed with unfamiliar uniform and a head full of insults, I was in. A member of the Senior Service. Junior Assistant Writer Second Class (JAWTR2) O'Rourke. It's a shame they didn't issue business cards. Has anyone ever reached the dizzy heights of 'Junior', 'Assistant' and 'Second Class' at the same time?

Basic training was as you'd expect, driven by huge amounts of testosterone with lots of young men being abused by lots of older men. For the record, all of this abuse was verbal and certainly not considered abusive at the time (by the abusers or the abused). Never in my Naval career did I ever encounter any form of physical abuse. The daily routine consisted of early mornings, physical activities, marching (like a fucking giraffe in my case), classroom lessons, three cooked meals and tremendous banter. I'd read Brendan Behan's 'Borstal Boy' a few weeks before joining up and it often struck me how similar my surroundings and routine were to those experienced by the young Brendan some decades earlier.

The six weeks of basic training warrant a book in itself but ask any ex-matelot what he or she remembers the most and it's usually the parade ground; being insulted and humiliated is always more joyful when carried out in public. On one occasion a particularly loud GI told me to put my legs together as the sight of daylight between one's legs when standing to attention is a sign of sloppiness. In my case it was a sign of bandy legs and when I pointed this out to the Petty Officer in question he looked at my name badge and remarked, "O'Rourke eh… Irish, I guess… in that case I'll let you off." When I attempted to point out that we Irish, or second-generation Irish in my case, weren't actually as stupid as some liked to make out, he bellowed at me in what turned out to be his native tongue… Gaelic. When he translated it was "Down for fifty, you spotty little wanker." Fifty press-ups for a spotty little wanker like me was a tough gig but as the bloke supervising my exertions was wielding a large stick I was incentivised to carry out the punishment without further debate.

Whilst I loved sport, particularly football, HMS Raleigh's gymnasium was not my favourite place. Five-a-side football yes, I could play that all day every day; but press-ups, star-jumps, squats, burpees, dorsals and rope-climbing were not my thing; I hated circuit training and I didn't care too much for the rather loud 'Clubswingers', Physical Training Instructors to give them their correct title; PTIs were always referred to as 'Staff' as in 'Yes Staff' and never 'Clubz' (not within their earshot at least). I didn't have any physical problems with any of this stuff, I just didn't enjoy it. At least I got through it which is more than can be said for a couple of lads who failed to complete basic training simply because they weren't fit enough. We were in the gym most days, all in the same uniform of t-shirts, shorts, socks and plimsolls, or pumps as they were referred to in the Navy.

Another challenge was the Royal Naval Swimming Test. Every sailor has to pass a test that includes swimming two lengths of the pool whilst wearing a set of standard issue overalls. I have always really enjoyed swimming despite not being very good at it. I can't actually swim more than a couple of lengths at a time and a set of heavy overalls didn't help. I enjoyed the weekly visits to the pool and did a bit extra in the evenings with a few of the lads. Despite much swimming later on in life I always struggled to swim more than a couple of lengths without taking a breather, something that nearly cost me my life many years later off the island of Boracay in the South China Sea but that's another story (thanks Bruv).

I learnt lots of new skills in basic training. I learnt how to clean toilets and bathrooms with a toothbrush. I learnt how to 'bull' boots (spit and polish). I learnt how to pretend that I'd had lots of girlfriends and loads of sex prior to joining up; kudos is only given for results, not effort; the latter rather than the former were the hallmark of my achievements in that particular department, or lack of. I learnt how to get out of one rig (clothes) and into another in the space of a few seconds. I learnt how to iron clothes. I learnt how to complete assault courses in soaking wet, muddy overalls. I learnt how to get on with a load of young lads from places I'd heard of and places I hadn't.

One particular training module that all wannabe matelots need to complete is 'damage control'. HMS Raleigh has a cutaway ship; well, a part of a ship to be precise, and this is filled with fire on some occasions and water on other occasions. Its beauty is the realism; from a trainer's perspective of course, not a trainee's. Obviously this training is simulated but fire is fire and water is water. Crawling along a ship's deck wearing overalls and breathing apparatus, in the dark, whilst fire rages, is not my idea of fun. Even less fun is trying to stem water flooding into a ship's cabin whilst that water, and the cabin's occupants, rise to the top rather quicker than anyone would have liked. Of course they will turn the water off when your head is touching the deckhead (ceiling), the water is touching your chin and you are shitting your pants. Of course they will. Of course they did. But none of us were ever too sure although one thing we WERE sure of was the enjoyment our discomfort gave to our trainers. I had few skills prior to joining the Royal Navy and to that short list I never added damage control whether it involved fire or water.

Another module where I excelled, not, was gunnery. Let's face it, I joined up as a Writer for good reason (essentially a process of elimination based on my personal skills, or lack of). I don't remember too much about the visits to the firing range other than on one particular occasion when I stood up with my rifle in the air, an 'SLR' back in those days, and the GI shouted, "Put that fucking thing down you fucking wanker!" Apparently waving a loaded rifle around is potentially dangerous. I didn't really appreciate this at the time although judging by Jock's white face, next to me, he certainly did.

Sundays were less intense than the other days and we were all given the opportunity to go to church; by opportunity I mean we were instructed to attend church. Prior to joining up I was a Catholic altar-boy and I attended church two or three times a week so the routine was familiar to me; this apparent devotion to the church was borne out of a keen teenage interest in choir-girls rather than some deep faith but as I mentioned earlier, there were no rewards for effort and results on my part, one charity disco in the local convent aside, were few and far between.

After church on the first Sunday a few of us were comparing notes in the NAAFI, essentially a canteen with loads of vending machines selling nutty (chocolate), crisps and fizzy drinks. I told Jock that we Catholics, or left-footers as we were referred to by our brothers-in-arms, were given tea and biscuits after mass. "Tea and fucking biscuits?" he shouted. "Tea and fucking biscuits? We were given fuck all by the Church of Scotland." Apparently when completing one of the myriad of joining-up forms Jock had answered 'none' to the question regarding religion. You're not allowed to not have a religion in the Royal Navy, or you weren't in those days, so Jock was allocated to the Church of Scotland (seemed to make sense given his accent). Anyway, turns out Jock was raised a Catholic so from the following Sunday he took his rightful place in HMS Raleigh's Catholic church; to say he enjoyed the tea and biscuits more than most is an understatement.

Classroom lessons involved a multitude of subjects including Naval history, rank structure, sex education, alcohol awareness and for those without the necessary 'O' Levels, basic Maths and English. Maths and English concluded with 'NAMET', the Naval Maths and English Test. An 'O' Level counted as zero and a 7 was a pass; anything more than 7 was civvie street (or the British Army). I had a zero courtesy of an English 'O' Level (two A grade English 'O' Levels actually but who's counting) but not having Maths 'O' Level I had to endure the Maths lessons. Perfection of course was 0:0 and I ended up with 4:0. Maths of course in those days included topics such as algebraic fractions, calculus, trigonometry and the like (nowadays I'm led to believe it's restricted to adding up and taking away).

Regarding rank structure and badges of rank, the Senior Service does things differently from the other two services (and just about every other service on the planet). Stripes are NOT badges of rank; in fact too many can mark you out as a bit of a non-achiever (we had other words to describe those in the slow lane). Someone with three stripes on their arm can have no rank and someone with one stripe can be more senior than someone with three stripes, not only in the Royal Navy but in the other services. Stripes are 'Good Conduct Badges' (GCBs) – nothing whatsoever to do with rank. If you have three but no rank, you have clearly served at least 12 years; if you are a Petty Officer with, say, one stripe, you're a whizz-kid as that indicates you've served between four and eight years and are already equivalent to a Sergeant in the other services. What happens when you get promoted to Chief Petty Officer? You lose all of your stripes. But to compensate you get buttons. As I said, the Royal Navy does things differently and is proud of it.

As for commissioned officers, a Lieutenant (pronounced

'Leftenant') is not the same as a Lieutenant in the British Army; a Royal Navy Lieutenant is the equivalent of an Army Captain. An Army Captain is much less senior than a Navy Captain who is equivalent to an Army Colonel. Got it?

Six weeks of basic training goes very slowly and essentially is a routine that involves lots of cleaning, lots of marching, lots of sport, lots of boasting, lots of swearing and lots of looking forward to getting the hell out of the place. On the sporting front the opportunities were endless. Like most things in life I missed out when talent was being dished out. But I was rather good at football, especially in the goalkeeping area. I spent the first 11 years of my life living in a Luton council house and we had one of those long hallways, or at least it appeared long to a scrawny little lad. My father, brother and I used to play football in the hallway with me in goal and my old fella and older brother trying to score as many goals as possible with a pair of rolled up socks, held together by several elastic bands. We also played football in the front and rear gardens of course. We also played football out on the street. We also played football at school. We also played football when we moved to a pub in Peterborough where my brother Patrick and I spent more time playing football in our conveniently shaped car-park than we spent inside with our family (we did venture in now and then to practise our pool and darts).

So whilst I wasn't good at many things I was particularly good at goalkeeping, particularly shot-stopping as my aerial ability left a lot to be desired. I was pretty competitive too and I have a primary school report that claims that I was "often disruptive" on the field of play. If I got pissed off for some reason during a game I would engineer a sending off, particularly if it was raining.

Prior to joining the Royal Navy I played for Peterborough's Catholic altar-boys' football team. Father Dennis and Father Tom took us all over the place playing football. It's worth mentioning here that despite all the accusations about Catholic priests, many well-founded and others not so, I never ever encountered anything of a sexual nature or sexual interest among our priests and never heard anything untoward from any of my fellow altar-boys. In addition to my duties as an altar-boy I was also a member of the St Vincent de Paul Society so I spent a lot of time with priests, in their bedrooms (which double as their personal study), in their cars and under canvas on camping trips. Unproven but widely reported allegations were made against Father Dennis some years later but I can honestly say those priests were great guys and like me and my mates, they loved football. Father Tom introduced me and others to White Hart Lane and Father Dennis introduced us to Portman Road (hence the time spent in their cars).

On one particular occasion when we played against Norwich Cathedral, a big game in the world of East Anglian Catholic football, I was sent off for being disruptive. Father Dennis was our coach and when I got to the sideline he asked, "Why did the ref send you off?"

To which I replied, "I called him a wanker."

Father Dennis replied, "Maybe he is a wanker but that's the Bishop of East Anglia." Sorry Bish.

Anyway, back to HMS Raleigh. The big game of the six-week training period was against the Artificers. In those days 'normal' ranks trained in HMS Raleigh and Artificers, engineering technicians in common parlance, trained across the road in HMS Fisgard (these guys didn't have to do NAMET for obvious reasons). Essentially Artificers joined up with more 'O' Levels than non-Artificers, Writers aside, although in the case of Writers our 'O' Levels were rarely if ever in any subject of a technical nature. Artificers or 'Tiffs' as they were known wore different uniforms to us, the same as those worn by Senior Ratings (SNCOs), complete with peaked caps, white shirts and black ties. We didn't particularly like Artificers and this dislike was formed before any of us had ever met any (the feeling turned out to be mutual). For some reason the Tiffs usually beat the non-Tiffs at football although Jock and I reversed the trend during our tenure. I probably played the best game of football I'd ever played, in goal of course, keeping out more shots on goal that I could count. Jock scored both of our goals and we won 2-1. That one game of football would live with me for the rest of my Naval career.

We were let out on a couple of occasions but only after four weeks when it was deemed safe to let us loose on the Devon/Cornish community. Apart from one trip in uniform across the water to Devon and the city of Plymouth our escapes involved visits to Torpoint's local pubs, usually the Standard Inn or the Jubilee Inn; there was also a club, the Harbour Club or something similar, that we would frequent. Whilst it was great to get out and have a beer in a pub, nights out in uniform and under curfew with few members of the fairer sex in attendance weren't of particular note. I've said for many years that I don't like going to pubs full of people like me and the Standard and the Jubilee were rammed full with people like me. Far more interesting runs ashore were to come.

We had a couple of 'expeds', outdoor expeditions which basically entailed a few days away under canvas. We spent a couple of days on Dartmoor and another couple of days at Pier Cellars, a former pilchard harbour not far from HMS Raleigh. Expeds consist of various team-building exercises, physical activity, navigation with compass and map, assault courses, singing around camp fires and loads of banter. I have yet to meet a Writer who ever mastered the skills of erecting a tent in a fashion that prevented water coming into the tent in the middle of the night; Seamen and Engineers of course, even trainees, had no problem with this particular task.

Probably the best day of basic training was the 'Call Round' (a visit to an operational warship). We were split into groups and visited different ships based in Plymouth's Devonport Naval Base, the largest naval base in Western Europe. I was in a group that visited

HMS *Andromeda*, a Leander Class frigate. We were shown around the ship but the primary purpose of the visit was to spend some time below decks with Junior Ratings to get a feel for life on board. We were treated to cans of CSB (Courage Sparkling Beer) and, for the smokers in the group, Royal Navy Blue Liners. A couple of hours in the mess made up my mind – I wanted my first ship to be a Devonport-based Leander.

Eventually we came to the end of our six-week training period; despite the scrawny kid from the pub in Peterborough whose father had let the best part of him run down his leg and who marched like a giraffe, our mess became 'The Guard'. There were 'intakes' other than ours who had joined up on the same day but as a group we were the best at marching and we got to wear the white belts and the white gaiters. The culmination of basic training is the 'Passing Out Parade' where all groups march to some particularly stirring music, courtesy of the resident Royal Marines band, in front of parents, wives, girlfriends, friends and family. Obviously there were 'Wrens' (Women's Royal Naval Service) in training with us but for the life of me I cannot recall if any passed out on the same day as us, hence me not mentioning any boyfriends watching. My mum and my youngest sister Tess were among the spectators; fair play to my mum coming down as she and my dad had divorced some months earlier and my Passing Out Parade coincided with the week in which she moved out of the family home (she'd move back again but that's another story).

On the subject of the absence of boyfriends, homosexuality was illegal in those days; it was a criminal offence contrary to Queen's Regulations for the Royal Navy. Many years later in the Sunday Times there was a letter from a retired Admiral which went something like this: "When I served in the Royal Navy homosexuality was illegal, then they decriminalised it, then they allowed it; fortunately I retired before they made it compulsory." A humorous letter but in the Royal Navy of today, an organisation so much more diverse than the Royal Navy of my day, diversity is king and no one currently serving who I've met cares a jot about their colleagues' sexual orientation.

So that was it, basic training complete. We'd been successfully bashed into shape and we all looked forward to taking our loved ones out for meals and drinks later. Once I'd given Mum and Tess the obligatory tour of HMS Raleigh we went out for the evening. I chose a delightful little pub called the Wilcove Inn down by the water; no idea why I chose this particular pub but its owner, Alfie Lang, became very well known to me in later years. Alfie is a top bloke who now lives in his homeland of Malta (an unusual name for a Maltese chap but his step-father was an English sailor). Alfie was one hell of a character and so too was his Maltese mother Helen; the last time I saw her was on her death-bed many years later and I was the last person to speak to her.

When a sailor leaves a ship or a shore establishment he or she is given what is referred to as a 'write-up', essentially a written 'reference' for that person's next Divisional Officer and Divisional Senior Rating. These were written on a form known as an S264A, colloquially known as '264s', and they followed sailors wherever they went. The first 264 would of course be the one written on completion of basic training and that would sit atop all others and form part of a sailor's 'Service Documents', sent to 'SC Offices' to be processed by those glorious men and women of the Writer branch. The first words of the first line on my very first 264 were: "A goalkeeper of some distinction, O'Rourke... blah blah blah." Nothing about any future potential as an Admiral but at least better than "you march like a fucking giraffe".

Most of the lads in my mess were members of the wider "Supply and Secretariat" branch so we were all off to the Royal Naval Supply School in Chatham. Now called the 'Logistics Branch' the S&S branch comprised Writers, Stores Accountants, Cooks, Caterers and

Stewards (in particular order). We couldn't wait to leave HMS Raleigh and crack on with our Naval careers. Most important of all was the opportunity to continue our training elsewhere, somewhere we were told would be a lot less 'strict' than Raleigh and somewhere where we would be allowed to go out at night as often and for as long as we wished. Chatham is very close to London and the prospect of weekend trips to the big smoke were particularly appealing.

2. PEN-PUSHING

After some leave in Peterborough and time to catch up with my beloved, the Eight Bells in Millfield, it was back on the train but this time a shorter trip via London to Chatham in north-west Kent. Chatham is situated 30-odd miles east of London and is a brilliant location for a dockyard (sadly 'was' given its closure in 1984 with the consequent loss of 17,000 jobs). Many years later the Daily Mirror described north Kent as a 'cultural wasteland' but in the early 1980s it had more than enough culture to keep young sailors occupied.

HMS Pembroke was indeed very different to HMS Raleigh. Whereas Raleigh was a collection of rather boring identikit buildings, predominantly white in colour, Pembroke looked more like a private school or a university (not that I'd ever visited a private school or a university). The buildings were quite splendid: large, Edwardian, ivy-clad, red-brick and just rather imposing. Once inside the main gate there was a long thoroughfare with the grandest buildings off to the right and the parade ground and other buildings down some steps and to the left. HMS Pembroke is no more but its buildings remain and they now form the University of Greenwich's Medway Campus. Whilst Raleigh was rather functional, Pembroke felt a bit special although Mountbatten Block where we would be housed, for sleeping purposes at least, wasn't one of its finest buildings, aesthetically at least.

The Royal Naval Supply School is actually a collection of different schools with the Royal Naval Writer School, clearly its best, about to become my place of work for the next 12 weeks or so. This is the 'professional' bit of training. All sailors start in Raleigh or Fisgard and after successful square-bashing, dependent upon one's specialisation, everyone moves on to different shore establishments in different parts of the country to continue their training. Weapons Engineers for example went to HMS Collingwood in Fareham, Marine Engineers went to HMS Sultan in Gosport and Seamen stayed in HMS Raleigh (for that we commiserated). Others went elsewhere.

Mountbatten Block was pretty functional but an improvement upon the large messes of HMS Raleigh. In my particular mess there were four of us: Jock, Trev, Roy and myself. We'd all got to know each other in Raleigh; Jock and I had become mates as had Trev and Roy. There was a social space in the block with a TV but we ate elsewhere, in the galley, and there was a bar and the obligatory NAAFI. We had the usual stuff of cleaning, night rounds and the like but our expectations were met; we all thought we were gonna like it here.

The Royal Naval Writer School is just that… a school. According to the official blurb Writers were (and still are) the Royal Navy's accountants and administrators, both seagoing and shore-based. This is where we'd train to manage the Royal Navy's accounts, its sailors' pay, personnel documentation, legal stuff, correspondence and everything else that involved a pen, ink and a typewriter. Yes, we still used fountain pen ink in those days, for certain documents at least; most if not all Writers have fond memories of Quink ink (other brands were not available).

As part of our training we learnt to type. All shore establishments have civilian typing pools and, not wishing to be sexist, in those days they were staffed exclusively by females. Women were not allowed to serve at sea in the 1980s and as the Navy ran on paper, particularly lots and lots of letters flying back and forth between ships, shore establishments and the Ministry of Defence, someone had to type the stuff that appeared on that paper. That someone was Writers. Incredible to think that with the passing of years and the advent of space-age technology, changing our lives immeasurably in the process, the QWERTY keyboard remains the mainstay of desktop and laptop computers and even now the smartphone (not that you can touch-type on a smartphone).

The typing room contained several rows of typewriters (quelle surprise), the manual/monospaced variety for the geeks among you, an illuminated board high up at the front with enlarged letters and symbols and of course the obligatory Senior Rate instructor. All instructors in the Writer School were Senior Rate Writers: Petty Officers, Chief Petty Officers and one or two Fleet Chief Petty Officers (or Warrant Officers as FCPOs are now called). All Writers were taught to touch-type and for a very particular reason, copy-type. From memory we had to achieve 40+ words per minute with 95% accuracy. It was a bit like learning to swim; no one thinks they're gonna crack it but almost everyone does. Some Writers leave Pembroke and when 'out in the fleet', far from the training environment, convert to two-fingered typing; others, the more pedantic among us, insist on continuing to touch-type as a matter of honour.

Whilst we still had elements of 'basic' training, including far too much time on the parade ground or in the gymnasium for my liking, our daily lives consisted of classroom, food, sport and beer. Each class consisted of around a dozen trainee Writers. My instructor, a Petty Officer known as Ginge to his mates, or PO to us, was a top bloke; we all got on great although of course we always knew our place and respected the instructors. Writers wear their pedantry as a badge of honour and Senior Rate Writers love to impart their knowledge and pedantry to wannabe pedants. In those days there were no computers other than the ones that operated radar, sonar, missile systems, etc. In the Writer world, other than the most basic of typewriters, everything was done by hand. The Navy seemed to run on 'C-Forms'. Knowledge of these forms and pedantic completion of said forms were the hallmark of a Writer's knowledge. Going on leave? There's a C-Form for that. Promoted? There's a C-Form for that. Fined by the Captain? There's a C-Form for that. Wanna set up a monthly allotment for a loved one? There's a C-Form for that. And if there wasn't a C-Form for it there was an S-Form for it. Do not believe anything ex-Engineers or ex-Seamen tell you. The Royal Navy did not rely upon engines or missiles, it relied upon forms and correctly completed forms at that.

The food was pretty good at Pembroke and the tea was so much better too. In Raleigh it was common knowledge, although it may have been Naval myth, that bromide was added to our tea to suppress sexual urges. I have never met anyone who disagrees with this although I cannot testify to its accuracy (the addition of bromide or its effects).

We worked hard at Pembroke but we played hard too. Young lads bursting with testosterone with a keen desire to see the world, well, Kent at least, had only one or two things on their minds after 'school'. Get fed, get showered and get out. Out of the main gate, turn left, walk up the hill and start at the Royal Marine pub. The landlord of this pub was a great fella and Jock and I would go and see him in later years at his next pub – the Grand Theatre in Plymouth's Union Street. Enough about Plymouth and Union Street – plenty of time for that later.

The Royal Marine was a friendly pub, frequented almost exclusively by residents of HMS Pembroke. Although on one notable occasion it wasn't particularly friendly. A French ship had berthed in Chatham's Royal Naval dockyard and a dozen or so of her sailors had taken over the public bar. Forget the world wars and the Germans; as my Naval career and excursions around different continents would teach me, it was only the French who British sailors disliked. All to do with history of course. Even the likes of me without a drop of English or British blood running through their veins possessed a keen sense of Naval history (not much knowledge but a keen sense nonetheless). After a few renditions of 'Rule Britannia' all hell broke loose. In common with most British/French naval battles there was only ever going to be one winner; after the rumble and with a few bruises but pride intact we carried on into town to sample the delights of a few more watering holes.

Second only to the Royal Marine in our affections was the Command House on Dock Road. Whilst weekends were reserved for trips to London, weekdays were reserved for the Royal Marine, the Command House and a selection of Chatham's other glorious pubs. My fondest memory of the Command House, as it often is with a plethora of other pubs and bars around the world, was of one particular barmaid. Every time I ordered a round she would roll her tongue around the top of one of the ale handpulls, rather phallic in their design it must be said. I have no recollection of how that pub's beer tasted but my abiding memory will always be of those handpulls and that particular tongue.

Going out drinking on a school night has its disadvantages of course. I recall one particular 'morning after' when we had 'Divisions'. That's the parade ground stuff although Divisions is a formal event when your kit has to be even more gleaming than usual and your marching so much better than the average giraffe. Just as I was about to keel over, Jock, sensing the signs, tried to grab hold of my arm. The Petty Officer GI, also sensing the signs, shouted, "Leave him fucking be!" My next memory was waking up with a couple of the said GI's rather thick fingers exploring my mouth looking for my tongue. There's a saying in the Royal Navy: "if you're looking for sympathy it's in the dictionary between shit and syphilis". There was no sympathy for my predicament on that particular morning although there was of course an abundance of merriment and piss-taking courtesy of my fellow trainees.

Training rolled on and we all became adept at form-filling, typing and the like. The rules of the Royal Navy were contained in 'BRs', short for 'Books of Reference'. Writers were exceptionally proud of their BR knowledge. One of our bibles was BR1950 – Naval Pay Regulations. This book was around 12 inches high, 9 inches wide and 3 inches thick (I'm a bloke so don't quote me on inches). In the Royal Navy you were never paid the same one month as you were the previous month and this was all down to the contents of BR1950 which most of us learnt to quote accurately even in our sleep or under the influence of the strongest beer. Other BRs with which we became intimately acquainted, to name but a few, were Queen's Regulations for the Royal Navy (BR31), Advancement Regulations (BR1066) and JSP101, the Manual of Service Writing (the bible for all true pedants). My biggest challenge whilst writing this book is trying to avoid double-spacing after full-stops; former students of the Royal Naval Writer School and anyone else taught to type on monospaced typewriters will know where I'm coming from and will share my pain.

The primary challenge in Writer training was not to get 'back-classed'. Every week we had exams and the pass mark for all was something like 90%. One or two were back-classed most weeks but Jock and I managed to pass everything. Being back-classed marked you out as a bit of a thicko; more importantly it meant that you would join a different class and would pass-out, subject to not getting thrown out, with a different bunch of blokes and after the guys you joined the Royal Navy with.

Another challenge, a challenge in all ships and establishments, was not to fall foul of the Regulating Branch (Royal Naval 'Police', or Crushers as we liked to call them). If Writers thrived on paying people correctly and getting their double-spacing correct, Regulators thrived on arranging for your pay to be reduced or your leave stopped. Any minor transgression of Queen's Regulations would see you hauled up in front of the Commanding Officer or another Senior Officer to whom he delegated (again, all 'hes' in those days). On one occasion Jock had three days of 'Number 9s'; the punishment of 'Number 9s' involved stoppage of leave plus additional jobs in the early morning and evening when everyone else was either sleeping or enjoying themselves (scrubbing pots in the galley was a favourite as was polishing the brass inside the main gate). Jock was 'trooped' for breaching the standard curfew one night – all to do with a woman of course. Luckily I escaped any punishment in training but my time would come later.

Most weekends Jock and I would venture into London. We always took enough money for beer and travel although we would frequently miss the last train and end up sleeping on Trafalgar Square close to a rather more famous matelot, long dead but immortalised in concrete. On one occasion I ventured into London with another oppo when Jock was on 9s; luckily we caught the last train with a minute to spare but unluckily we both fell asleep and woke up in Dover. Dover train station is not the most comfortable place I've ever slept but neither is it the worst.

Jock and I were teenage sailors, let loose on the world. We weren't into theatres or museums, although we did visit a few museums as part of our training at HMS Pembroke (the Imperial War Museum, the National Maritime Museum and HMS Belfast spring to mind). No, women and beer occupied our minds and not much else. In those days Soho wasn't the cool, hip place it is today; no, it was much more fun, it was a den of iniquity and it needed to be explored.

On our first cultural evening in Soho we got chatting to two lovely young women who we arranged to spend a few hours with in a nearby flat. Lovely though they were there was a requirement to hand over some of our hard-earned dollar in advance; but we were promised an evening to remember with some very special 'equipment'. They had to head off to set up the room and the equipment so Jock and I went for another beer before we met them at the appointed spot half an hour later. We never saw them half an hour later as they failed the rendezvous and we never saw them again.

On another occasion we came across the world-famous Raymond

RevueBar. Actually neither of us had ever heard of it until we'd come across it in a porn mag (no iPads in those days). For some reason or other we believed we were entitled to some sort of military discount so we showed our Royal Navy ID cards on entry and were quickly shown to the best seats in the house. Fuck me, we were thrilled. This is what we joined up for; there was nothing like this in Alloa or Peterborough. Just as the performance was about to start a couple of burly security blokes turned up and asked us to come back to the foyer. They asked to see our ID cards once again and whilst I was unconvinced either had the ability to read one remarked, "We thought you were coppers, not sailors, and you're not even 18. Fuck off, the pair of you."

Undeterred by scheming women and tough doorstaff, Jock and I continued to visit London most weekends. On a couple of occasions we went to Luton so that I could introduce Jock to the delights of Kenilworth Road and Luton Town FC. In the 1980s the home end was the Oak Road, nowadays the away end. Like most first-time visitors to the mecca of football Jock was impressed by the grand entrance in the Oak Road; there aren't many football stadiums where you have to walk under someone's bedroom to get in. To be fair to Jock he got into the spirit of things although he did insist on shouting, "Come on, Luton!" when the correct pronunciation is actually "Come on Loo…un". Jock returned the favour many times in the future by introducing me to the delights of Alloa Athletic and his beloved Dundee (not to be confused with Dundee United under any circumstances).

One of the delights of training is receiving mail from loved ones; a bit like being in prison I guess. Rather unexpectedly I received a letter from one of my sisters telling me that she had been approached by a girl in Sixth Form who wanted to know my address so that she could write to me. Amazingly this was Yvonne, the Polish girl and one of the reasons why I joined the Navy (not the main reason but I was frustrated with her apparent lack of interest and I certainly wasn't interested in anyone else).

At one point I did think I'd hit the jackpot with Yvonne. I didn't get to many parties at school, just the one from memory, but it was around the corner from school and lo and behold Yvonne was going (the only reason why I went). It was just before I applied to join the Royal Navy; Yvonne and I were both members of 'Lower Sixth' studying 'A' Levels. Somehow I managed to sit next to Yvonne on the floor in a room crammed full with other teenage party-goers; I recall Yvonne wearing a bright pink jumpsuit – she was the most gorgeous thing on the planet at that moment in time. I actually plucked up the courage to 'ask her out' and she said she'd think about it. She was sitting next to me for Christ's sake... surely she was interested? The evening came to an abrupt halt when my older brother turned up, unannounced, unexpected and unwelcome. "Come on, Hughie," he said, "Mum's outside in the car, time to go home." Embarrassed? You bet.

I did spend quite a bit of time with Yvonne, both in the Sixth Form Common Room and also in class as we both studied English (having sat next to each other for two years prior during English Literature 'O' Level we carried on sitting next to each other during our 'A' Level studies). Yvonne and I also went to see the Pope together at Ninian Park in Cardiff in June 1982. We went as part of an organised school trip, sleeping out in a school in Bristol the night before; we were both really looking forward to seeing the Pope, Yvonne especially given Pope John Paul II was Polish. Yvonne and I sat next to each other on the coach and we also stood side by side on the terrace behind the goal. I've visited many, many football grounds throughout my life and I have experienced some amazing atmospheres but not many can match the atmosphere that day in Cardiff City's football stadium when not a ball was kicked. Yvonne wore her Polish 'Solidarity' t-shirt with 'Solidarność' emblazoned across it in bright red lettering (the Solidarity union being the movement that ultimately brought down the Iron Curtain and reunited Europe). Yvonne took a photo of the Pope as he stopped in front of our terrace. When she showed me the photo a few weeks later she remarked, "See how he's staring straight at my t-shirt?" Yep, no surprise there, I spent a lot of time staring at it myself that day.

Yvonne and I exchanged scores of letters, maybe hundreds, over the next few years. We also went out together a couple of times whilst I was on leave but one kiss aside, nothing of note happened (despite much hope and effort on my part). Yvonne and I continued to write to each other on a frequent basis right up until I married some years later but I've never heard of or from her since.

Despite the relative freedoms we were still in the Royal Navy and we were still in training. Marching, boot-polishing, Captain's Rounds and similar delights remained a daily feature of our lives. Whilst a tad more benign than their counterparts in HMS Raleigh, Pembroke's instructors still had a job to do and, like their counterparts in Raleigh, a feature of this was to frequently remind us that we were all shit and we were the worst intake they'd ever seen (the worst intake since the previous intake but not as bad as the next would turn out to be).

Captain's Rounds are what it says on the tin: the Captain would do his rounds of the accommodation block, visiting all messes, whilst his junior officers and Senior Rate instructors would rub their hands and swipe their fingers across all surfaces in the hope of finding dust or some other offensive foreign being. The Captain's team would wear white gloves and they would rub their hands and fingers across the tops of wardrobes, underneath beds, in far corners and anywhere else that would accommodate a finger (now, now). If anything untoward were found, dust particles or anything similarly offensive, in the officers' or instructors' opinion rather than the trainees' opinion of course, then that invariably led to a 'rescrub' which involved stoppage of leave and an evening of cleaning on hands and knees to compensate.

As we were considered 'one team' and all in it together Captain's Rounds meant that if one mess failed we all failed. 'Awarded' a rescrub one particular evening we were all on our hands and knees, bemoaning our loss of leave and wondering how on earth Chatham's publicans and young girls would cope in our absence. Well, not all. Turned out one of our fellow trainees, Barry Mellor, was absent. Barry had been earmarked as a future commissioned officer very early in training and rumour had it he was playing golf with the Commander or someone of similar importance. Whether this were true or not I never found out; Barry did make officer and a few years later he and I would work side-by-side and on a couple of occasions we socialised together; I even visited his flat near Langstone Harbour but I never referred back to that evening in Chatham. One man missing did not do our morale any favours on that particular night. On the bright side Chatham's girls and publicans all coped admirably in our absence.

As a youngster I often talked in my sleep and on occasion went for the odd walk too. When you live with a bunch of piss-taking males this is not a good idea. After lights out the CPO on duty would do his rounds to ensure that everyone was in their pit and getting their heads down. It became a bit of a nightly routine that if I fell asleep before the others Jock would wake me slightly and get me talking in my half-sleep. He usually timed it for the Chief's rounds. They say a drunk man never lies and neither does a teenager with a sleep-talking problem. I do remember what Jock told me I told him and others but some things are best not repeated. This would also happen outside of HMS Pembroke, much to my embarrassment and much to the amusement of others.

One particular occasion of note was during an exped. We were somewhere in Kent, 12 men per tent complete with belongings most sacred of which were our tin 'billy cans' and cutlery, essential for the enjoyment of the 24-hour 'rat-pack' (ration pack). This was early 1983, less than a year after the Falklands War, something that was embedded in the DNA of every serving member of the Royal Navy, including those of us who had joined up a few weeks or months after the war had finished (some call it a 'conflict' but it was most definitely a war). I woke up on the first morning on one side of the tent with my 11 comrades squashed together on the other side. When I asked what was going on Jock told me that after I'd fallen asleep some Army types who were camped in a nearby field had decided to play with their guns and create some noise (it's what Pongos do). Apparently I stirred slightly and Jock whispered in my ear, "It's the Argies… they're coming," I responded by picking up my knife, a normal knife of the type usually accompanied by a fork, and started waving it around and jabbing it at my mates; apparently I 'chased' Jock and others around the tent on my hands and knees screaming obscenities. Whilst the lads had quite an uncomfortable night huddled together on one side of the tent sheltering from the maniacal JAWTR with the knife, at least they had some fun at my expense.

Football was obviously a feature at Pembroke and Jock and I played for a couple of teams. The pitches at Chatham seemed miles away from the accommodation and I have memories of trudging across fields, especially in the wet, to indulge in our footballing passion. Similar to the game at Raleigh against the Tiffs from Fisgard, Pembroke had a showpiece football match and this was against the Royal Hospital School in Holbrook near Ipswich. I cannot recall much about this school other than it was a posh place with some sort of Naval link (an independent boarding school where students wore Naval uniforms). A bit like Raleigh's match versus Fisgard, once again this was a case of the oiks versus the posh twats. It was a wet and mucky match but once again the goalkeeper and the centre-forward stole the show; I saved the opposition's shots and Jock converted ours. The oiks won.

All in all Chatham, Pembroke and the Writer School were a pleasant experience. I'd learnt to type, I'd learnt to complete C and S Forms, I'd learnt how to calculate pay (Naval pay is more complex than military missile systems), I'd solidified friendships, I'd enhanced my cleaning, ironing and polishing skills, I'd got my first but not last taste of North Kent and, most importantly, I'd passed every exam averaging 94.9% and passed out with Jock, Trev, Roy and the rest of the lads on time and on budget. I'd never cross paths with Trev again, a shame as I liked him, but I would bump into Roy at a later date (or rather I'd be lying at the bottom of the stairs of a Gibraltarian night-club as he was leaving in a more conventional manner but more of that later). I was, however, still a virgin, much to my frustration and despite much effort on my part, but that was about to change.

After leaving HMS Pembroke I had a few weeks' leave so I went home to Peterborough to catch up with the oldies. I didn't keep in touch with school friends other than Yvonne and a mate called Shaun whose parents owned a pub about 50 yards from my parents' pub (the Hand and Heart which, unusually for Peterborough and particularly Millfield, remains a pub to this day). Shaun apart and occasionally Yvonne, far too occasionally for my liking, I rarely ventured away from our pub other than for away pool and darts matches and of course home and away Peterborough United football matches; Luton Town was, is and always will be my number one team but I loved football and I loved matchdays so Peterborough was a satisfactory substitute.

On this particular period of leave and rather unusually my brother Patrick and I went out on the sauce together. I sported a very obvious scar close to my left eye, so distinctive it was noted on my Royal Navy ID card as a 'Distinguishing Mark'. This was a sporting injury suffered during a charity table-tennis tournament in the year before I joined the Royal Navy (who knew table-tennis could be so physical?). I recall my brother saying, "Don't hit him," after a little Welshman from the year below had belted me with his bat, splitting it in two. Hit him? I couldn't even see him.

Anyway, roll on a year or so to this period of leave; Patrick and I were having a jar or two in the 'Wortley Almshouses' in the city centre. Patrick went to the toilet and on his return said, "Remember that little Welsh guy who gave you that scar? Well, he's in the pub and he's by the toilets." Off I went to seek revenge for the scar but the little Welsh guy was no more; the guy had turned into a brick shithouse and he had a number of equally large mates with him. When I returned to my brother he remarked, "I'm guessing you let him off." Yep, I let him off.

3. ON THE JOB

Having completed both basic and professional training it was now time to join the Royal Navy proper for 'on-job' training. Basic training at Raleigh constituted 'Part One' training and professional training at the Writer School constituted 'Part Two' training. It was now time for 'Part Four' training. Don't ask me what happened to 'Part Three' training as no one knew and in any case Part Four training would be in two parts (the Navy does things differently).

'Part Fours' are trainees who have completed basic training and, for all practical purposes, are fully-paid up members of the 'Fleet'. However, to join the seagoing fleet Part Fours had to complete task books 'on the job', under the close supervision of a Senior Rate Writer (normally a Petty Officer). Back in the day Wren Writers, female Writers, were divided into 'P' and 'G' Writers; the former specialised in matters relating to 'Pay' and accountancy matters and the latter specialised in 'General' matters which essentially saw them employed in senior officers' registries or 'Service Certificate Offices' ('SC Offices' for short). SC offices were to all intents and purposes 'Personnel Offices', or 'HR Offices' as they tend to be known nowadays in Civvie Street. Male Writers did the lot as we had to go to sea (female Writers now do the lot as the 'split', if you pardon the pun, was later abolished).

For my Part Four training I was drafted to HMS Osprey on the Isle of Portland in Dorset. Ratings are drafted, officers are appointed; ratings serve ON ships, officers serve IN them. Portland is located around five miles south of the coastal resort of Weymouth and is connected to the mainland by Chesil Beach. I was drafted in March 1983 and by now I had been 'advanced' from 'Junior Assistant Writer Second Class' to 'Assistant Writer', courtesy of having completed my basic training and reaching the glorious age of 17 and a half years old. It was anticipated that I would spend around six months in HMS Osprey; on completion I would be drafted elsewhere to complete the second half of my 'on-job' training. Six months with Weymouth on the doorstep – whatever would I do with myself during the summer months?

The objective of the first part of my on-job training was to complete my 'Pay' task book and for this I would work alongside experienced colleagues in the Pay Office, situated in Osprey's 'Admin Block' which directly faced the airfield (noisy but a great view). HMS Osprey was a helicopter base and most of its inhabitants were members of the Royal Navy's Fleet Air Arm, affectionately known as 'WAFUS' throughout the Service (Wet And Fucking Useless). I have little memory of travelling to Weymouth from Peterborough other than it seemed to take a very long time.

The Pay Office consisted of two rows of very old fashioned wooden desks where the top part formed a shelf where 'customers', not that we ever referred to them as customers, could lean or complete paperwork and the lower part formed the desk proper where we Writers would ply our trade. One row ran from the front door towards the end of the office on the right-hand side and the other row, directly opposite, ran from the left-hand side down towards the end of the office, leaving a large space in the middle with the two rows of desks and accompanying Writers facing each other. At the end of the office was the 'Service Certificate Office', staffed by Writers of course. On my left closest to the door was Leading Writer Paul Campbell and on my right was Petty Officer Wren Writer (Pay) Catriona Paton. Paul and Catriona were blunt-speaking Scots and it became obvious very quickly that there was nothing they didn't know about pay accounting in the Royal Navy.

In 1983 we had calculators but that was about it – no computers. Naval pay accounting was part science and part art. Every member of HMS Osprey's Ship's Company had a pay account and every Writer in the Pay Office looked after approximately 200 accounts. Courtesy of BR 1950 (Naval Pay Regulations) and a Scottish sandwich, it didn't take me too long to learn the ropes. Catriona and Paul were superb trainers and if I did something wrong, I knew about it (but I never made the same mistake twice). My daily routine consisted of working in the Pay Office and my evening routine consisted of visits to various hostelries in Portland and Weymouth. I also played football as often as I could.

Whilst I worked in the Admin Block on the Naval Air Station, referred to as RNAS Portland, living quarters for the Ship's Company were in a different part of the base; this part of the base, HMS Osprey proper, consisted of several multi-storey accommodation blocks, the galley, gymnasium, a few other buildings and, rather importantly of course, the Ship's Company bar. My mess was on the top floor of one accommodation block, at the front of the building where the windows looked out to sea with the entrance to Portland Harbour and Weymouth to the left and the English Channel to the right. It was a truly fantastic view, especially in the summer months of 1983 with the sun frequently streaming through the window. One of my favourite memories was waking up one day and seeing one of the Royal Navy's aircraft carriers, HMS *Illustrious* or her sister HMS *Invincible*, completely filling my window. Whilst it was my desire to be drafted to a Plymouth-based Leander-class frigate on completion of my Part Four training, I vowed one day to serve on an aircraft carrier. Whilst not aircraft carriers in the purest sense, CVSAs/CVSGs to Naval geeks, they were truly wonderful ships and the best we had (and in my view any ship that carried helicopters and jet fighters was indeed an aircraft carrier).

Most of the lads who I befriended in HMS Osprey were a couple of years older than me and all had completed their first sea drafts, something I could look forward to on completion of my Part Four training. It didn't take them long to show me the delights of Portland and Weymouth. Only problem was that before going on a run ashore we had to start with a few in the Flying Fish, HMS Osprey's very own bar. My overriding memory of the Flying Fish was a plastic tub of lumpy cider situated on the bar counter. Whenever I drink 'proper' cider nowadays, Scrumpy by any other name, I am taken back to that bar on board HMS Osprey (note: it is always on board and never onboard or on-board). After a few pints of those warm lumps we would head out towards HMS Osprey's main gate and the taverns just outside, the Green Shutters and the Jolly Sailor soon becoming my personal favourites. After a few more wets we would walk down to Victoria Square, situated just outside the main entrance to the Naval Air Station. There was a pub on the square, from memory it may have been called The Ship or something similar, and of course we had to have a couple in there too. So, full to the brim with fizzy lager, we would board the bus around 2000; the challenge of further drinking on an already full stomach (and bladder) lay ahead.

In the 1980s most of the pubs in the local area sold a lager called 'Faust', brewed by the Dorchester brewers Eldridge Pope; this beer was truly foul and almost as bad as HMS Osprey's warm and lumpy cider. I was a young lad and wanted to fit in so I went with the older lads and drank what they drank; unfortunately for me these lads had completed their drinking apprenticeships long before me; I was a mere sprog.

The bus journey from Portland to Weymouth took us along Chesil Beach, the shingle strip that joins the island to the mainland, described by author John Fowles as "an elemental place, made of sea, shingle and sky, its dominant sound always that of waves on moving stone: from the great surf and pounding ... of sou'westers, to the delicate laps and back-gurgling of the rare dead calm..." The view from the bus was certainly beautiful which was always more than could be said for the feeling in my stomach. Our evening routine always consisted of a pub crawl which took in the likes of the iconic Black Dog and invariably ended up at one or both of Weymouth's night-clubs, the Steering Wheel and the Harbour Lights. This was my introduction to drinking proper; this was my apprenticeship; this was my real on-job training.

One of my most memorable days during that six-month period was Saturday 14 May 1983. If anyone reading this recalls the football manager David Pleat famously running onto a football pitch wearing a brown suit and frantically waving his arms in unbridled joy, and also apparently his legs, this was it, this was the day. A football clip that would be replayed many thousands of times. It was the last day of the football season and in Division One, England's top division, nowadays rather more grandly entitled the 'Premier League', Luton Town were third from bottom and Manchester City were fourth from bottom. In order to avoid relegation to the second tier Luton Town had to beat Manchester City away from home and, in so doing, leapfrog them in the table and relegate the mighty City instead. It couldn't be done... could it?

After a few too many in the Black Dog opposite I was on the beach with a few mates, transistor radio in hand. With only a few minutes left on the clock and Luton about to be relegated, up popped Radomir Antić with a goal out of nowhere. Cue wild celebrations in the away end at Maine Road. Cue wild celebrations across Luton. Cue wild celebrations on Weymouth beach – a drunken 17-year-old with shiny white Irish skin jumping up and down waving a tranny around (not that kind of tranny). Our hero Raddy went on to become the only man to manage Barcelona, Real Madrid and Atlético Madrid – an absolute legend in more ways than one.

Unfortunately my wild exertions on the beach resulted in the loss of my wallet which contained my Royal Navy ID card, all of my cash and a few other items. Not untypically for me I ended up leaving my mates, wandering around the streets of Weymouth on my own. Failing to find my wallet and having no money for a bus or a taxi, I decided to head back to base, walking several miles back across Chesil Beach to reach Portland and then on to HMS Osprey. On the way back nature called so I decided to have a quick pee outside a huge house on the main road close to the air station. Despite my inebriation I had enough sense, just, to realise that I had been spotted as two chaps in Royal Navy uniform suddenly appeared hurtling down the long driveway towards me. I may have been pissed but I was pretty fit in those days and I could run fast, drunk or sober. You don't spend the first 11 years of your life as a skinny little gobshite on a Luton council estate without learning to leg it when the odds are stacked against you. Unbeknown to me at the time, the huge house was the official residence of the local Admiral and the two guys in question were members of the Regulating Branch, our very own Police Force.

Rather than tackle the main gate without an ID card with two uniforms hot on my heels, knowing the consequences of such a foolhardy act, I decided to take a path that I knew led to the back of HMS Osprey. It was a long walk, more in time than distance, especially as I spent half of it hiding in bushes and behind trees. Once I knew I'd outpaced my less fit if rather more sober and senior colleagues I clambered up a large fence and over some barbed wire. I'd become pretty adept at this as a kid but on this occasion I was full of lager and I failed to get over the fence unscathed; my face was cut in several places from its unwelcome introduction to the barbed wire.

On Monday morning I was sat quietly at my desk nursing my pay accounts, affording them the usual tender love, care and attention. In walked one of the Regulating Petty Officers from a nearby office (RPOs are the equivalent of Military Police Sergeants in the lesser services). "O'Rourke – a word," he summoned. I could cope with a word, any word, but I suspected he wanted more than a word. "Where's your ID card?" he enquired with a look of thunder.

"I lost it on Saturday," I replied. "I was going to report it at stand easy."

"Where did you lose it?" he growled, now sitting behind his desk.

"On Weymouth beach, RPO."

"Did you by any chance stop by FOST's residence on the way home?" he enquired ('FOST' being the Flag Officer Sea Training, a Rear Admiral who headed up the Royal Navy's operational sea training unit based at HMS Osprey).

"I don't know where he lives, RPO," I replied meekly.

"Right, let's cut this short, smart-arse, why were you in Threshers yesterday?"

Fuck, was I in Threshers? I thought to myself without answering the question.

"How old are you, Writer O'Rourke?" he further enquired.

"Seventeen," I replied.

"So I ask you again, what the fuck were you doing in an off-licence under the age of 18?"

"I was buying a packet of salted peanuts, RPO."

"You really are a smart fucker; how did you get all those marks on your face?"

"I was playing football on the beach, RPO, and I fell on some old bits of metal."

At this point he brought his right hand up from underneath the desk and threw my wallet at me, shouting, "Fuck off, smart lad, and consider yourself lucky... I'm in a good mood today." I got off lightly and later found out my Scottish sandwich of Paul Campbell and Catriona Paton were responsible for the RPO's self-styled good mood, both of whom had put in a good word for me. I wasn't so lucky the next time I transgressed Queen's Regulations. Or the time after that.

A few days later I was walking on the road that led from HMS Osprey's main gate to the side gate that I used to access the Royal Naval Air Station. I noticed a rather large black car with a flag on the bonnet coming towards me which I assumed to be carrying a senior officer so I got ready to salute. I was staring at the car, expecting to catch sight of a peaked cap emblazoned with a load of gold, but all I could see were a few guys wearing blue berets. I carried on walking as the car passed me but stopped when I heard it screech to a halt. A Leading Regulator, one down from a Regulating Petty Officer in the rank structure, got out of the car and screeched almost as loudly, "Are you fucking blind… why didn't you salute the Admiral?"

I replied, honestly, "I didn't see any admiral." I was 17, I'd been in the Royal Navy for less than one year, I thought admirals had three feet of gold in front of their noses. "Everyone was wearing berets," I muttered in self-defence.

"Of course he's wearing a fucking beret you fucking moron, he's fucking FOST you fucking retard." I quote this not out of some simple pleasure from using foul language but out of a very vivid recollection of the event, word for word.

The consequence of my not saluting the Flag Officer Sea Training, a grave offence, was an appearance at 'Captain's Table' the following day. This isn't a quaint invite to brunch or tea. Rather it is the Navy's disciplinary process. You queue up with other miscreants, get called in, stand to attention, remove your cap and a bit of dialogue ensues (not much). My Divisional Officer defended me as best he could but I was found guilty as charged and fined £10. Could have been worse, could have been a few days' Number 9s; potential loss of leave would have been a bigger loss than a tenner.

A couple of weeks later, together with a few others, I was walking from our accommodation block towards the galley for our evening meal. We all noticed an officer of Lieutenant rank (two gold rings) walking towards us on the other side of the road. If an officer doesn't want to salute you, which sometimes happens outside of 'normal' working hours, he or she will either ignore you or remove their cap (or beret although clearly admirals keep those things firmly attached to their heads, even when they're in a car). We all decided that this chap was ignoring us for a reason so we carried on towards the galley for some well-earned scran. The Lieutenant continued to walk past us on the other side of the road but stopped after a few yards and screamed at the top of his voice "Oi, you lot, are you fucking blind?" As you will have gathered, the F-word and all of its relations, close and distant, are in frequent use in the Royal Navy. He strode across the road and introduced himself, not in any amiable way, as the 'RCO'. All four of us thought, simultaneously and without speaking to each other – *What the fuck is an RCO?* Our new friend explained, ever so gently, not, that the RCO is the 'Regulating Control Officer', only the commissioned officer in charge of all Regulators in HMS Osprey (like God but more senior apparently). "You, I recognise you," he said to me. "What the fuck is wrong with you?"

Because there was clearly something the fuck wrong with me, I was summoned to the Captain's Table once again whilst all of my colleagues were let off; their explanations were accepted but mine, despite being the same explanation, was disregarded because I had form. Once again my Divisional Officer did his best, stating, "O'Rourke is a very bright young man with great potential… but why he doesn't salute Naval officers I really don't know." Thanks, boss. I was 'awarded' three days' Number 9 punishment.

Coming from a reasonably large Irish family I was fairly proficient at washing pots and pans. Sibling rivalry and an Irish mother who owned more than one wooden spoon ensured that all pots and pans were cleaned to an exceptionally high standard in our kitchen. The benefit of this extensive practice over the years came in handy for my visits to HMS Osprey's galley as part of my punishment. In fact the Petty Officer Cook asked for me to spend more time in the galley than originally allocated as even the biggest pots and pans I had ever seen in my life were no match for my well-developed elbow grease. On balance scrubbing pots and pans was better than polishing the brass inside the main gate, or clearing weeds, as the galley had a more limited audience; that said I did have the brass job every morning at 0600 but my experience of cleaning the urinal pipes in the gents' toilet of my parents' pub every morning before school stood me in good stead for this job. The three days passed relatively quickly and I was soon able to reacquaint myself with my two loves – the Steering Wheel and the Harbour Lights.

Sport, football, keep-fit and general exercise were, as ever, a big part of my Naval life and I even took up running; the views across the English Channel from the cliff road that ran from the back gate of HMS Osprey were absolutely stunning. But football was my passion and I played as much as I could. When you live with a load of young lads it's very easy to ask, "Who fancies a game of five-a-side?" and to be playing within half an hour. My most memorable match came courtesy of the annual air station sports day – Royal Naval Air Station Yeovilton vs Royal Naval Air Station Portland. Whilst I have another very good reason for disliking RNAS Yeovilton, which I won't bore you with, this particular day and my first visit to Yeovil gave me my first reason. I remember little of the game itself but I do recall being sent off. For some reason I wasn't in goal and played outfield; some oaf of a WAFU took every opportunity to kick me so I kicked him back. I only kicked him once but it was a bloody good one.

In common with all other Writers I formed part of the 'Duty Writer' roster which didn't involve much to be honest, other than making tea/coffee for the whole office and manning the Captain's Office during lunch-breaks. On one such occasion a junior officer, a Lieutenant, asked to see the Captain. Now I recognised this guy and had been told he was around and that he might pop in to see the Captain. He was none other than Prince Andrew, the Queen's second son. After a couple of minutes waiting he asked in a very condescending and patronising manner "How long will he be? I've got a very busy day."

I replied, "He's the Captain, sir; he's the busiest man here." He gave me a shitty look and continued to pace impatiently around the office until the Captain appeared; with his usual grace and politeness, characteristics the Queen's son clearly lacked, the Captain invited the junior officer into his personal office.

Prince Andrew had served on board HMS *Invincible* during the Falklands War the previous year. It was said, possibly unkindly, that he was kept so far from the action that he should have been awarded the Africa Star rather than the South Atlantic Medal. The popular press seemed to love Andy in those days, revelling in his playboy image, referring to him as 'Randy Andy'. He was cast as a 'normal bloke' for preferring to be called 'H' by officers more senior than himself. Maybe these journalists had served in the Royal Navy although I very much doubt it. Those who I met who had served with Andrew, and those who I met much later in life who had served on board HMY *Britannia*, had other names for him. Let's just say he wasn't as popular as he or the press made out. In short he was considered a complete narcissist although there were much shorter words used to describe him.

I'd started driving lessons in Peterborough at the age of 17 but I only managed to squeeze in a handful as I joined up around seven weeks after my 17th birthday. I decided to continue with my lessons and signed up with a local driving school. Learning to drive on Portland is a challenge; its roads are full of bends and there are far too many hills for a novice driver. My instructor would often say "next left" or "next right" but as every left or right was always a few yards after a bend I often missed the turning completely. My driving lessons came to an abrupt halt one day when my instructor asked if I'd been drinking. Sure, I'd had a couple of pints of lumpy cider in the mess bar before my lesson which in those days wasn't something that would be considered unacceptable (whilst quite rightly it is today). My instructor refused to take me on my lesson so I never spoke to him again.

There was a girl in the Service Certificate section of our office, let's call her Louise. Louise was in her early 20s so around four or five years older than me which seemed like quite an age gap, relatively speaking at least. Louise had fucked at least three of my mates and I wondered when it would be my turn. Louise and a few of the girls had arranged to meet some of the lads from the office, myself included, in a local pub one Sunday. I've been to many pubs for a Sunday sesh but this would be one Sunday that I would never forget.

After a few beers I was standing in the bar eating a classic of 1980s pub grub, chicken in a basket, when Louise came over to me and said, "I want a piece of your meat," with a look in her eye that suggested she had a particular fondness for meat. I gave her some chicken, being the gentleman that I am, and after eating it she said, "I'll be back for more of your meat later." We ended up back at one of her friends who lived off the base and in one of the bedrooms. I'd waited a long time for this. Despite much effort on my part to correct my ways I was still a virgin. Losing one's virginity is a spectacular event but this wasn't spectacular sex, for me or for Louise. When she got undressed and lay on the bed she said, "Oops, I nearly forgot," reached down and removed a blood-red tampon from between her legs. I'd waited nearly 18 years for this moment so I decided not to let that put me off although I'd argue that it did as my coming of age lasted only a couple of minutes and I came before

Louise had realised I'd even started. But practice makes perfect as they say and you have to start somewhere.

Talking of coming of age, I hit the grand old age of 18 in the July of 1983 and I arranged to meet up with Jock who, after HMS Pembroke, had been drafted to HMS Centurion in Gosport to commence his own Part Four training. We'd arranged to spend the weekend in Great Yarmouth with his mother, father and sister. Jock and I arranged to meet in London's Union Jack Club as we'd planned a night on the lash before meeting up with his folks the following day. We'd agreed not to drink on the train, me coming up from Portland and Jock coming up from Gosport, so that we'd commence drinking at the same time. I stuck by the agreement and after checking in at the UJC I waited, sober, in the reception area for my Scottish oppo. After an hour or so in walked Jock. I say 'walked' but he was completely bladdered and could barely stand upright; he'd had a few wets on the train... more than a few. Despite not keeping to our agreement and being some way ahead in the drinking stakes, we nonetheless had a great evening in London.

On the train to Great Yarmouth the following day I went up to the buffet car to get some wets in for me, Jock and his old fella (a prison offer and a great character). I was refused service which I took as a personal insult and argued the toss with the guy behind the counter, telling him in no uncertain terms that I was 18 and would prove it. As I reached into my pocket for my ID card which contained my date of birth Jock whispered in my ear, "You're still 17, mate, you're 18 tomorrow." It was the first and last time that I'd ever been refused service or asked my age. The rest of that weekend was a bit of a blur but I do remember that we all thoroughly enjoyed it.

I completed my task book with little difficulty having benefited from the immense experience and expert mentoring of my Scottish sandwich. Catriona Paton was, to most people, quite a fierce PO Wren but I admired and respected her enormously. Whilst Catriona was my 'Divisional Senior Rate', Paul Campbell was also hugely instrumental in giving me the best start in life as a young Writer. I was to move on to complete the second phase of my Part Four training and my next draft couldn't have been more different. Having spent the past six months on a helicopter base on the south coast of England I was drafted to HMS Neptune, a nuclear submarine base on the west coast of Scotland, some 500 miles away.

4. SPORTAHOLIC OR ALCOHOLIC

Situated towards the top of the Gare Loch at Faslane in the west of Scotland is the Clyde Submarine Base, otherwise known as HMS Neptune. The base is headed up by a Commodore, a 'temporary' rank in between Captain and Rear Admiral; if my memory serves me correct 'COMCLYDE' during my period was Commodore Morse, a true gentleman. The Clyde Submarine Base was the home of 'Polaris' SSBNs, the UK's ballistic nuclear submarines. Faslane is around five miles north of the town of Helensburgh and around twenty five miles west of Glasgow.

Not everyone was a fan of Polaris submarines, particularly the CND camp situated outside the base. The Campaign for Nuclear Disarmament was a big thing in the 1980s and we were all under the strictest of instructions not to befriend any of the women who inhabited this camp; I say 'camp' but essentially it was a collection of scruffy caravans close to the base and if you'd ever met any of the women you would understand that it was no hardship being banned from befriending any of them.

I was drafted for a period of between six and twelve months, dependent upon the availability of a seagoing ship on completion of my Part Four training. I was allocated to the CRO, the Combined Registry Office and the pen-pushing nerve centre of the base ('combined' because it also housed submarine squadron staff). Once again I was to be under the close supervision of a Petty Officer Wren Writer, Heather Pugsley. PO Wren Pugsley was in the same mould as PO Wren Paton in HMS Osprey, supremely knowledgeable and the best that a young Writer could wish for. I became 'CC4' which meant that in that section of the office I was subordinate to CC1 (Heather), CC2 and CC3. There was no CC5.

The job of the CRO was to process all of the Commodore's correspondence, including all classified information up to and including 'Secret'; squadron staff processed correspondence and classified material for the two submarine squadrons and the nearby 'X Registry', staffed by Writers, processed all 'Top Secret' material. The Navy ran on paperwork and I became intimately acquainted with 'packs' (Naval files), the Kalamazoo (pack numbering system), a manual typewriter, filing cabinets and other such delights. There were around a dozen people in the office consisting primarily of Naval Writers but also a couple of civil servants, to all intents and purposes civilian Writers. There was also an elderly couple, a lady and a gent who ran the postal section; whilst I couldn't understand most of what they said, they were very funny and absolutely delightful. All of the civil servants called me 'Shuggy' (or 'Shug'), Scottish for Hugh.

The CRO was a very busy place to work but also very enjoyable. It was six months since I had completed my professional training at HMS Pembroke and six months since I had done anything except pay accounting; this was no issue, however, as Heather Pugsley was as good a trainer as Catriona Paton.

I was allocated to a four-man mess although the other three beds changed frequently and on occasion I was the only person in my mess. Oppos had told me that HMS Neptune turns people into sportaholics or alcoholics, given the fantastic sporting facilities and plethora of drinking establishments in nearby Helensburgh, Dumbarton and Glasgow. HMS Neptune even had its very own dry ski slope! Sportaholic or alcoholic? Which would I become?

I quickly settled into a routine: office during the day, football during lunch break, a run after work and beer in the evening. The Writer branch is a sub-branch of the wider 'Supply and Secretariat' branch and the Chief Writer, Keith Hudson, managed the S&S football team. We had a pretty good team and as I grow older that football team has become better and better. Keith was a top bloke, despite being a Sunderland fan. Actually being a Sunderland fan was no problem; rather a fellow Writer called Tony was a problem; he supported a small, insignificant club in Hertfordshire; I can never remember its name but it begins with a W and, rather appropriately, they wear yellow.

Most evenings were spent in HMS Neptune's bar or in one of Helensburgh's hostelries. The bar on the base was pretty good and well used as there were no pubs outside the base within walking distance. Whilst there were quite a few Wrens based at HMS Neptune, my mates and I were only interested in civvies. Helensburgh had a handful of busy pubs but Dumbarton was where the action was. Actually the real action was a lot closer to home but we'll come on to that.

I joined HMS Neptune in September 1983 and as I had been 'volunteered' for Christmas and New Year duty I set off home to Peterborough in early December for a rather premature 'festive' leave period. My leave always consisted of working in the pub, drinking in the pub and going to watch Peterborough United play home and away. On one evening, pretty early on, there was a young girl in the pub playing pool. Sharon was the daughter of one of our regulars, not exceptionally pretty but young and friendly. A couple of my pub friends were playing with her, pool that is, and to start with I wasn't particularly interested. However a competitive edge kicked in, my interest increased and Sharon and I hit it off. It had taken me nearly 18 years to lose my cherry and I certainly didn't want to wait another 18 years for my second experience in that department.

A couple of days later Sharon and I were in the bar playing pool; the pub was closed as all-day opening was not permitted in England in those days, unlike Scotland which was far more civilised. We started mucking around and we ended up in the lounge bar with Sharon on the floor and me on top of her putting lumps of ice down her top (I had no particular ice fetish but we had a machine full of the stuff a yard or so away and it seemed like a good idea at the time). Things started getting interesting until my six-year-old sister Tess turned up. In an effort to shake her off I suggested we play hide and seek; I told Tess to count to one hundred whilst Sharon and I found somewhere to hide. I chose the ladies' toilets as I had an urgent need for a door with a lock on it. This was 1983 when pub toilets weren't as well appointed as they are now. The toilets in the Eight Bells were cold and they had hard, tiled floors. Sharon and I locked ourselves in one of the cubicles and commenced where we had left off before Tess had arrived in the lounge bar a few minutes earlier.

Sharon was lying on her back on the floor and shortly after I entered her, Tess started banging on the door shouting, "I know you're in there, I know you're in there Hughie, I'm telling Mum." I tried to carry on for as long as possible but as I had to slow down and keep quiet I decided to give up; silencing my little sis was now of more importance. So my second sexual experience, much like the first, was a lot shorter than I would have liked but it was so much more pleasurable than the first and as the painters weren't in there was no hint of the red stuff. Sharon and I got dressed sharpish and legged it after Tess who I wanted to silence before she got to my mother. Tess clearly didn't know what we were up to but I got to my mother first with my excuse of hiding in the toilet during hide and seek with my little sister; what a good brother was I for entertaining the little tyke?

On another occasion just after closing time and a little before midnight Sharon and I decided to have a chat in her car which was parked in our car park. A few minutes later we were hard at it, windows steamed up, when there was a knock on the window. I heard my old fella say, "You OK in there?" – cue for me to withdraw quickly and get dressed. Nothing was ever said about this, by my old man or myself, until around 20 years later when we were having a beer in his home town of Boyle in the west of Ireland. He had known all along what I was up to. Needless to say Sharon and I continued our close acquaintance until my leave finished when it was time for me to head off back to Scotland. Sharon and I never continued our 'relationship' but that was no bother as that particular leave period was very productive for this young, horny teenager.

About once a week I would form part of HMS Neptune's 'Duty Watch'. This consisted of routine patrols around the base and when submarines entered the base 'out of hours' I had to play my part in helping to bring them alongside. For someone who is not very good with ropes this was something of a challenge. I would stand on the jetty alongside other members of the Duty Watch whilst submariners would throw huge ropes towards us, ropes which had to be secured to the jetty on which we stood; our task was to pull the submarines in gently towards the jetty (with the aid of a tug on the other side of the submarine). I was never shown how to do this, quite incredibly when you consider what was on the other end of the rope, and on every occasion I shat myself. If I knew anything about ropes or wanted to play with them in any way I would have joined the Seamanship branch, not the Writer branch; pens yes, ropes no.

Over the Christmas and New Year, as mentioned, I was a member of the Duty Watch. In general it was a very quiet period and on every other day I was duty. On the alternative days life was pretty quiet as there were few people on the base, service or civilian. I had never spent New Year's Eve in Scotland and, despite being duty, I was actually looking forward to New Year's Eve this year.

All military bases were on alert in the 1980s due to the antics of the Irish Republican Army. Whilst they never attacked Naval bases we were all at risk to some extent, particularly HMS Neptune owing to its high profile. All military bases were subject to 'security states', the normal state of alert being 'Bikini Black'. A slightly higher state was 'Bikini Black Alpha' which was a fairly non-specific threat, above that was 'Bikini Amber' which meant an attack was imminent and above that, the top threat, was 'Bikini Red' which probably meant it was too late and you were already dead. We also had a 'Bandit Alarm' which referred to a base-specific threat, generally an illegal incursion and something that probably only ever sounded in HMS Neptune. The Bandit Alarm consisted of a very loud alarm accompanied by the words "BANDIT, BANDIT, BANDIT". Effectively this paralysed the base for the duration of the incursion which could last several hours.

An hour or so before midnight on 31 December the base received a telephone call informing us that there was a bomb on the nuclear jetty and that it was timed to explode at midnight. The Duty Watch, together with the Officer of the Day and members of the Ministry of Defence Police, legged it down to the jetty. We searched for any suspicious packages with the single instruction of not to touch anything we found. Nothing was found so a few minutes before midnight we retreated a hundred yards or so back from the jetty. At the stroke of midnight a bell sounded throughout the base, courtesy of HMS Neptune's PA system, followed by a rendition of Auld Lang Syne; I was crouched down almost on my knees behind a wheelie bin next to a Ministry of Defence Constable who offered me his hand and in a very strong west of Scotland accent chirped, "Happy New Year, son." This was not how I expected to see in the New Year.

A couple of minutes after midnight the Bandit Alarm sounded – the local caravan dwellers, our CND friends, had secured entry into the base via the perimeter fence using bolt cutters to cut a large hole. They were clearly responsible for the hoax bomb call knowing it would ensure that the skeleton Duty Watch would be at the opposite end of the base, down on the jetty. To be fair to the great unwashed they were not a significant security threat; all they wanted was to cause maximum disruption; the consequent court appearances and fines were of no concern to them. A few members of the Duty Watch and a Ministry of Defence Constable escorted them to and out of the main gate. I and another member of the Duty Watch were given the coveted job of guarding the hole in the fence against any further incursions. I spent four hours in the dark, between 0100 and 0500, looking at that hole; my comrade in arms, actually we weren't trusted with arms, had about as much personality as the hole in question so conversation was limited. My first few hours of the New Year, spent in a country that knows how to celebrate New Year properly, were not how I had imagined them to be.

The Bandit Alarms were too frequent for our liking – at least one every couple of weeks. As these alarms were established for incursions from the likes of the IRA, the Base Commander decided that we needed a new alarm to reflect the fact that the threat posed was very minimal. It wasn't as if these ladies were storming the nuclear submarines armed with AK-47s and Armalites; they just wanted to disrupt our day-to-day activities and piss us off. The Base Commander decided to replace the Bandit Alarm with an alternative alarm to be known as the Vermin Alarm, 'vermin' being short for 'very minimal' to reflect the minimal threat posed. So for a few weeks, on every occasion that our peace-loving neighbours decided to breach the perimeter fence and enter the base, the PA system would blare out, "VERMIN, VERMIN, VERMIN." Not sure who complained but even in those days, less PC than the days of today, this was considered unacceptable. After a few weeks we reverted back to the Bandit Alarm. It was fun while it lasted.

Sometime in January 1984 a request came into the base for volunteers to appear as extras in the Scottish soap opera 'Take The High Road' (Emmerdale but with Scottish accents and lots more water). I had never heard of this particular programme but was well up for a day out of the office on location courtesy of STV. Around a dozen of us headed off to Loch Lomond and the scene we were to appear in centred around a sponsored swim in that rather famous loch. Scotland is a cold country; it is particularly cold in January; in fact it is bloody freezing in January. On the way down to the loch after the bus dropped us off I walked past a priest and, given my Catholic upbringing, it was only natural and polite to say, "Hello Father."

He looked at me oddly, smirking, whilst one of my oppos remarked, "You're a twat mate, he's an actor, not a fucking priest." How was I to know?

Apparently the members of a local scout group were meant to be playing the extras in this scene but they withdrew because of the cold and the potential for adverse health consequences. By fuck it was cold. Later on in my career I would be 'awarded' the 'Blue Nose' certificate for crossing the Arctic Circle but that was a sauna compared to Loch Lomond in January. We had to cover ourselves from head to toe with Vaseline to protect from the cold and jump in when instructed. The scene was edited to appear as if we were swimming the full length of the loch but we only swam for a few minutes in one direction and then to the side. We were 'on location' for several hours and the cold aside we all had a great time. STV fed and watered us; in fact the 'water' was that famous Scottish stuff normally sold in bottles but today it was mixed with tea and coffee. We were given a number of STV mementoes + £30 each which was the standard fee for extras at the time; they weren't allowed to pay us any less as that would incur the wrath of the actors' union Equity.

A few weeks later the girls in the office were chatting about the scene in which I appeared as it had aired the previous evening; apparently the camera had focused on me for a few seconds as I was swimming immediately behind the star actress. The local paper carried a story on its front page (clearly a quiet news week) of said actress losing the top half of her bikini whilst swimming; apparently this caused much merriment amongst those around her and those on the side of the loch with good eyesight; given I wasn't a particularly strong swimmer all of my concentration was on getting back to land alive so despite being closest to the action I missed the best part.

Most of my weekends were now spent further afield either in Dumbarton or Glasgow; I will be forever grateful to the west of Scotland for the opportunities it afforded. It was much easier to trap (pull) in Scotland. It wasn't that girls were easier than in England, far from it, but they were friendlier and would always say yes if you asked them to dance in a night-club. Jock had told me this would be the case and he was right; if they didn't want to progress they would make that clear but as I was never confident in asking girls to dance for fear of rejection, Scotland was the ideal place for me to live. Dumbarton was good, Glasgow was better but even better was somewhere much closer to home.

5. WASHING POWDER

One of the civil servants who worked in the CRO asked why I didn't go to the Drumfork Club. When I asked what town that was in he answered, "It's on the Naval estate, where all the wives live." Initially I couldn't see the relevance of this until he pointed out the obvious, I suppose: "Where do you think the wives go when their husbands are at sea?" At any one time there was a Polaris submarine at sea – the other three would be doing other stuff but one was guaranteed to be at sea 24/7. One hundred and forty blokes at sea for six months with no contact with their loved ones and guaranteed not to pop up in the Gare Loch without warning. The following weekend I headed to the Churchill Estate with an oppo and located the Drumfork Club, a building so lacking in any sort of character or appeal it screamed at you to walk on by; we walked in.

I was with an oppo called Lee, one of the smoothest operators I had ever met, and we trapped within five minutes of sitting down. Lee was the most upfront bloke with women that I had ever met: polite, to the point and most important of all, good looking. He was great to go ashore with and on this particular evening he started chatting to the two women closest to us; within a minute one of them said, "Our husbands are on the Repulse... Port Watch." They were telling us their husbands were at sea. Polaris submarines don't suddenly reappear; if they go away for six months they go away for six months; in fact they disappear for six months, that is their raison d'être. Some of the wives would display OMO washing powder boxes in their windows, meaning variously 'Old Man Out', 'On My

Own' or 'Old Man Overseas'. Lee and I had a good night; we went back to the same house, him with the good-looking one and me with the other (she wasn't too bad to be fair and I wasn't complaining – I was still serving my apprenticeship). It was often like that, particularly when we went clubbing in Dumbarton, but feeding off Lee's leftovers was very productive for me; I never once objected.

Myself, Lee and another mate Steve spent a weekend in Kirkcudbright (pronounced 'Ki...coo...bree' or something like that). Kirkcudbright is a small town in the south west of Scotland, close to the larger and better known town of Dumfries. Steve owned a Vauxhall Opel so he did the driving. I have no idea why we chose Kirkcudbright but we had a fantastic weekend. Whilst most Scots are naturally wary of English accents they are strangely drawn to them, especially in small towns; they want to know what the fuck you're doing there, in the nicest way possible of course. The people of Scotland are very friendly, none more so than the townsfolk of Kirkcudbright, especially the girls. We all made good use of our B&B accommodation that weekend and certainly got our money's worth.

Not sure why but Lee and I never went to Glasgow together. I tended to go with football mates to watch either Celtic or Rangers, depending on who was playing at home. Coming from an Irish family my footballing preference in those parts was Celtic although being military most of my mates were fans of Rangers. We tended to visit Glasgow at least once or twice a month. All-day opening in Scottish pubs was a huge novelty for us English lads and that novelty never wore off. Mind you, I soon discovered than in 50% of Glasgow's pubs I was hated for my Irish ethnicity and in the other 50% I was hated for my choice of career.

We would also go to occasional concerts in Glasgow. On one such occasion a few of us went to see a fellow townie of mine, Paul Young. From memory he performed in the Glasgow Palace, although it might have been called the Glasgow Palais. Either way the place was jammed full with squealing teenage girls, most of whom were far too young for us. I lost count of how many I saw faint but it was well into double figures. Much as I liked Paul Young our machismo took over so we disappeared into a neighbouring watering hole well before the concert finished.

In early 1984 Jock broke his leg whilst playing football and as a consequence spent a couple of months at home in Alloa on sick leave. On a number of weekends I would go across to Alloa, a particularly unattractive town located very close to the considerably more attractive Ochil Hills. Jock and his family would often remark, "If you can see the Ochils it's gonna rain; if you can't see them it's pashing doon." Jock's father 'Big Martin' was a serving prison officer at nearby Glenochil prison, in those days a Young Offenders' Institution.

One afternoon the two Martins and I decided to watch a film, a film that they had both seen before. 'Scum' starred a very young Ray Winstone and portrayed life in an exceptionally tough borstal. Before we started watching it the older Martin went into the kitchen to make a cup of tea and the younger Martin remarked to me, "We'll get another cuppa halfway through, you'll see." Scum is a very powerful film and contains many quite brutal scenes. Halfway through the film, or at least a good way through, a group of lads went into the prison greenhouse. Big Martin got up and asked, "Tea, lads?" The scene that followed was a brutal, graphic portrayal of male rape. Our tea arrived just as the scene ended, which the older Martin missed. Prison officers may be tough, particularly the Scottish variety, but they're still human.

Martin senior rarely talked of daily life as a prison officer. However his son often told me stuff, in particularly of how his father worked in the punishment wing. Glenochil held some of the worst, possibly THE worst, young offenders in Scotland, many of whom were transferred to Glenochil as they couldn't be tamed elsewhere. Those who ended up in the punishment wing were often the baddest of the bad. I recall Jock telling me of how on occasion his father would return home with his uniform covered in blood, the result of having to deal with a suicide victim; the clothes would go in the washing machine and nothing would be said. Martin senior was a great bloke who I admired immensely and I take my hat off to him and his colleagues for doing a job that most of us wouldn't be able to do for an hour, let alone a full career.

Jock and I would spend our weekends in Alloa or nearby Stirling drinking and chasing girls; we were always successful at the former and occasionally successful at the latter. Jock had one leg covered in plaster but that didn't hinder him or our efforts. One 'morning after' I woke up in Jock's bed, wondering what the hell I was doing there and where the hell my oppo was. I made some comment and Jock appeared from the floor on the other side of the bed, head just visible mumbling, "Ya pashed ma bed, ya fucker." Now I rather liked Jock's younger sister and I particularly liked his parents so the potential embarrassment was of enormous concern to me. I asked Jock not to tell his sister or his parents and he promised faithfully that he wouldn't. Big Martin explained that Jock and I had arrived home bladdered, went up into his bedroom, got undressed and then started arguing and almost fighting. The older Martin broke up the argument and told us to go to bed; I guess he was rather skilled in dealing with gobby teenagers albeit normally sober (and tougher) ones.

Half an hour or so later we were all sat at the kitchen table eating breakfast. We chatted away and during one rare moment of silence Jock's lovely mum said to me, "Don't worry, Porky," (O'Rourke... Pork), "I've put the sheets in the washing machine... they'll soon be clean." My embarrassment was complete and I said little else for the remainder of the meal.

My weekends in central Scotland would end on a Sunday evening when I would catch a train from Alloa to get to Glasgow in time to catch the last train back to Helensburgh. If I missed the train I would be late for work the following morning and on Captain's Table for being 'adrift', something I wanted to avoid at all costs. Jock and I would spend a few hours drinking in Alloa's finest taverns before I would catch my train. On one particular Sunday the weather was awful – freezing cold with snow blizzards the like of which I had never experienced. As my departure time neared a number of locals advised me not to travel, telling me that there were problems with the trains, particularly those departing from Glasgow. Jock and I had had a lot of beer and took the brave decision for me to stay another night. No mobile phones or internet in those days and I decided not to bother looking for a public phone to ring the base; I would make my excuses early the next morning.

Jock and I then hit the vodka really hard. I don't like spirits and this was my first introduction to vodka. The pair of us got absolutely bladdered and decided to visit the Chinese takeaway prior to heading back to his. Girls not saying no when asked to dance and all-day licensing hours were two of my favourite things about Scotland; another was the ability to order chicken curry and fried rice in one pot so that you could mix them together and eat in the taxi on the way home (so much more civilised than in England where you have two pots, one with curry and one with rice, which are difficult to balance at the best of times let alone after a night on the beer). We didn't have enough money for the food so I offered to leave my kit bag, something clearly I would have to collect in the morning prior to setting off back to Helensburgh. The Chinese lady agreed and off Jock and I went with our curries.

The next morning I collected my kit bag, paid for our meals and headed back west (for the following 20+ years the Chinese lady always remembered me and my kit bag). Getting to Glasgow was problematic and getting from there to Helensburgh was even more problematic but achieved nonetheless. There were no buses and no taxis due to the iced-up roads so I had to walk the five miles up the loch to HMS Neptune with a large, heavy kit bag (if I wanted to do this sort of stuff I would have joined the Royal Marines). I was absolutely shitting myself as I was late for work already and I hadn't let anyone know; clearly I was going to blame the weather but in the military there is no excuse for being adrift. Eventually I got back to base – freezing, knackered and cacking myself. When I got to the main gate I started to splutter my excuses to the Chief Petty Officer on duty, shivering with cold and with the expectation that I was in very serious trouble. "You needn't have bothered, young fella," he remarked, "the base is shut today… fucking weather is shite."

I decided to restart my driving lessons and enrolled with a local driving school. There were no roundabouts in Helensburgh and very few traffic lights, hence all of my lessons were 'double' lessons as they involved driving the eight or nine miles to Dumbarton, practising there and returning to Faslane on completion. My instructor was great although I do not recall him giving me much actual instruction. He would often look out of his window and upon spotting an attractive member of the opposite sex would say, "Would you have a look at that." As soon as I complied with the instruction he would shout, "For fuck's sake…concentrate on the road will you!"

On the subject of driving Steve, Lee and I would often drive around the west of Scotland in the Vauxhall Opel (Steve driving of course but to be fair he did own the car). Inveraray on the western shore of Loch Fyne and the surrounding area were particular favourites of ours. Scotland is a beautiful country, particularly the west; western Scotland's hills and water are quite breathtaking in their beauty and combined they are truly spectacular. It wasn't all beer, football and girls.

One of my more memorable evenings in Scotland was spent in a pub in Rhu, a small village situated on the eastern shore of the Gare Loch on the road towards Helensburgh from Faslane. It was Sunday 10 June 1984, not really a day for going too far afield. England were playing Brazil in Rio de Janeiro, a friendly which England amazingly won 2-0. The match will always be remembered for THAT goal, a wonderful solo effort scored by the incredibly talented John Barnes. Watching England beat Brazil in a Scottish pub, alongside English mates and outnumbered by Brazil-supporting Scotsmen, was an event worth paying for. Priceless.

Whilst Glasgow attracted much of our attention we also paid several visits to Edinburgh. I went a couple of times to watch Hibernian and Hearts at their respective home grounds of Easter Road and Tynecastle; as a football fan I wanted to visit as many football grounds as possible. Jock also introduced me to the delights of Alloa Athletic and, more frequently, Dundee. A particularly memorable weekend was a visit towards the end of my time in HMS Neptune and that was with a couple of mates to attend the Edinburgh Military Tattoo. We booked into a cheap hotel and spent the evening, after a few beers of course, in Edinburgh Castle. Edinburgh is a wonderful city and its majestic castle combined with the Military Tattoo makes for a quite awesome event. More beer followed of course, courtesy of the huge number of watering holes in nearby Rose Street. Whatever else happened that night, truthfully, is not in the memory (it never was).

Talking of Jock and Dundee I vividly remember one 'Derby Weekend'. The football schedulers used to organise all of the respective derbies for the same day – Celtic v Rangers, Hibernian v Hearts and Dundee v Dundee United among others. I'd arranged to meet Jock at Glasgow Central to catch a train to Dundee. I was really looking forward to my first taste of a Dundee derby as Jock had mentioned the atmosphere a couple of hundred times in the short time that I'd known him.

So there we were, standing minding our own business on the platform, waiting for the Dundee train. Across the platform a train pulled in and a huge number of Celtic fans swarmed out. Now Jock was wearing his red, white and blue Dundee scarf. Some Celtic fans spotted this colour combination, anathema to the green half of Glasgow, and proceeded to hurl insults towards us. The sensible thing to do of course would have been to ignore the jibes and hope their owners would remain on the other side. Jock proceeded to hurl his own insults across the platform and in response around ten or so Celtic fans decided to make their way across the bridge to where we were standing. As they approached their aggression appeared to diminish a little; as they got close they realised that the blue in Jock's scarf was a different, darker shade of blue to the blue of Rangers, the subject of their hate (Dundee are known as the 'Dark Blues' for a reason).

One of the Celtic lads said, "Sorry pal, we thought you were the Hun, good luck today."

Jock replied, "I fucking hate Rangers, even more than you."

As the lads walked away a couple gave Jock the thumbs up and one remarked, "Good man."

Jock responded, "And I fucking hate you lot too, more than Rangers hate you."

I shat myself. This is where I would die, on the platform of Glasgow Central railway station, courtesy of fans from what hitherto had been my favourite Scottish football club. One lad, a big specimen, walked back towards us and up against Jock's face said, "Bet you don't hate them more than we do," and walked off. The rest of the day proved to be more peaceful and ended up as expected – Dundee lost to the team they call 'the Arabs', or 'fucking Arabs' to be more precise. It's worth mentioning that whilst the footballing rivalry in Dundee is intense on derby day, the atmosphere in the pubs amongst the two different sets of supporters is second to none, before and after the match. To this day, every weekend, I still look out for the Dee's results.

I completed my training by working the various sections of the office and was duly signed off as competent to join the seagoing fleet. I had requested a Plymouth-based Leander-class frigate and I got my wish – I was to join HMS *Charybdis* in the September of 1984. I absolutely loved Scotland and as expected I had become something of a sportaholic AND an alcoholic. My draft came too soon for me to complete my driving lessons but that was something I could restart after my 18-month sea draft; I did actually sit a driving test but it was far too early and I failed (who knew you weren't allowed to drive across a zebra crossing whilst an old lady was still using it?). Actually the test started as it went on; I drove out of the Test Centre, turned left into the main road and stopped immediately behind a lorry that appeared, to me at least, to be waiting behind a few other vehicles at traffic lights. After a couple of minutes the examiner asked, "Are you going to pull out at some stage?"

I replied, "But he's in the queue behind the lights."

To which the examiner replied, correctly as it turned out, "He's parked up, son, you're in a lay-by."

Scotland had been fabulous but I had joined the Royal Navy to go to sea and to see the world; I'd never been abroad and I couldn't wait to get going.

6. HANDS TO HARBOUR STATIONS

Prior to joining HMS *Charybdis* I had to complete a few 'PJTs' (pre-joining training). My PJTs consisted of Fire-Fighting at HMS Cochrane on the east coast of Scotland, Damage Control back at HMS Raleigh, First Aid at HMS Excellent on Whale Island in Portsmouth and Naval Military Training at HMS Cambridge on the south coast of Devon. I learnt once again that fire, floods and guns are not my forte and that lesson was also learnt by the Leading Regulator who drove me across to HMS Cochrane as he too was off to sea and had to complete the same training course. We chatted continuously on the way across from west to east but on the way back, after I'd singed his hair after opening a hatch too early, he never spoke to me.

'Naval Military Training' might sound a tad oxymoronic to some, especially any Army types reading this, but every ship had a small team of sailors from different branches who were given additional instruction in the use of SLR rifles (above and beyond what was taught in basic training) and also riot control, should it ever be required in a foreign port. The training only lasted a week and took place at HMS Cambridge, the Royal Navy's Gunnery School in Wembury, just along the coast from Plymouth. Actually a bit more practice gave me much more confidence in handling and using SLRs; a shame they couldn't be self-cleaning as well as self-loading but never mind. I particularly enjoyed the 'riot control', especially playing the part of a rioter; I just pretended I was on the streets of the Creggan in Derry and got into character (I reckon I would have been a far better rioter than a soldier).

HMS *Charybdis* was a Leander-class frigate, one of 26 in the class and the workhorses of the Royal Navy in the 1980s. Originally Leanders were fitted with a large 4.5-inch gun and the Seacat missile system. Refitted Leanders such as HMS *Charybdis* were armed with the latest anti-aircraft (Seawolf) and anti-ship (Exocet) missile systems; the large guns were removed as the Royal Navy had believed such beasts were a thing of the past (costly lessons learnt during the Falklands proved otherwise). Leanders carried one aircraft, the incredibly versatile Lynx helicopter and the hangar and flight deck were located at the back of the ship (stern).

On the day I joined the *Cherry B*, as she was affectionately known, I located my messdeck and, kit bag in tow, I fumbled my way through the hatch on 2 Deck and down the metal ladder into 3EZ mess, my home for the next 18 months. A Cook (always known as Cooks rather than chefs in those days) was sat opposite on a bench and with a friendly face looked up and in a strong Liverpool accent said, "Hello mate, who are you?" I introduced myself as Hugh O'Rourke and he replied, "Ah, Rocky O'Rourke eh? I'm Scouse – pleased to meet you." Phil McCann, Scouse to you and me, was a Leading Cook (equivalent to a corporal in the lesser services) and, as I would soon find out, was one of the leading lights of '3 Easy' mess. Only Scousers and O'Rourkes remember the character Rocky O'Rourke from the kids' TV drama of the same name in the 1970s; Rocky was a cheeky young scally who lived in Liverpool and the TV series was based on the book *A Pair of Jesus Boots* by Sylvia Sherry. This young Rocky didn't own a pair of Jesus boots (sandals) but I did own a couple of pairs of steaming boots, shortened on board simply to 'bats'.

The Junior Rates' messdecks on Leander-class frigates were all pretty similar, consisting as they did of a small 'mess square' at one end with bunks, referred to by all and sundry as 'pits', running back from the communal space in threes. The middle bunks folded to create a seat with the bottom bunks which was a massive disadvantage if you were allocated one of the bottom two bunks in the mess square. I was allocated the top bunk in the mess square, not good for privacy or peace and quiet but great for watching the continuous supply of porn on the telly. Most of 3EZ's inhabitants smoked and this was another disadvantage of having a bed in the mess square; passive smoking wasn't talked about back then but over the following 18 months I must have smoked as many Blue Liners as the most hardened of smokers.

The mess square consisted of a red upholstered bench along the bulkhead (wall), similar to the type of bench that you will find in a traditional pub. Opposite this bench were the three nearest beds and a couple of lockers. Other than a TV, a video tape recorder, a few chairs and a small table, that was about it. The fridge was full of beer and the stowage underneath the bench seating was full of pornographic magazines, or 'scud mags' as they were known.

3EZ housed all members of the 'Supply and Secretariat' branch other than Senior Ratings (Petty Officers and above) who had their own messes. Stokers, Seamen, Communicators and the rest all had their own messdecks whilst commissioned officers, of all ranks and branches, shared the 'Wardroom' (although they all slept in individual cabins on a higher deck).

As the ship was due to sail the following day for two weeks' exercise off Portland, to be overseen by my old mate the Flag Officer Sea Training and his staff, my first evening was very busy with lads returning from leave and new arrivals such as myself. Everyone seemed to have a nickname – Scouse, Jack (Daw), Brum, Jan, Chuck, Soapy, Jock, Buck, Smudge, Tommo, Taff, Larry and of course a new baby Scribes called Rocky. I was introduced by Scouse to everyone as Rocky and to the 220 members of *Cherry B*'s Ship's Company, I would never be known by any other name. Actually that isn't quite precise; Stevie Milne, a Scot, always called me Shug.

The following morning, before, during and after breakfast, there was a huge amount of activity. The ship prepared for sea, 'sailing' as it is always referred to. Men were scurrying around everywhere in the narrow corridors known as 'flats' that ran the length of the ship. The noise, the smell and later the movement are what I remember most from my first day and week at sea. I couldn't wait to go to sea – this is what I'd been waiting for.

The Ship's Office was very small and contained two bench-like desks secured to the bulkheads on either side, one on the left for two men and one on the right for two others. Taking up a great deal of space, given its scarcity, was a photocopier on top of a small filing cabinet up against the bulkhead opposite the door, a door that had a top part and a bottom part. The top part of the door could be swung back and secured to the bulkhead in the flat whilst the bottom part had a small shelf at the top for members of the Ship's Company to complete any necessary paperwork, or simply lean on whilst loafing if they had a minute or two to stop by for a chat.

The office was managed by a Petty Officer Writer by the name of Bill Bailey (Bill being a nickname) and my fellow Writer was a bearded chap by the name of Paul Davey. One of the ship's junior seamanship officers, Sub Lieutenant Smith, a very pleasant Scot, held the part-time job of 'Corro', short for 'Correspondence Officer'; it was his job to liaise with the Supply Officer and the Captain on all matters of official correspondence (most junior officers held additional roles in addition to their full-time roles). Paul and I sat together on the left-hand side of the office, pretty much side by side if you ignore the filing cabinet underneath the desk between us, whilst Bill and S/Lt Smith, when he was there, sat on the other side with a filing cabinet between them; Paul and I faced one bulkhead and had our backs to Bill and the Corro who faced the opposite bulkhead. The Corro's job was a bit of an odd one as he had no real management responsibility for us Writers; the POWTR reported to the Supply Officer whilst Paul and I also reported to the Supply Officer albeit via the POWTR. Paul and I split the pay accounts between us and also the correspondence and service record duties.

"Special Sea Dutymen close up; assume Damage Control State 3 Condition Yankee; hands to Harbour Stations, hands out of the rig of the day clear off the upper deck; close all screen doors and hatches." Those immortal words were piped throughout every single ship prior to sailing. This was it, this was sea time, this is what it was all about.

A couple of hours later I was in the toilets, referred to as 'heads' in every ship and shore establishment throughout the Royal Navy (and also in every sailor's home as it happens). This was it. This was seasickness and I did not like it one bit.

The ship's movement was very hard to contend with, as were the noise and smell, so I spent much of the first day, and indeed the next couple of weeks, in the heads puking up. When it was very rough, it was very rough. The Ship's Office was located in '2D', the deck above my mess and a bit further forward. Working and sleeping at the front end of a Leander isn't ideal because when the ship moves in rough weather the front bounces up and down more violently than the middle. When it got really rough we would stow everything away and go to bed as all pits contained thick leather straps that were used to prevent sailors from falling out. Whilst many of our shipmates would take the piss out of us Writers for disappearing when it got rough, my usual response would be, "You don't see any Dabbers (Seamen) in the Paint Shop during roughers do you?" The Paint Shop was even more forward than the Ship's Office; no idea why it was called a 'shop' as it was a store rather than a shop but it wasn't a place that I ever visited or cared to.

Movement was constant – ships move (kind of the point) and the combination of Naval exercises and rough seas amplified that movement. Noise was constant courtesy of the ship's machinery, 220 men and the sea. Smells were constant, primarily the combination of men, machinery and fuel. That combination of constant movement, constant noise and constant smell was very difficult to contend with and for the first time in my short Naval career I felt really under the weather.

The food on board was pretty good and from what I hear so much better than the fayre served up in today's Navy. There were two galleys, the Junior Rates' galley and the Senior Rates' galley (the food was cooked by the same Cooks but Senior Rates and Junior Rates were not allowed to eat together). In addition to three cooked meals of breakfast, lunch and dinner we also had 'Stand Easy' in mid-morning and '9 O'Clockers' in the evening. We had a NAAFI on board that sold nutty, crisps and the usual snacks plus a number of other essentials; essentially the NAAFI was a small shop but so small it only had a counter. Two civilians managed the NAAFI: the Canteen Manager known as the 'Canman' who lived with the Petty Officers and his Canteen Assistant who lived with us S&S (never quite sure why it was called a 'canteen' but it served its purpose). We weren't wanting for food and the benefit of sharing the same mess as the Cooks is that we knew what to eat and, more importantly, what not to eat (if anyone pissed them off, Stokers usually, they would add extra 'ingredients' for the offending mess members). As with most things matelots had nicknames for their favourite foods among which were 'babies' heads' (steak and kidney suet pudding), 'cheesy hammy eggy' (cheese, ham and egg on toast), 'shit on a raft' (kidneys on toast) and 'snorkers' (sausages). Food was simply referred to as 'scran'.

Talking of nicknames, matelots also had nicknames for the various branches and sub-branches. Marine Engineers were known as Stokers or Spanner Wankers, Electrical Engineers were Greenies, Seamen were Dabbers, Electronic Warfare specialists were Gollies, Stewards were Flunkies, Stores Accountants were Jack Dusties, Medics were Scablifters, Aircraft Handlers were Chockheads, Regulators were Crushers, Sonar Specialists were Tas-Apes, Radio/Radar types were

Pinkies, the PTI was a Clubswinger and the Padre was a God Botherer. Writers were simply known as 'Scribes' or, less frequently, Scribblers. Most of these I learnt in basic training as they are used throughout the Royal Navy, not just on seagoing ships.

Every Junior Rates' mess had a fridge containing small cans of beer (the Petty Officers and Chief Petty Officers' messes had draught beer as did the Wardroom). The allowance was 'three cans, per day, per man, perhaps' and the allowance and the associated payment were administered by the mess 'Beer Bosun'. There were 25 lads in our mess so we were allowed 75 cans of beer per day. If there were, say, 60 cans of beer in the fridge at the beginning of the day, only 15 could be issued as 75 was the maximum. Of course 75 cans were purchased every day by our Beer Bosun and the Beer Bosuns of every other mess; the 'excess' was stowed underneath the mess seating with the porn where it would remain until such time as it was consumed or, horror of horrors, confiscated in punishment for any beer related transgression or other misdemeanour (how on earth did the Reggies know where we stored our illicit beer?). Courage Sparkling Beer (CSB as it was known) and McEwan's Export were the options – nothing else.

The 'Reggies' on board consisted of a 'Master At Arms' (CPO rank) and a Leading Regulator. The 'Jossman' or simply the 'Joss' as the MAA was colloquially known (not to his face) and his Leading Reg, Nobby Noble, occupied the office adjacent to the Ship's Office. MAA Joss Murfin was a frequent visitor to our office, for both 'official' business and, more often, just to chew the fat with the POWTR. In addition to their disciplinary duties the Regulators administered all shore leave, such as issuing travel warrants, so the proximity of their office to ours made sense as we dealt with the financial side of travel and allowances. In later years the Writer branch would assume the Regulators' travel responsibilities, leaving them free to concentrate on the disciplinary stuff, hence their modern name of Royal Navy Police.

Washing was referred to as 'dhobey' and we had the obligatory Chinese laundry on board where two natives of Hong Kong washed and ironed all clothes, for a price of course (all ships had Chinese laundries). All members of the Ship's Company had a 'dhobey number' which was the last four digits of one's service number (decades after leaving the Royal Navy ex-matelots will always remember their service numbers, even if they're out on the lash and too pissed to remember their own names). The Chinese lads lived right at the arse end of the ship, far more uncomfortable than the front end and certainly a lot noisier. Their command of the English language was reasonably good, unless you had a query with your bill or some crushed buttons in which case they reverted to Cantonese.

Captain's Rounds occurred every night although these rounds were carried out by the Officer of the Day (OOD) and the Duty Senior Rate. These were much less formal than in training establishments and so long as the mess decks were clean and tidy, that was it. On rare occasions the Captain would conduct rounds personally and on these occasions the toothbrushes would come out to clean all mess decks and heads (toilets/bathrooms).

A warship's 'Captain' isn't necessarily of Captain rank (four gold rings). Leander-class frigates were commanded by Commanders (three gold rings) whilst aircraft carriers were commanded by Captains and ships smaller than Leanders were commanded by Lieutenant Commanders (two and a 'half' gold rings) and even smaller ships by Lieutenants (two gold rings). The Captain's deputy on board was the 'First Lieutenant', an officer of Lieutenant Commander rank who was universally known as 'The Jimmy', the case on all ships. The Supply Department was headed up by a Supply Officer, my Divisional Officer, an officer of Lieutenant rank. My SO was Simon Whalley, a tremendous boss who managed the Supply Department with great efficiency and exemplary fairness.

During the day we wore 'Number 8' uniform which comprised thick blue woolly pullys, rough blue shirts, rough blue trousers and steaming bats/boots. 'Evening Rig' consisted of white fronts, black No. 2 trousers and steaming boots/bats (no shoes for safety reasons). Everyone showered twice a day, before breakfast and before dinner; peer pressure ensured that this practice was universal. The heads containing the sinks, showers, etc. lacked any sort of privacy but no one cared – this was life at sea.

The day-to-day routine in the office was of course similar to what I had experienced in HMS Osprey and HMS Neptune, although accompanied by more noise, more smell and more movement. It isn't easy working when your workplace is constantly moving, side to side, up and down, often violently and without notice; this of course also applied to eating, showering (no baths on board) and just about everything else including toilet activities. But I would get used to it, as I was assured by everyone with whom I came into contact.

On occasion the office was quiet as we industriously plied our trade. However most of the time we chatted as we worked and the office had lots of visitors, during official times of opening for queries and at all other times, mainly fellow Senior Rates who came to have a chat with our POWTR, Bill Bailey. Bill was a great character and he seemed to attract other great characters from the Petty Officer and Chief Petty Officer messes. One of our most frequent visitors was Petty Officer Cook 'General Grant'. POCK Grant was a big man with a big beard and a big character. More about General later – and also his daughter Connie.

My seasickness carried on for the whole two weeks and despite having waited two years to actually go to sea, I was very happy to berth alongside in Devonport Dockyard a couple of weeks after leaving; the cessation of movement came as some relief to me and I guess a few other newbies. We all had a weekend's leave and I travelled to Luton where my mother now lived after splitting up (again) from my father who remained in Peterborough. By the time I got 'home', I say home although it was my first visit to this particular house, I was feeling very ill. My mother took me to see a doctor the following day and it turned out I had some sort of virus and a mouth full of ulcers; whether or not I was ill when I joined the ship or whether the uncomfortable surroundings had made me ill no one knew. The doctor signed me off for a week which later became two weeks. In one sense I wanted to return to my ship as soon as possible as that was where I should be but in another sense I dreaded going back to sea with all the associated discomfort. Maybe I'd feel better once the ulcers had disappeared and I'd had a couple of weeks' rest.

I informed the ship of my illness as soon as possible but thereafter I had to liaise with the Regulators in HMS Drake, the shore establishment that forms part of Plymouth's Devonport Dockyard. Once I was fit to return to the *Cherry B* there was a slight problem – the ship had sailed and the good folk of HMS Drake weren't quite sure where she was (somewhere in or around the Irish Sea apparently). As a consequence I had to return to Devonport and report to the Regulating Office.

When I duly reported to the Reg Office I was informed that the *Cherry B* was on its way up to the west of Scotland and I would rejoin her in Loch Fyne. A travel warrant was issued for me to travel from Plymouth to Tarbet in the west of Scotland. When I suggested to the RPO that Tarbet was a village on the banks of the landlocked Loch Lomond, a loch that I had previously been rather closely acquainted with, he replied, "Piss off, smartarse." When I suggested that maybe he meant Tarbert which was situated adjacent to Loch Fyne, further south west and rather crucially a sea loch accessible to ships, he scratched his head, muttered the word 'fuck' a number of times, ripped up the warrant, wrote out a new one and wished me a safe journey, or something not like that. Had I not possessed a decent knowledge of Scottish lochs and their whereabouts, courtesy of Steve Pugh and his

Vauxhall Opel, not to mention that famous Scottish soap opera, I would have ended up standing on the shores of a landlocked lake staring into the distance looking for a Royal Navy warship.

Armed with the correct travel warrant I made my way up to the west of Scotland, something that I did not expect to happen so soon after leaving HMS Neptune. After a long train journey and a short taxi ride from the nearest railway station I arrived on the banks of Loch Fyne, staring out at the *Cherry B* anchored off in the middle of the lake. A local chap offered me a lift in his boat and around 20 minutes later I was clambering up a rope ladder, Naval suitcase in hand, and back on board. Loch Fyne was serene and beautiful and its waters moved not an inch. HMS *Charybdis* was also serene and beautiful and her 2,500+ tonnes sat peacefully in the middle of this Scottish splendour. A world away from the rough seas off Portland.

We remained in or rather on Loch Fyne for a week, during which time we were granted a couple of nights' shore leave which was spent in local pubs (courtesy of one of *Cherry B*'s small boats which was used to 'taxi' us back and forth across the water). The ship's daily routine continued as normal: work, scran, rounds, etc. When we sailed to return to Plymouth I was somewhat hesitant that my seasickness would return in the Irish Sea. It didn't and neither did it ever return in the future, even in seas much more violent than what I had experienced off the coast of Portland a few weeks earlier.

7. THE STRIP

Back in Plymouth and returned to full health I was introduced to the joys of Plymouth's Union Street, known throughout the Royal Navy as 'The Strip'. This street housed most of the bars, clubs and dens of iniquity back in the day and every sailor worth his salt became acquainted with each and every one of them. Particular favourites included pubs such as the Tube, the Malthouse, the Two Trees and the Prince Regent; favourite clubs included Diamond Lil's, the Academy and Boobs. There were no hybrid late-night bars/clubs in those days – there were pubs and there were clubs and the latter opened much later than the former (normally until 0200).

One of the 'perks' of seagoing Writers is that we didn't do 'duties'. We were known as 'Blue Card' although I never actually saw a blue card and have no idea if they even existed. What this meant is that I could go ashore every night if I pleased and my social life was never restricted by being a member of the 'Duty Watch', something the majority of my fellow shipmates had to endure. When alongside in Devonport Dockyard, or any other dockyard for that matter, we would rarely stay on board in the evenings; single, teenage matelots had better things to do.

I loved Plymouth and I loved the Strip. Every night the bars and clubs would be full of servicemen as all three services were represented in Plymouth – the Royal Navy, Royal Marines (part of the Royal Navy I hasten to add), the Army and the Royal Air Force. The Armed Forces were much bigger in the 1980s than they are today, courtesy of the Cold War, and culturally things were much different – pubs and clubs were where young people went, it's what we did. Oh, and there were girls, more girls than I had ever seen in my whole life.

If I had been a slow starter in matters relating to girls and sex Plymouth afforded the perfect opportunity to catch up. How on earth the prostitutes around Millbay Docks ever earned any money remains a mystery; obtaining sex in Plymouth was not a difficult challenge. Plymouth was very different to Helensburgh, Dumbarton and Glasgow; most girls I asked to dance declined but more importantly it was easier to 'trap' (or 'pull' in civilian parlance).

'Boobs' night-club, long since demolished, is the stuff of legend (known amongst civvies as the 'Royal Naval School of Dancing' and among matelots as 'Home of the Steaming Bat Shuffle'). Every Guzz-based matelot of a certain era has fond memories of the place. Rubbish beer, sticky carpets and loose women – what else could a young teenage matelot want? I'm pretty sure many marriages were made in Boobs and I'm also sure many more may also have been broken in that wonderful establishment.

One of my favourite nights in Boobs ended with me in a car with three females. When I asked the driver where we were going he replied, "Exeter." Now I had never been to Exeter but my 'mate' for the night seemed pretty good looking, quite stunning in fact, and I wasn't about to argue. Carol's two mates disappeared (you can't have everything) but we ended up in her house. The following morning, after a rather pleasant wake-up call, Carol asked if I wanted breakfast. She was rather less attractive than the evening before but I was hungry and she had bacon. In the kitchen she noticed she'd run out of bread so she asked if I'd pop down to the corner shop. As I was about to leave I noticed a framed photograph of a soldier on her sideboard and a pretty mean-looking soldier at that. "Who's that?" I enquired.

"My old man, the kids' father," she replied.

"He looks hard," I said.

"He's well fucking hard, a violent bastard," she replied. Cue squeaky bum time.

"So what time is he back?" I further enquired.

"Oh don't worry, he doesn't live with me anymore."

"Where does he live?" I asked, hoping the answer would be somewhere like Norwich, Wick or Aberystwyth.

She walked to the window and pointed to a house over the road, saying, "Over there."

I refused Carol's offer of money for the bread and left the house after she gave me directions for the local shop. I walked to the shop, I walked around the corner and I then legged it, as fast as I could. I stopped briefly to ask for directions to the nearest railway station and ended up at St David's (every time I visit St David's, nowadays quite frequently, the memory of Carol, the never-eaten bacon sandwich and a violent squaddie spring to mind). I didn't eat breakfast that morning and I never saw Carol again. However, I remained in one piece and that mattered more than anything else. As I would often remark to friends and foes alike: "I'm a Writer, not a fighter." (I was much better at one than the other.)

Alongside in Devonport Dockyard my familiarity with Plymouth and its watering holes grew. I was introduced to the 'Barbican', an old harbour area in Plymouth, not far from the city centre. The Barbican was home to a plethora of great hostelries, my favourite being the legendary Dolphin Inn ran by the even more legendary Billy Holmes, a big Irishman originally from Bandon in County Cork. Just down from the Dolphin there was the famous Cap'n Jaspers; Jaspers was a little shack by the water (less of a little shack today) and it served up amongst other fine treats first-class bacon rolls (there's not much I wouldn't do for a decent bacon buttie, getting beaten up by a potentially violent squaddie aside of course). The Barbican was known as the area where the 'nice' girls would go, nurses and the like. My evenings would involve lots of beer in a number of pubs including the Admiral MacBride, the Navy and the Dolphin; all cracking boozers but the Dolphin was the best of all. With a bellyful of lager and the pubs shut for the night it would be time for a bacon buttie and a mug of tea from Jaspers before heading off to the Strip and Boobs (never knowingly frequented by nice nurses).

Union Street had its own clubs where 'nice' girls would frequent. OK, probably just a couple, one being Dance Academy or simply 'the Academy' as we knew it. On one evening I spotted three girls chatting to each other so I asked the most attractive if she would like to dance. She refused. I asked the next most attractive if she would like to dance and she refused too (clearly both lesbians). I asked the third most attractive, an Irish girl, and she accepted; we danced, not very well in my case, we had a few drinks and we arranged to meet up to go to the cinema the following weekend. She had a very nice Irish name which I have never forgotten but for the sake of this dit let's call her Bridget Mary Kelly. We arranged to meet outside Jumping Jacks or the Corner House as the pub was also known, at the bottom of New George Street.

As agreed, a few days later, I was stood outside Jumping Jacks but I couldn't for the life of me recall what Bridget looked like. Every time an attractive girl approached I moved out of the doorway on to the pavement in anticipation of a smile and a hello; they walked on by, all of them. Whilst I was looking elsewhere a girl approached, not particularly attractive but I don't wish to be too unkind, and said hello. It was Bridget. *Oh well,* I thought, *I bet she has a lovely personality.* We ventured off to the cinema, the Drake (Odeon) on the roundabout at Derry's Cross. I was wrong on the personality front and fell asleep during the film, woken only by my own loud snoring. Bridget and I left the cinema together, said goodbye and never saw one another again. I'm pretty sure the opinion on personality was a mutual one.

By now we knew we had a six-month deployment to the Indian Ocean planned for the second half of 1985 – Armilla Patrol. Armilla Patrol was a continuous presence in the turbulence of the Middle East and consisted of a Type 42 destroyer, a Leander-class frigate and a replenishment ship known as an 'RFA' (Royal Fleet Auxiliary). Before then we would have a period in Devonport Dockyard for extended maintenance (DED), two weeks' operational sea training (COST) and various joint maritime courses/exercises (JMCs) in coastal waters off the UK. 1985 was shaping up to be a pretty busy and hopefully memorable year.

Alongside in Devonport the noise and the smells continued, although I was well used to both by now. But the ship didn't move and we had pubs aplenty on our doorstep. The day-to-day routine was pretty similar to being at sea, during the day at least. Writers continued to ply our trade – the lads needed to get paid and the Navy ran on paperwork. Much of the typing involved copy-typing. The Ship's Office would receive and process all mail addressed to the Commanding Officer (Captain). This involved allocating letters to appropriate packs (files) and distributing them to relevant officers. Nine times out of ten a reply would be required and the replying officer would write up a reply, by hand, and give it to the Ship's Office to type. A Writer would type up the reply, without even looking at the keys of course, and leave it in a tray for the relevant officer to pick up and sign. Letters for signature by the Captain would be taken up by the Corro for approval and signature. We would often have to type up the same letter several times – there were no electronic typewriters or word processors in those days. The typewriter sat 'underneath' one desk and via a clever device that effectively turned part of the desk upside down, it could be pulled up to do its stuff.

Typing at sea can be difficult. Even a simple word such as 'and' could be problematic. On one occasion I was typing an important and somewhat lengthy document for the Captain's signature when the ship 'jumped' violently. The 'n' in 'and' ended up a few millimetres above the 'a' and the 'd'. As the Corro was busy doing something else, probably his full-time and rather more important job, the POWTR asked me to take the letter up to the bridge for the Captain to sign. The Captain asked me to type the letter again, or rather the offending page containing the misplaced 'n'; when I say 'asked' it was a request that invited no refusal or debate. "But that was your fault, sir," I remarked.

"In what way was it my fault, Scribes? You're the typist, not me," he replied.

"But you were driving, sir, not me."

I re-typed the offending page.

One of the highlights of dockyard routine was the mid-morning 'Stand Easy'. A wagon from Ivor Dewdney's would pull up on the jetty and load up the NAAFI with proper Devon pasties (better than the version sold across the Tamar). I would sit astride the office bin eating my pasty every morning, trying but failing not to spill bits of it into the bin or onto the floor. They say an apple a day is good for you but pasties are better, especially the Devon variety.

By now we also had a new addition to the mess – a young lady named Doris, made of rubber and the property of Larry Lamb, a baby Cook about the same age as myself. Doris became very much a part of the mess; she didn't talk much but she did as she was told and always dressed in her Cook's uniform for evening rounds.

Talking of 'ladies', every mess on board every ship had what is known as a 'Gronk Board'. Apologies if some might find this non-PC or even a tad offensive but this was the 1980s and this was the Royal Navy and history is history. The idea was to fill the Gronk Board with as many photos as possible of young women 'trapped' by mess members; particular pleasure was gained from those not blessed in the looks department. I never contributed any photos solely because I didn't possess any. Yvonne and I continued to write to each other but I never owned a photo of her and if I had I most certainly wouldn't have put it on that board (far too good-looking).

Whilst Larry owned the mess doll and contributed much to the Gronk Board he wasn't just into rubber. I recall him shagging a Wren Officer, literally. He brought her on board one day and after a few cans took her to one of the gulches, the areas of messdeck between the bunks further back from the mess square. They were quite noisy and we were quite jealous. Larry was a big character and he quickly became one of the mess characters.

As for mess characters, Scouse McCann and Larry Lamb aside, we had Gerry Moonan, a Scot from some place near Glasgow named after a tie, Stevie Milne, another Scot, Brum Cotton from England's second city, Aids Clode from Devon, Tommo from Dorset and Adrian Childs from God knows where. We also had the quiz legend that is Budgie Burgess. The evening quizzes at sea with questions piped through the ship's PA system were won by 3EZ more often than any other mess. Budgie was a walking encyclopaedia – no Google or Wikipedia in those days. I hear Budgie appeared on Mastermind many years later but I have no idea of how he fared. Whilst the mess contained a huge amount of testosterone and no end of banter there was never any bullying; some didn't get on so well with others but in the main we all rubbed along just fine. I only recall ever having one argument and that was with Tommo, a good mate of mine. Tommo was from Dorchester and I spent one cracking weekend in that famous town with him, staying with his parents. One argument does not break a friendship, certainly when you're living together in a very small space.

One evening whilst alongside in Devonport Bill Bailey, my POWTR, invited me down to the Petty Officers' mess after work.

This was a rare privilege, especially for a young lad who was a bit in awe of those older and more senior (Prince Andrew aside of course). I was lashed up with beer, sea stories and the like. Bill Bailey and General Grant were an entertaining double act and General mentioned his daughter on a number of occasions. As Bill and General had wives and marital homes in Plymouth, in common with other 'RAs' on the ship, i.e. those who lived out whilst the ship was alongside, they had to go home after our drinking session ended. General told me I was going home with him to meet his daughter Connie Francis (not that Connie Francis). So off we trotted to get a bus from Devonport to Mutley, the area of Plymouth where General lived with his wife and his rather attractive daughter.

Connie and I became rather close and we started seeing each other on a regular basis, my first proper girlfriend I guess. I would often leave the ship with General and come back with him the following morning. Whilst Connie had her own room I slept downstairs on a camp bed. We would sneak between her room and the living room but General and his wife knew all of this of course. On one occasion General and I were walking along Mutley Plain early one morning to catch a bus back to the dockyard and my hand touched something in my pocket that shouldn't have been there. I took out the foreign object and realised it was Connie's knickers from the night before. I panicked a bit and threw them over the nearest wall, into a churchyard. Knowing Plymouth I'm sure that wasn't the first or last pair of knickers that the local vicar had to contend with (read that how you wish).

Whilst I really liked Connie I started to miss nights out with the lads. I still had some of course but I felt constrained; I couldn't cheat on Connie because General would find out and I'd probably end up in a large pot in the galley to be served up to the Stokers on the next occasion that they pissed off one of his team. I decided to call it a day with Connie and arranged to meet her in the Fortescue pub on

Mutley Plain (a pub that got better and better over the years – RIP Steve Smith, a true legend of Plymouth's pub scene).

Connie put some tunes on the juke box which wasn't helpful. After I'd explained my decision there were a lot of tears. It would have been easier if she'd slapped my face, told me to fuck off and stormed out. She sat there quietly dabbing away at the tears whilst love songs played in the background. She was a lovely girl but I wasn't ready for a girlfriend at 19 years of age with a lengthy deployment on the horizon.

Fair play to General, he never judged me and he never criticised. On the contrary. On one occasion at sea he was leaning on the shelf on the bottom half of the door chatting away to Bill. Paul and I were quietly working away when General asked, "What are you doing this weekend, Rocky, when we get back to Guzz?"

"Out on the piss with the lads, PO," I replied.

"Fucking idiot," he replied. "You could come home with me and be up to your nuts in guts all night." Matelots are matelots and always will be.

The Cooks were always talking of General – he was an immense character. I remember Scouse telling me about having to shake (wake) him early one morning with a cup of tea: "He slept in the middle bunk of his gulch – it was pitch black and I slid the curtain open and reached out for his bunk light. The fucker sat up and as he yawned my outstretched hand went right down his throat. He gagged, I shit myself and threw the tea over the bloke in the bottom bunk who screamed in pain; General fell out of bed, retching and rolling around on the deck with the other bloke screaming at the top of his voice. The mess lights went on with everyone thinking an epic disaster had occurred but I'd scarpered; no one ever knew it was me."

A lot of the lads on board had been to the Gulf in 1984, just before I joined the ship. I heard some fantastic 'dits' (matelots' sea stories) about African ports and I couldn't wait until we deployed. Throughout my training period I'd heard lots of stories about certain places, matelots' favourite fleshpots, one of which was Mombasa in Kenya where we would visit about halfway through our deployment. Other places that I wanted to visit at some point included Hamburg, Amsterdam and the Far East, particularly the Philippines.

On a night out in Plymouth I met a lovely girl called Julie in one of the city's better night-clubs just off Union Street (most certainly not Boobs). Julie was a particularly 'nice' girl and there was definitely no sex on the first night (or any other night for that matter). But I really fell for Julie which wasn't ideal in terms of timing, a couple of months before our deployment. Julie lived with her family in Cornwall, close to the Devon border. We started to spend a lot of time together and I would often stay at her house; however, unlike Connie there was no mucking about in different rooms. Julie's parents were lovely and she had a sister Fiona who was going out with a Royal Naval Officer, a Supply Officer who had started Naval life as a Writer. Julie's family were lovely; I wasn't used to middle-class English families and it was pretty obvious they weren't used to someone from a working-class Irish family. I did introduce them to Brendan Shine and top tracks such as 'Spuds' and 'Carrots' but I think their smiles were smiles of confused amusement rather than enjoyment.

In preparation for our forthcoming deployment and after our maintenance period we headed to Portland for two weeks' 'COST' which stood for 'Continuous Operational Sea Training', as opposed to the lengthier 'BOST' which stood for 'Basic Operational Sea Training' for ships coming out of build or refit. No one looked forward to COST; it was an opportunity for FOST and his team to put the ship and her company through its paces and it was going to be two weeks of hell.

We spent most of the two weeks in 'Defence Watches'. I enjoyed my daily routine as a Writer even though I worked longer hours than the majority who worked the 'watch' system (but give me 'day routine' every day). Defence Watches entailed 'six on, six off' on a continuous basis. At least I could work in the Ship's Office and crack on with my normal work. Food is always important on board and the midnight meal during Defence Watches was a particular highlight. Apart from one evening when I'd just sat down to eat my chicken supreme, a particular delight on board the *Cherry B*, when the ship moved violently and I ended up on my back on the deck with chicken and piping hot sauce all over me. The other lads all commiserated with my predicament and no one laughed or took the piss. No one. Of course not.

Whilst Defence Watches involved a period of heightened alert, Action Stations meant just that – action was imminent or ongoing. No more accounting or administering for me – Action Stations meant I had to report to the Petty Officers' mess where I became a member of the First Aid team and the said mess became a casualty treatment area. FOST and his staff were genuine world leaders in their field and they knew how to simulate war. This was the nearest thing to real action and whilst I couldn't see what was going on with ships and aircraft around us in the waters off Portland, the noise and the activity on board was intense to say the least. Casualties were made up with incredibly realistic injuries by the medical team and we had to recover these casualties and treat them. Experience from the Falklands ensured that casualties were made up to look like genuine casualties and simulated exercises were as close to the real thing as possible. Fucking about in a hot engine room with everyone around screaming and shouting was not my idea of fun; you can't just pull a sailor up a ladder if his face is covered in burns and both his legs are broken. That said, whenever I had my turn playing a casualty it was great fun. I would get into character and pretend that those bits of made-up flesh falling off my body were real bits of flesh. I would shout for England until someone would shout louder: "Shut the fuck up, Rocky, for Christ's sake!"

COST was pretty awful but at least there was no seasickness, unlike my first visit to those waters on the *Cherry B*. Every day was intense. Every single department was inspected and every single action was interrogated. The Ship's Office was inspected from top to bottom by FOST's Writer staff who, alongside their colleagues, just wanted to put you through your paces and give you as much shit as possible. Every account, every ledger, every piece of paper, every process – there were no exceptions. Rounds were a nightmare despite every mess, every toilet, every sink and every shower being cleaned to within an inch of its life with a toothbrush. Office and mess floors had to be scrubbed and every inch had to sparkle. I kid you not, if one square inch failed to sparkle, anywhere in the ship, a 'rescrub' would be announced and you had to go through the whole thing again.

We kept our spirits up and we got through it; we knew we had a fantastic deployment planned with some exciting foreign runs ashore so FOST and his staff couldn't break us; but they tried and they often very nearly succeeded.

Sea time continued with various maritime exercises, sometimes on our own and at other times with other RN and NATO ships. At sea there was no live television – no satellite TV in those days. We had a video recorder and there was various stuff on the ship's radio courtesy of the BBC's World Service and we also had BFBS, the British Forces Broadcasting Service. Quite apart from official stand easys, I would often pop down the mess for a cup of tea and a chat with the lads. Whilst most members of the S&S were day workers, some worked odd shifts such as Cooks and Stewards so there was always someone down there. In the evenings one or two of the Cooks would bring down some extra stuff from the galley, not available to the other messes; one of the lads would cook mini pizzas which was a particular favourite although not for me, the only mess member not to like cheese.

Although a day-worker I would often go back to work in the

evenings after dinner. Paperwork in the Royal Navy doesn't stop at 1700; rather it tends to accelerate in the evenings as officers catch up with admin duties. If it was the time of the month for pay we were often working against the clock. 'Pay Statements', semi-completed, would arrive by post from HMS Centurion, the Navy's pay and records centre in Gosport; we had limited time to manually reconcile each account, calculate that month's pay and return the necessary paperwork to Centurion so that everyone would be paid correctly and on time. If the helicopter stopped working for a few days it wasn't a major problem (unless it was due to pick up some post). If a boiler broke down that too wasn't a major problem, particularly as we had two. Being fed and being paid are what matelots care about most and for that reason Dabbers, Stokers and the like would rarely upset Cooks or Writers.

On some routine evenings at sea I would do an hour or so in the office, pop down the mess for a bit and then return to the office. Work aside, I had started studying for Leading Writer; a huge incentive was immediate promotion on successful completion of the exam as the Leading Writers' roster was 'dry' at the time. A dry roster was one where the number of available billets exceeded the number of qualified candidates. The opposite was not good and there were some branches such as Cooks where the waiting list for Leading Rate after successful completion of the qualifying exam was up to seven years. But that didn't concern me, I was in the right branch at the right time and I wanted to make the most of it.

Leading Rates are the equivalent of Corporals in the lesser services although as you may recall any stripes worn were a coincidence. The badge of rank for a Leading Rate, known as 'Killicks' in the Navy, was an anchor (two crossed anchors for Petty Officers). Given the Writers' branch badge consisted of a star with a 'W' in the middle, I aspired to wear a uniform with a W on one arm and an anchor on the other.

More often than not there would be a porn movie on the tellybox when I popped down the mess. Mess members would often remark, "Fucking hell... not again," when porn was suggested but the mess was at its quietest when scud was on the box. If anyone not in the mess at the start of the movie started talking when they got to the bottom of the ladder they'd be told in no uncertain terms to shut the fuck up. 'Debbie Does Dallas' was a particular favourite in the mess and this movie got more than its fair showing.

A difficulty whilst watching porn was leaving the mess to go to the toilet; you weren't allowed a call of nature whilst watching porn – you obviously wanted to do something else (pretty uncomfortable if you genuinely wanted a piss). When a movie wasn't being played but you needed a porn fix a 'Shithouse Shinpad' was required, a method of transporting an appropriate magazine to the heads without being noticed. No one ever admitted to wanking but everyone did it. Not me though. Never.

Despite a significant stash of hard porn underneath the mess seating, collected from some of the world's finest ports, matelots still liked the not knowing, leaving something to the imagination. One afternoon when I popped down the mess for a cuppa and a break from the office there were five or six lads stood up staring at the television; they were watching a recording of some show or film featuring the singer Shirley Bassey. They thought they'd caught sight of her 'snatch' which I thought was pretty difficult given her skin colour, the black dress she was wearing, the probable colour of her snatch and the poor quality television that we owned. Despite the easy availability of the hard-core stuff, the unexpected albeit unconfirmed sighting of Shirley Bassey's you-know-what produced significant excitement which led to a long debate and frequent reruns of that particular clip.

Work, scran, porn, beer and banter – the daily routine of a matelot at sea.

8. WANKING MONKEYS

Due to the ship's commitments I didn't get as many opportunities in 1985 to watch the mighty Hatters as I would have liked, a shame given the Luton team of the 1980s was the most successful in our history. However I did get to the FA Cup semi-final at Villa Park against treble-chasing Everton which we lost and also the home match versus Millwall in the previous round which became famous for all the wrong reasons; Millwall fans rioted before, during and after their defeat.

Of that fateful night in March I can honestly say it was the only time that I was genuinely scared at a football match; I am not embarrassed to say I was shaking with fear even though I'd witnessed more than my fair share of football violence in the 1980s; this was violence on a different level. Before the match Millwall's thugs invaded the pitch and tried to get into our end opposite theirs; they threw bottles, nails, coins and other objects at home supporters which included women and children; one bottle missed my head by an inch or so and a couple of coins hit me on the arm. Unbeknown to me at the time a cousin was also at the game and he was hit on the back of the head with a plastic seat. During the game Millwall's thugs threw missiles onto the pitch and they even threw a knife at our goalkeeper. After the match they invaded the pitch; many invaded a neighbouring stand used by home supporters – they ripped up plastic seats and they used those seats and the dislodged lumps of concrete as missiles which they threw at the police. Many were injured that night, over 80, including 31 police officers.

Not only did Millwall's thugs smash up our stadium but they smashed up the neighbourhood surrounding the ground; they smashed up our neighbours' cars, they smashed our neighbours' windows and they smashed up our town centre. Luton banned away fans as a result and introduced a membership scheme. How did the football authorities respond? The Football League expelled us from the 'League Cup', their annual cup competition (which we won two seasons later when the expulsion ended) and the Football Association fined Millwall £7,500 which was withdrawn on appeal. In court the following morning most of the thugs identified as fans of other clubs, mainly West Ham United and Chelsea, although of course the truth of those claims were never substantiated.

1985 was a very dark year in football terms. I recall watching the Heysel tragedy unfold on the mess television in late May, only days before we deployed to the Middle East; 39 people were killed on that horrific day, mostly Juventus fans, and more than 600 were injured. The tragedy was caused by Liverpool supporters and as a result all English teams were banned from European competition; quite unexpectedly this would affect Luton Town and deprive us of our place in the UEFA Cup competition three years later. A couple of weeks earlier we also witnessed via our TV screens the horror of the Bradford City stadium fire which claimed the lives of 56 football supporters (265 were also injured in this accidental tragedy). 1985 was a difficult place for football fans and fatal for many.

By now Bill Bailey and Paul Davey had left the ship and were replaced by POWTR Paul Edwards and WTR Paul Wasilkowski (pronounced 'Vashilkofski' or something like that). The new POWTR didn't appear to have the same endearing personality as Bill and whilst I liked Paul Davey, I was looking forward to having a younger single Writer to work alongside (Paul Davey was a thoroughly nice chap but he was married so his priorities didn't include getting laid and pissed at every opportunity, unlike many of

Cherry B's married men, it has got to be said). Paul Wasilkowski quickly became known as 'Waz'; a top lad from Carlisle and a cracking footballer to boot so a great addition to the mess.

Before he left the ship Paul Davey and his wife, together with Julie and I, went to the 'Cornwall Coliseum' in St Austell to see the comedian Chubby Brown; Chubby quite accurately described the venue as "Cornwall's biggest cowshed". Paul had a vague idea of Chubby Brown's humour but the girls had no idea. I on the other hand had previously seen him perform in the Flying Fish Club at HMS Osprey so I knew what to expect. I was sat with an aisle on my right-hand side, Julie on my left and Paul and his wife to her left. Julie was a bit prim and proper to say the least and so was Paul's wife. Chubby's humour isn't to everyone's liking – he is most definitely a Marmite character. I was literally falling into the aisle laughing. The girls didn't laugh once. Paul was clearly very embarrassed.

Julie and I continued to see each other and whilst I was excited at the prospect of a six-month deployment with numerous visits in far-flung lands, she didn't share that sense of excitement. On our final evening together prior to the ship's deployment we went for a drink at the Holland Inn close to where she lived in Cornwall, just over the border from Plymouth. The pub had a piano and on that particular evening there was a professional pianist performing. Minutes before my taxi arrived to take me back to the dockyard the pianist started singing Rod Stewart's 'Sailing', a recording that would soon become synonymous with the *Cherry B* and our Armilla deployment. I kissed Julie goodbye and left her in tears with strains of 'Sailing' still ringing in my ears as I got into the taxi. It would be six months before I had any chance of seeing Julie again but I promised to write and at some point call (no mobile phones, email or social media in those days).

In the days and weeks immediately prior to our deployment it was frantic. We had lots of 'Store Ship' where even Writers had to get involved (yes, even Writers). 'Store Ship' is what it says, getting the ship stored up with food and other essentials such as CSB, McEwan's and Blue Liners. Sailors from all branches would form a continuous single line from the dockyard jetty, up the gangway, along the ship's corridors and into the stores. Store Ship would last for hours and the obligatory banter aside, it was an entirely necessary exercise if somewhat boring; if I'd wanted to be a Jack Dusty I'd have joined as one.

Fully stored with food, fuel, beer and the like we sailed on 3 June for Armilla. We joined up with the Portsmouth-based Type 42 destroyer HMS *Exeter* and a Royal Fleet Auxiliary support ship laden with fuel, food and other stores (RFA *Bayleaf*). We sailed for Gibraltar which was not the 'plain sailing' that I had expected. The Bay of Biscay was truly awful with some of the roughest seas that I had ever encountered, before or since; Waz and I would often disappear down the mess and into the safety of our pits, fully strapped in. It was impossible to work at times but to my immense relief I didn't get sick although a few of the lads did. That's not to say I didn't feel bloody awful and on the verge of vomiting most of the time.

But we did do some work of course and daily routine was pretty similar to daily routine in the waters around the United Kingdom, or anywhere else in the world for that matter. It became clear very quickly that our new POWTR's relationship with the Supply Officer was going to be a problem and Waz and I were always conscious of this. Unlike his predecessor Bill Bailey, Paul was unable to combine time for his fellow Senior Rates and others who would call by for a chat with his work – he had a real problem achieving deadlines. It wasn't a lack of knowledge; on the contrary Paul had a lot of it and never resisted an opportunity to impart it, in great detail. Combine Coronation Street's Roy Cropper with David Brent from The Office and you have Paul Edwards. The Supply Officer would often come into the office asking where something was or why something hadn't been done. As the Office Manager Paul was solely responsible to the

Supply Officer for the management of the ship's cash account; this was not something that Writers below the rank of Leading Writer were allowed to get involved in. The SO would often tell Paul in no uncertain terms that he had an hour or so to complete something, more often than not the cash account, but as soon as someone knocked on the office door, even if we were shut for enquiries, Paul couldn't help himself. Paul was exceptionally helpful and would give very long answers to very short questions. Sometimes you had to tell people to fuck off – you were busy. Bill Bailey was good at this and Waz and I would often try and do it on Paul's behalf. Whilst the Ship's Office was still a great place to work the dynamic had changed and there were frequent periods of tension that needn't have been there.

Whilst at sea my messmates managed to find time to repaint the mess-square in a truly unique style. Wood-panelling, scuttles and sea-views were all incorporated into the general scene. All who were given the honour to view the eye-catching work were thoroughly impressed, none more so than the Captain himself. Of course no one wanted Writers armed and dangerous with paintbrushes so Paul and I kept our distance, viewing proceedings with some degree of amusement. Writers and paint do not go together – everyone in the Royal Navy knows that.

As Gibraltar beckoned, the first visit of our deployment only a week after leaving the UK, I wrote letters to Yvonne, Julie and my mum. All port visits involved ingoing and outgoing mail so I never lost an opportunity to write. Looking back I suppose it was a bit strange that I wrote so often to two girls who I'd never had sex with; not that sex was everything of course but I was a horny teenage matelot and it was always front of mind.

There are three procedures for leaving or entering harbour: Procedure Alpha, Procedure Bravo and Procedure Charlie. Charlie is routine, Bravo involves all personnel who are not Special Sea Dutymen and Alpha involves the whole Ship's Company lining the upper deck wearing Number Ones. Writers only participated in Procedure Alpha, never Bravo or Charlie, except when we could get out of it. It wasn't just because this could be a long, drawn-out affair, often in the cold, but more a question of priorities. We wanted to get ashore as much as anyone and we usually had foreign currency and the Captain's official mail to sort; sometimes this would arrive the night before but often it would arrive as we were sailing into port. We entered Gibraltar via Procedure Bravo so I had no need to waste my time on the upper deck.

Gibraltar was a little piece of Britain, a 2.6 square mile little piece of Britain to be precise; it was often the last piece of Britain before months away at sea and it was also the first piece of Britain on the way back. In 1985 the border with Spain was shut so no one, supposedly, was allowed across it. As a British Overseas Territory Gibraltar was very much a 'part' of the United Kingdom and one quick view of the map demonstrates the strategic importance of this tiny bit of land to the UK and its Royal Navy. Whilst Gibraltar's strategic importance to the United Kingdom has declined over the years, especially in military terms, half of the world's seaborne trade passes through the narrow straits which link the Atlantic Ocean to the Mediterranean Sea; at its narrowest and separating Europe from Africa the straits are less than eight miles wide.

Gibraltar was considered a 'routine' visit and most members of the Ship's Company had visited before, either on the *Cherry B* the previous year or on different ships. As soon as I left the dockyard I was struck by the feeling of still being in the UK, albeit with the hot Mediterranean sun beating down. Red telephone boxes, cars driving on the left, fish and chip shops, British pubs and shops, bobbies on the beat and UK banknotes (no need for money-changing prior to this particular overseas visit) all made us feel somewhat at home. British writer Laurie Lee once commented: "Gibraltar is a piece of Portsmouth sliced off and towed 500 miles south" (I'm pretty sure he got his miles wrong but his point is well made). Mind you, Gibraltar's eclectic architecture, a mix of Palladian, Moorish and many other styles with an abundance of Genoese shutters thrown in for good measure, was definitely more Mediterranean than British; a wander down Gibraltar's attractive Main Street is a far more pleasant experience than a wander down Portsmouth's Commercial Road which is many things but most certainly not attractive.

Gibraltar is well known for its bars and rightly so. The only disappointment was the lack of women. The bars were great but very 'blokey', not helped of course by the addition of a few hundred matelots from the *Cherry B* and HMS *Exeter*. A few of the lads allegedly crossed the border to La Línea and found a particularly good whorehouse by all accounts but no one from 3 Easy mess got across so maybe that was a *Cherry B* myth – Stokers making things up as usual. I did come across one whore, not literally, whilst playing pool with Tommo in the London Bar; she was the only female in the bar and she spoke to every one of us in turn, touting for business. Whilst an amusing source of entertainment she was a particularly ugly whore and clearly an unsuccessful one, for good reason.

Gibraltar is dominated by a massive 1,400-foot-high limestone rock, named the Rock of Gibraltar for some obscure reason. I spent quite a bit of time wandering around this big lump which, via cable car to the top, afforded fantastic views of Spain, North Africa and of course both the Atlantic Ocean and the Mediterranean Sea. The Rock is inhabited by hundreds of Gibraltar's famous Barbary macaque monkeys, known locally as 'rock apes'. Semi-wild with a penchant for eating, drinking and wanking, these monkeys bear striking similarities to many matelots although, that said, I've never seen a matelot wank in public.

One memorable if rather unpleasant memory of Gibraltar relates to toilet roll, or rather lack of. I was wandering around away from the main hustle and bustle of the town with one of the lads from the mess, Stevie from memory. We'd eaten and drunk quite a bit and I was suddenly taken with the need to go to the toilet. Unusually we were some way from a bar but I was desperate and beginning to think I would have to use the same toilet as the rock apes. In the distance I spotted a bar and walked as fast as I could; if I'd run things would have become messy and I would have had no need for the bar or its toilet.

As soon as we entered the bar, a particularly small bar with only a handful of customers, I said to Stevie, "Order a couple of halves, mate, once I've had a shit we'll get out of here pronto." The toilet was at the end of the small bar and had only a single door separating it from the bar itself. I couldn't get my jeans down fast enough but with milliseconds to spare it was job done; this was up there with the best of them. I was rather conscious of the smell, especially given the toilet's close proximity to the bar and its inhabitants, so I got up as quickly as possible to do the necessary. Disaster – no toilet roll. With no substitutes for loo roll in the loo itself I had to improvise. I used my underpants (no boxers in those days) and whilst not man enough for the job, they did their best. Not wishing to block the toilet and with no other option I placed my underpants, covered in the dirty brown stuff, in the corner behind the toilet. When I opened the door everyone stared at me as the smell was somewhat overwhelming. I went to the bar and said to the barman, "That toilet is disgusting, mate, absolutely disgusting, whoever was in there before me has got a problem." Stevie and I downed our half-pints with as few gulps as possible, left the bar and legged it. My jeans were a bit of a mess but the boys from Hong Kong would soon sort that.

Whilst we were only in Gibraltar for a few days we made the most of its bars, of which there were plenty. Whilst always a Writer rather than a fighter I did get thrown out of one bar after an argument with an obnoxious barman. Actually I was thrown down the stairs but the momentum took me out onto the pavement. A few seconds later Roy Caitlin appeared from the club; I hadn't seen Roy since HMS

Pembroke and I had no idea why he was in Gibraltar as he wasn't one of HMS *Exeter*'s Writers. We exchanged pleasantries and walked off in separate directions. I never did find out why Roy was in Gibraltar.

On another evening, or to be more precise early one morning, I wandered back to the ship on my tod; leaving my mates after a sesh and wandering around on my own is a habit that I developed at a young age and one that has never left me. I got back to the dockyard and saw the *Cherry B* in the distance. After some time I realised that I had taken a wrong turn and I ended up beside a jetty that was separated from the *Cherry B* by what seemed, in my inebriated state at least, to be a relatively small body of water. I had a choice. The obvious and sensible choice was to walk all the way back around the quay and find the correct route to the ship but I was tired and needed my pit. The less obvious and less sensible choice was to jump into one of the small boats moored to the jetty and row back to the ship – so much quicker. I selected a boat that had oars, removed the mooring rope from the bollard to which it was secured and started to row towards the ship. I was often reminded of why I chose the Writer branch and this was one of those moments. Fifty yards out from the jetty into what now felt like a body of water greater than the Mediterranean, the boat overturned and I was completely submerged.

As I've previously mentioned I'm not a strong swimmer. I struggled to swim back to the jetty but made it with some difficulty. Luckily no one was around to witness my misfortune so I walked the long way around in soaking wet clothes. In what seemed an age I finally clambered up the gangway and onto the ship. The Quartermaster and his oppos were all in tears; I assumed one of those bright sparks had just spun a rather scintillating dit. "You daft fucker, Rocky, you had us in fucking stitches," the QM remarked, tears rolling down his face.

"What, you saw me?" I replied.

"Every step of the fucking way, mate. We watched you walk down the wrong jetty, we watched you take the boat and we watched you go for a swim. Fucking hilarious." Doing the 'middle watch' during an overseas visit isn't much fun when your oppos are ashore on the piss but the guys on the gangway were thoroughly enjoying their middle at that particular moment; glad to be of service, guys.

Gibraltar done, it was time to set sail and head across the Med to the Suez Canal for our journey south to the Indian Ocean. Shitting my pants and late-night swimming apart, I'd thoroughly enjoyed Gib and was glad that we'd call in again on our way home in a few months' time.

9. SUEZ AND BEYOND

As we sailed across the Mediterranean we were joined by a number of uninvited but very welcome guests. They were very interested in us and we were very interested in them. Dolphins. Dozens and dozens of them. At any one time there would be at least a dozen or so swimming alongside the ship as we made our way east. Dolphins are truly beautiful creatures and to see them in their natural habitat was something quite special.

The Med was calm and peaceful so life at sea was productive. I'd taken on the role of 'Welfare Secretary' and sat on the committee that oversaw the ship's Welfare Fund. I enjoyed this role and everyone seemed to enjoy the minutes of the meetings that I produced; I was surprised that I was given carte blanche to write what I wanted so I made the most of it and injected as much humour as possible. I was also getting into my studies for the Leading Writer 'Professional Qualifying Examination' which I intended to sit in October.

The ship's routine continued as normal – in addition to our own specific branch duties there were always daily fire exercises, evening rounds, three square meals, physical exercise, etc. Most of us liked to keep fit and I participated in circuit training on the flight deck most evenings although I preferred running around the upper deck to all those squats and burpees. Not everyone kept fit though and there was certainly no compulsion to participate in physical activity. Everyone on board was under 40 with most in their late teens or 20s so the vast majority were slim and fit. That said, there were a few you wouldn't want to be behind climbing up a ladder to escape a burning or flooding compartment.

There was always loads of banter on board and rarely did anyone take offence. Mind you, Waz would sometimes take offence when we queued for scran. Being of Polish origin and given the dire situation in Poland at the time we'd often say stuff like, "You must be used to queuing for food, eh Waz?" and, "Do you queue for dinner at home?" But everyone took the piss out of everyone. In my case my Irish origin was the subject of a lot of piss-taking and I was frequently referred to as a 'Boggie', 'Left-Footer', 'Terrorist' or 'Fenian Bastard'. We all gave as good as we got – it was part and parcel of life at sea.

When we arrived at Port Said at the northern end of the Suez Canal we had to hang around for a couple of days before we could continue south. We were joined by dozens of small boats with very cheerful men trying to sell us all sorts of trinkets, ornaments and the like. After lots of banter and bartering deals would be done with goods and cash exchanged by rope. I didn't buy anything but many did; whilst the merchandise looked a load of tat to me, the sight of so many boats and so many locals energetically plying their trade made for a great scene looking down from the upper deck – so much colour, noise and laughter.

During our time at Port Said a party of lads were lucky enough to fly off for an overnight trip to visit the Pyramids at Giza on the outskirts of Cairo. My name was in the hat for the trip but unfortunately it wasn't pulled out. Whilst disappointed I knew that I would have an opportunity to see the Pyramids on the way home as our penultimate visit would be the Mediterranean port city of Alexandria on Egypt's northern coast and a further trip to Cairo, next time by road, was planned.

As we completed our transit of the Suez Canal and continued south via the Red Sea we'd talk of our fast approaching first foreign visit (Gibraltar didn't count as a 'foreign' run ashore). Djibouti, home to a large contingent of the French Foreign Legion, is situated at the bottom of the Red Sea (or the entrance to the Red Sea if you're coming from the other direction). Its location on the Horn of Africa gives Djibouti, a small country, some significance as the shipping lanes in the area are very busy indeed. Serving as the port for its larger but landlocked neighbour Ethiopia, Djibouti saw even more trade than usual in 1985 due to the awful famine ravaging the country at the time; grain and other foodstuffs were routed to the starving country via the port.

We would talk of women and sex. We sometimes talked about other stuff. The lads would ask, "Have you ever fucked a black bird, Rocky?" to which my honest answer was "no" and, to clarify, "no way". I'd never considered it. I'd only ever had sex with white women and given my experience in Scotland, some particularly pale white women at that.

"Ah, but you will," they would respond.

"No chance," I would retort.

"Wait 'til you get to Africa, mate," they would reply in unison.

An essential job prior to any foreign run ashore was 'money-changing' and my first experience of this was the night before we arrived in Djibouti. All messes had been furnished a couple of days before with mess lists and all members of the Ship's Company, including Senior Ratings and officers, had to write down beside their names how many Djiboutian francs they required. The Ship's Office would be open every morning for money-changing but this routine of arranging the bulk of foreign currency the night before was a tried and tested method of avoiding a queue of 220 sailors outside the Ship's Office on the first day of a foreign visit. As soon as the money arrived on board it was divided by mess and given to a delegated mess representative for further division.

Money-changing was always a bit of a challenge in terms of balancing both cash and paperwork – there was an awful lot of both.

But if we Writers were good at anything it was cash and paperwork so we rarely had problems. Sailors wouldn't physically exchange UK sterling as we would make the appropriate deductions from their pay accounts. Foreign currency amongst sailors was variously known as 'ickies' or 'spondoolies' although the latter was more of a general term for any money including our own currency.

Money-changing before our entry to Djibouti was a pretty mucky affair as the piles of Djiboutian banknotes that we sorted through were so dirty our hands were left completely black. But we didn't complain, not that that would get us anywhere; this was foreign money, ickies, spondoolies, beer tokens.

Prior to any foreign visit a 'Ship's Visit Memorandum' would be produced; once drafted by the delegated officer for that particular visit, approved by the First Lieutenant, typed up by the Ship's Office and signed off by the Captain, numerous copies would be distributed to all messdecks. This would contain a plethora of essential information, general guidance, advice and tips. Most sailors started with the section regarding bars and would always bear in mind those bars that we were advised to avoid (invariably we visited them first). In his address the night before via the ship's PA system the 'Jimmy', the First Lieutenant or Executive Officer to give him his proper title(s), would back up the contents of the memo, particularly with regard to dos and don'ts.

Once we entered the port I couldn't wait to get ashore. The ship was buzzing with activity and excitement on the morning of entry. Once we'd sorted through the official mail and conducted last-minute 'additional' money-changing it was off for a shower and then a change into civvies for our first run ashore. We'd all read the Captain's Ship's Visit Memorandum and we'd all paid attention to the First Lieutenant's verbal brief the evening before. Those who had visited before described Djibouti as a 'shithole' but I'd never been to a foreign shithole so I couldn't wait to get going.

The first thing that struck me on leaving the ship's gangway was the size and quantity of the grain sacks stacked up in the dockyard and further away in the distance. Closer inspection revealed that many of these contained UK markings and were obviously awaiting further transit to neighbouring Ethiopia. Luckily I didn't climb any of the sacks but one Able Seaman did. He climbed the highest stack that he could find and sung Live Aid's 'Feed the World' from the top. He fell off, broke both his wrists in a vain attempt to break his fall and was subsequently flown back to the UK. Not so 'able' now – daft twat.

There wasn't a huge amount of 'cultural' stuff to do in Djibouti so we confined ourselves to wandering around the city visiting bazaars, souks and small local 'restaurants' with their limited menus focused on rather delicious spicy soup, seafood and other French/African delights. Oh, and we visited bars... lots of them. We did have one game of football against a contingent from the French Foreign Legion which we won by a single goal; apart from that it was mainly beer and food.

The bars were a great craic. Unlike Gibraltar there were loads of women in the bars. Very black women; not brown but black, very black, all whores and all good fun. Every night we had a great laugh with the girls who in my view and the view of most of my oppos were quite unattractive, particularly given most of them were rather skinny, skeletal in fact. But they had great personalities and they tried hard to sell their wares. A few of the lads did their bit and contributed to the upkeep of their homes and their children but I resisted, not that I found it difficult. If I was gonna pay for it, it had to be worthwhile.

On one evening we decided to nick the national flag from one of the bars; seemed like a good idea at the time. I say 'we' but it was Larry Lamb, always up for a laugh, who removed it from the wall. We legged it out of the bar as we'd been spotted; luckily we got a good headstart as a few of the locals chased us. Somehow we escaped and we flagged down a taxi to take us back to the ship where we hid the flag in the mess. The next day all hell broke loose as the whole Ship's Company was threatened with complete stoppage of shore leave unless the flag was returned within one hour. The flag mysteriously turned up on the flight-deck a few hours later and the threat to keep all on board was lifted.

One of my most vivid memories of Djibouti is the dockyard water, almost as black as the local whores and smellier than the local banknotes (or was it the other way around?). We were playing football on the flight-deck and I kicked the ball off the deck into the water. Wearing only shorts I jumped off the quarterdeck below the flight-deck into the grimy water with the applause and shouts from my oppos ringing in my ears. I swallowed a load of the oil-infused muck but I retrieved the ball and clambered back up to the ship via the jetty. Covered in black gunge I continued with the game until we decided to go ashore. A huge bowl of local spicy soup and copious amounts of lager couldn't get rid of the acrid taste which remained in my mouth for several days.

So that was it, first foreign run ashore complete. I was very pleased to have visited Africa and even more pleased that I'd proved my messmates wrong; I didn't find black women attractive and I didn't fuck any of them, despite a huge intake of alcohol over several days. "Wait until you get to Mombers," they would retort. I'm sure the girls in Mombasa would turn out to be no more attractive than the girls in Djibouti.

10. ELEPHANTS, HORSES
AND THE DOG

We left Djibouti and proceeded east out of the Gulf of Aden into the Arabian Sea. Together with our companion HMS *Exeter* we 'relieved' the outgoing Armilla patrol of HMS *Andromeda* and HMS *Manchester* and enjoyed the Naval tradition of lining the upper decks and spraying water at each other from high-powered ships' hoses. We steamed towards the Gulf of Oman, the subject of our patrol. Depending on who you talk to this area is known as either the Persian Gulf or the Arabian Gulf; to us it was simply 'the Gulf'.

In 1985 Iran was flinging missiles across the Strait of Hormuz in an effort to disrupt merchant shipping, particularly oil tankers. The Strait of Hormuz is a strategically important choke point at the entrance to the Persian Gulf where around a third of the world's oil production is moved every day (more according to some estimates). The aim of the Royal Navy's Armilla Patrol was to protect British interests, to give comfort and, if required, to provide assistance to British shipping. The permanent presence of a destroyer and a frigate was also aimed at providing a deterrent to the Iranians – we had the firepower to strike back at any aircraft or ship that interfered with merchant ships going about their lawful business. The *Cherry B* was equipped with the Exocet surface-to-surface (anti-ship) missile system and the Seawolf surface-to-air (anti-aircraft) missile system whilst HMS *Exeter* was equipped with Sea Dart anti-aircraft missiles and a 4.5" multi-use gun system. We knew this stuff worked; Exeter's Sea Dart system alone was responsible for taking out three Argentine aircraft in 1982, aircraft hell-bent on destroying British ships and killing British sailors. Mind you, not all systems worked at the same time and this was a constant challenge for both ships' Weapons Engineering Departments.

Whilst we had plans to spend a lot of time in this area we only planned to transit the Strait twice, to visit the Gulf states of Bahrain and Dubai. Whilst it was our intention to 'fly the flag' and let everyone know we were here we had no intention of inflaming a very tense situation, a situation that had prevailed for a considerable length of time given Iran and Iraq had been at war for around five years.

Whilst daily life at sea continued as normal we stepped up our exercises, particularly in relation to 'NBCD' or Nuclear, Biological, Chemical Defence to give it its full title. The ship had a system of 'pre-wetting' installed which meant that in the event of a chemical attack, something that was a distinct possibility given the protagonists in this region, our water jet system would create an 'umbrella' of water on the upper deck whilst the interior would be sealed off to create a pressurised, locked area known as a 'citadel'. To make this system work every sailor had to know his duty as a breach of the citadel, in the event of chemical attack, could result in many deaths and potentially the loss of the ship.

During NBCD exercises my duty was to man the 'After Decontamination Area' – essentially the after shithouse (the heads at the rear of the ship). Those who had no choice but to be exposed to chemicals would enter the citadel via airlocks and go through a process of decontamination before being allowed to proceed elsewhere within the protected confines of the ship. We wore thick charcoal-lined suits over a set of thick overalls which in turn were worn over a set of Number 8 uniform (yep, they were pretty thick too). We also wore thick anti-flash hoods and AGRs, Anti-Gas Respirators or gas masks to you and me. The ship's air-conditioning would be turned off for obvious reasons. So three heavy layers of clothing with head and face covered in an airless ship's shithouse in the heat of the Persian Gulf. It was hot, stuffy and quite unbearable. On one occasion I was so hot, unable to stand or move, so I lay down on the deck on my back and moved not an inch for more than three hours. Whenever anyone came into the decontamination area I'd say, "You know the routine, mate, crack on." It wasn't that I didn't take my duties seriously, I was physically unable. How on earth the guys on the upper deck coped in the searing heat I will never know.

Safely completing our first transit of the Strait of Hormuz into the Persian Gulf we arrived in Bahrain on 10 July. Manama, the capital, would be our home for the next five days. Bahrain is an exceptionally affluent Muslim nation and for a number of reasons this would clearly be a different visit from Djibouti and Gibraltar. Beer and women would be in short supply. Or so we thought.

Walking around Manama was certainly different from walking around Djibouti – you couldn't visit two more contrasting cities. My pockets were full of Bahraini dinars and it was clear that it wouldn't take long to empty them. We wandered around the city and visited several souks, admiring the humongous amount of gold on sale. I wanted to buy a bracelet for Julie but a couple of the old salts on board told me the souks were even better in Dubai so I thought I'd wait until then. We visited art galleries, admired the Islamic architecture on every street and visited the world famous La Fontaine Centre. We came across a Hindu temple and, rather unexpectedly, a Catholic church. We ate in local cafés and hotel restaurants where we enjoyed the delicious local cuisine of grilled meats, curry, seafood and of course rice.

We were surprised to find that it was easy to find beer, albeit in the Western hotels and at an exorbitant price. But those hotels had hidden treasures. On one particular evening, myself and one of the lads from the Stokers' mess ended up chatting away to a couple of gorgeous German women, both probably around ten years older than the two of us. Neither of us was trying to 'trap' so it was very easy pleasant conversation; they were way out of our league. They were in the Gulf with their husbands who were both currently in Abu Dhabi on business so they were in the hotel restaurant having a meal and a few drinks. Anyway, one thing led to another and we went up to their rooms. Annette, not the first girl that I would have sex with of that name, was something else. She taught me things about sex I hadn't come across in our mess wank-mags or seen on our mess videos. I didn't stay overnight, just in case an unwanted husband turned up unexpectedly, and the following morning I discovered my shipmate had also decided not to stay the whole night, for the same reason as I (great minds think alike and all that). Turns out his partner had been to the same school of sex as mine so we'd both enjoyed the best run ashore of the trip so far.

On another evening Aids and I met a load of Filipino girls in the Holiday Inn who were some of the sexiest, funniest girls I'd ever met. On my suggestion Aids and I took a couple of the girls back to the complex where they lived but on arrival at their living quarters we were greeted by an armed guard who wouldn't let Aids and I in. Cue no sex and massive disappointment. If you'd told me before our visit that I'd shag either a German or a Filipino, I'm sure my money would have been on a Filipino. But alas no, I would not experience that pleasure until many years later.

We visited the American Navy Club where we played table tennis and went swimming and we also visited the Sherlock Homes Pub in the Gulf Hotel where the 'Happy Hour' was a particular favourite.

We left Manama, went straight into Defence Watches and exited the Strait of Hormuz to the relative safety of the Gulf of Oman and the wider Arabian Sea. We'd had a cracking run ashore in Bahrain and, more importantly to the Royal Navy and HM Government, we'd flown the flag inside the Persian Gulf and demonstrated that our warships were prepared to go anywhere to protect our legitimate maritime and commercial interests.

Before our next visit to Sri Lanka in ten or eleven days we exercised at sea with the usual mix of Defence Watches and Action Stations. This routine of a few days in a foreign port followed by a week or so on patrol suited me and most of my shipmates just fine. The first few days or so would be 'recovery mode' with everyone chatting and laughing about what we'd got up to and the next few days would be eager anticipation of the next run and what we intended getting up to there (more of the same obviously).

For some reason I always knew Sri Lanka was going to be a special run ashore, especially as I'd signed up for an overnight visit to the ancient capital of Kandy. This visit would coincide with Esala Perahera, a Buddhist festival held annually in late July and early August. The festival is centred on the Buddhist temple of Sri Dalada Maligawa, the Temple of the Sacred Tooth Relic. The visit was oversubscribed but I was one of the lucky ones out of the hat so I was guaranteed a bit of culture in addition to the usual shenanigans associated with a port visit.

Before entry to Colombo on 26 July we had the usual routine of sorting foreign currency and mail, both brought on by boat the night before. Despite a civil war breaking out on the island a couple of years before, a war that would rage for the next 26 years and cause incredible hardship for the general population, we were assured that Colombo and Kandy were safe cities to visit.

On my first wander around Colombo I was struck by the city's eclectic architecture, a real mix of different styles and eras. Whilst no architect (that was my brother's choice of career) it was obvious that this mix was a result of various colonialists including the British, Dutch and Portuguese adding to the styles created by Buddhists, Hindus and others. There were some truly stunning buildings, most notably from my point of view the imposing Red Mosque (Jami Ul-Alfar Masjid) with its tall swirling minarets and striking red and white patterns.

Unsurprisingly the city was an absolute hive of human activity containing a real buzz, vibrancy and frenetic pace. Most of the food that I ate was purchased from local street vendors and whilst I had little idea of what I was eating at the time, or concern, it generally contained a mix of curry and seafood with quite a lot of spicy crab thrown in; absolutely delicious. Each evening we would eat out at one of the hotels but my preference was always the street vendors, invariably little old ladies with their more authentic and basic offerings; in fact I topped up on these several hours after every evening meal before going back to the ship (how great would it be if we could swap our own boring burger and kebab joints back in the UK for these wonderful street vendors?).

I took advantage of a guided tour to a tea plantation up in the hills, somewhat cooler and less stuffy than the hot, noisy, polluted Colombo. Having been brought up by Irish parents in Irish communities, both in Luton and Peterborough, tea had always been an integral part of my life and no visit to a plantation would be complete without purchasing a few boxes for my Irish mother and grandmothers. On the way back to the ship we were dropped off in town; how I managed to maintain possession of my treasured boxes of tea after visits to numerous bars remains a mystery.

The day of the Kandy visit arrived and with some excitement I boarded the bus that would take us east inland to Kandy. On the way we stopped a couple of times, once to buy some coconuts which were taken off the trees as they were ordered and a second time to view some elephants. Elephants are truly wonderful creatures; here some were lying on their sides in dirty 'ponds' cooling themselves after the effects of the blazing sun and some gave us rides, not that they had much choice in the matter of course and in exchange for the requisite number of ickies given to their beaming owners. We were paired up with elephants and I rode in front with a Chief Petty Officer sat immediately behind me.

When we arrived at the hotel I was astonished at the beauty of its surroundings. I hadn't stayed in many hotels and certainly nothing like this. The hotel was of very traditional design, most definitely not a Hilton or a Sheraton, and located up in the hills with quite stunning panoramic views of the neighbouring hills and mountains. Stood on my balcony admiring this incredible panorama with its multitude of varying colours of green, around me and in the distance, I thought, *This is why I joined the Navy.*

As for the festival itself, there are few words that can do it justice. Esala Perahera is a Buddhist festival that lasts for ten days, the highlight of which is a torchlit procession of over one hundred elephants, each festooned with bright silk garments, bright lights and other bright decorations (did I mention 'bright'?). Accompanying the elephants were drummers and other musicians, dancers, acrobats, fire jugglers and of course thousands of onlookers, including a few pasty-looking lads from a far-flung country several thousand miles away. All of this in the shadow of the illuminated Buddhist temple of Sri Dalada Maligawa, the Temple of the Sacred Tooth Relic. The combination of incredible light, colour and music made for a truly magnificent scene.

The people of Sri Lanka are amazingly cheerful and friendly. It was such a shame that there was a civil war raging in the northern part of the island; it was incredible to think that people with so many similarities could be killing each other in cold blood; unfortunately that is an enduring feature of humankind and of course isn't confined to this part of the world.

A shame this was a sex-free visit on my part although Aids and Andy did find a whorehouse in Colombo where they bumped into the Jimmy off HMS *Exeter*. When it comes to sexual needs and desires, rank is of no relevance.

On my 20th birthday, on the last day of July, we set sail from Colombo with memories that would last a lifetime.

We were only at sea for a few days before our next visit and we arrived in Karachi, Pakistan in early August. The ship had visited Karachi the previous year and by all accounts it was a shithole. Given my own experience of Pakistanis in Peterborough I wasn't expecting too much but the lads who'd been on board the previous year told me the locals were an exceptionally friendly bunch. I used to play football for Peterborough Sikhs prior to joining the Royal Navy and my memory of Peterborough Pakistanis, especially on the football pitch, wasn't of a particularly friendly bunch (although of course Peterborough Sikhs vs Peterborough Pakistanis was always a bit of a grudge match).

Money-changing the night before was similar to Djibouti in that the Pakistani banknotes were absolutely filthy. We'd received the usual pre-visit advice and in particular were warned in no uncertain terms not to eat any food other than from the large, branded hotels and certainly not to buy any food from local street vendors. Even in the hotels we were to avoid the likes of lettuce as Karachi's sanitation system at the best of times was pretty rubbish but the day before we entered harbour it had effectively broken down. So no women, no beer and the likelihood of illness or death – this wasn't going to be a great visit.

As Gerry and I walked out of the dockyard on the first morning, together with scores of other lads off both our own ship and also HMS *Exeter*, we were confronted by what seemed like hundreds of screaming taxi drivers. By taxi drivers I'm talking of the horse-drawn variety. All I could see was a throng of Pakistani men screaming, "TAXI?!" at us – not sure if it was a command or a question. One chap came right up to us and started screaming, "Gerry, Gerry!" Fuck me, it was only the guy who Gerry had used the previous year and he recognised Gerry as soon as he saw him. Ali helped us up into the carriage, more of a glorified cart, got on his horse and started screaming at the animal in his native tongue (the driver's, not the horse's, although the latter appeared to understand Urdu). Gerry told me that Ali was a top man and that he'd drive us about all day every day and we would pay him whatever we thought he was worth at the end of each day.

Being driven around Karachi's pot-holed streets and narrow alleys on a horse-drawn carriage was a great experience, albeit heart-stopping and death-defying in equal measure. Ali would park up whilst Gerry and I would get out and wander around shops and cafés and even if we'd been gone for a couple of hours Ali would always be where we'd left him. In the evenings we could be in a hotel for several hours and he'd always be waiting for us. If we'd bought presents for loved ones back home we would leave them with Ali. On one afternoon I'd bought an onyx lamp and vase for my mother and I left these with Ali whilst Gerry and I continued on in to the evening. There was no question of the presents or Ali disappearing. He would always be there, just where he'd parked up. We would always pay him at the end of the day when he dropped us back at the ship and he'd always complain that we were giving him too much. Given average earnings in Karachi at the time, the money that we gave him was certainly a lot. But compared to what we had in our pockets and the service that Ali provided it wasn't a rupee too much. Ali was the first Pakistani that I met in Pakistan itself and, like every other Pakistani I met after him, he was an exceptionally likeable bloke. He clearly didn't have much in material terms but he had great integrity and a fabulous sense of humour, commentating with wonderful comedy on our surroundings as we clattered through the teeming streets of Pakistan's largest city.

Competing for space on Karachi's clogged roads were small buses, all decorated in vivid bright colours and filled to the brim with passengers. Actually they were more than full as passengers would also sit on top of the buses. I never sussed out whether or not there were actually seats on top of these buses but there appeared to be as many passengers literally on the bus as there were inside.

There was an awful lot of poverty in Karachi with beggars on pavements and in the late evenings on our way back to the ship we saw men and women sleeping rough everywhere. One little old lady with her arm in plaster will always be in my memory. On the first occasion that I came across her I gave her a few rupees; I came across her on two further occasions but on both occasions when I offered her money she declined.

Not forgetting the advice to avoid purchasing food from street vendors, I purchased food from street vendors a couple of times every day. Whilst the majority of my shipmates swerved these vendors I couldn't resist them. Even after we'd had evening meals in the hotel restaurants I'd have a snack from one of these street stalls before going back to the ship. The food was what we term 'Indian' food back in the UK, Pakistan being part of the Indian sub-continent of course, and it was quite delicious. The only time I'd enjoyed Indian food this much was when I used to babysit for a Sikh family back home in Peterborough. Every time I babysat for Jack Singh his lovely wife would leave food cooking for me on the stove; authentic homemade Punjabi food consisting more often than not of some sort of spicy curried chicken. India is a massive sub-continent and whilst the cuisines from its various regions have their differences they share a real intensity of taste and flavour, so much greater than the offerings in 'Indian' restaurants back home in the UK (almost always Bangladeshi and cooked to suit European tastes). The lads all told me that I would die as the 'Karachi Dog' would take hold of me in a few days but I considered it a fair exchange for all those delicious chicken rolls and equally delicious behari tikka.

One thing that did surprise me in this Muslim country was the number of men who walked around hand-in-hand. One of the lads told me that "Pakistani men fuck women to reproduce and fuck their mates for fun". I have no idea if this was true but I'd never seen so many men showing affection towards each other in public. But that was all part and parcel of Karachi's street scene. A scene that was quite chaotic in its vibrancy with people, horses and vehicles competing vigorously for the same limited, noisy, dirty space.

One afternoon Aids and I were walking along the beach when we were approached by a local chap who told us his name was Atif; he had a couple of horses in tow and asked if we fancied a ride, in exchange for a handful of rupees of course. Now the last time I'd been on a horse was on my Uncle John's farm in the west of Ireland many moons ago. This Pakistani horse was a bit more excitable than the Irish horse and took off at great speed, galloping across a busy dual carriageway with its owner in hot pursuit. A bit like the one and only occasion that I rode a motorbike, I hadn't been told how to bring the thing to a halt and shouting, "Whoa, ya bastard!" failed miserably as a tactic. We got across the road in one piece although two cars had to swerve to avoid us; as I looked behind I could see Atif frantically trying to keep up and I could also see Aids in the distance, trotting calmly towards us on his rather more peaceful horse.

Eventually the horse came to a standstill and Atif started berating me. As soon as he saw how much I was sweating from pure panic he calmed down and realised that I had no intention of stealing his beloved horse. His attention soon turned to something in the undergrowth a few feet away and he started kicking at what turned out to be a male, dead or asleep I had no idea what. Despite numerous shouts and kicks the prostrate male never moved and Atif motioned me back towards the road and the approaching Aids on the other horse. I asked several times if the bloke in the undergrowth was dead or alive but I never understood Atif's answer, delivered I suspect in Urdu rather than English. Aids and I enjoyed the experience, him more than me, and we buggered off back into town to find a bar and the rest of the lads.

A number of us were invited by the British Embassy to eat a

traditional meal in one of the large city centre hotels. When I entered the room where we were to eat all that I could see was a massive narrow cloth stretched out on the floor; the cloth was laid end to end and stretched from one wall to another. On the cloth there were 40 to 50 plates, half on one side and half on the other with an additional two at each end. There were no tables and no chairs. We each took a position on the floor and the food arrived on plates and bowls arranged along the length of the cloth, accessible to diners on both sides. Whilst cutlery was provided we were encouraged to adopt the traditional method and eat with our hands; the technique being to reach into a large bowl and take some rice, gently roll it between fingers and thumb into a self-sticking ball, dip it into the sauce, mix with a vegetable or a piece of chicken and then, the most important part, pop the whole thing into one's mouth. Easier said than done but a massively pleasant experience nonetheless.

Our visit to Karachi at an end, many of the lads bought presents made of wood – chess boards, ornaments and the like. I only had my onyx lamp and onyx vase and a few of the other lads had opted for onyx too. Let's just say that when we got back to the UK a few months later the onyx was in much better condition than the wood…

Back at sea the 'Karachi Dog' hit us with a vengeance – a literal shitstorm. I say 'us' but I was absolutely fine – no Dog, no sickness and no symptoms. It was so bad some of the heads were reserved for those with the Dog and others for those without the Dog. I found it somewhat amusing that so many of my shipmates who'd only eaten in the large western-owned hotels were some of the Dog's biggest casualties. Despite probably being the street vendors' biggest customer I never had a visit from the Dog. Not that I mentioned this at all to the Dog's casualties. Not once. Of course not.

11. MOMBERS

Back at sea we looked forward to our next run ashore although we had to crack on with the day job for a couple of weeks – patrolling the Strait of Hormuz once again. Mombasa in Kenya would mark the halfway point of our deployment and we had a 17-day stay scheduled; time for some much needed ship maintenance and, of far more importance to the inhabitants of 3EZ mess and every other mess, extended shore leave for the Ship's Company. As with all other visits we would operate 'Tropical Routine' which essentially involved mornings at work with the rest of the day reserved for time ashore; however, Mombasa would also include 'Station Leave' whereby all members of the Ship's Company would be granted seven days' leave to do as they pleased; for the married men, well most at least, this would involve flying their wives out to stay with them in a hotel; for the rest of us it would involve staying in a hotel without the encumbrance of wives.

Life at sea wasn't all about daily routine, exercises, Defence Watches, Action Stations and the like. There was lots of that of course but we were also given time to amuse ourselves with organised events such as the 'Mr and Mrs Contest' and the 'Tramps and Tarts Disco', both held on the flight deck on Saturday evenings. We also held a 'Song Contest' which was won by our very own 3EZ mess. Clad in leather jackets, skirts made from plastic bags and a liberal supply of make-up (where did that come from?), the 'Chamois Leathers' led by Leading Cook Scouse McCann trounced the competition. My voice and legs were entirely inappropriate for the group – I left that to those better qualified.

We would also use the upper deck, when available of course, for keep-fit, circuit training, deck hockey and other sporty stuff. I loved deck hockey; we would make up around a hundred 'balls' in advance, made entirely of black masking tape. When the last ball flew over the deck into the sea the game ended and the side with the most points won.

Whilst the weather outside was always very hot, it was relatively comfortable between decks. Most of us wore white fronts, white shorts and sandals so we were dressed for comfort. When time and operations permitted we were allowed to sunbathe on the upper deck but my Irish skin never reacted well to the sun so I generally avoided sunbathing, save for a couple of occasions. Whilst most of the lads were morphing into bronzed gods, I resembled a pale Pakistani with a bright red nose.

On a couple of occasions we enjoyed 'Hands to Bathe', an event unique to the Royal Navy. Where else can you jump into a swimming pool as large as the Indian Ocean? The first time I jumped off the deck into the sea was a tad scary, not being a great lover of jumping into water at the best of times, let alone water that contained other living creatures much larger than myself. Hands to Bathe was popular with the Ship's Company and whilst I participated, I never swam far from the ship.

On one occasion an inhabitant of 3EZ decided to have his very own Hands to Bathe. Whilst we always topped up with fuel and stores when alongside in port, we would sometimes replenish whilst actually at sea, via an exercise known as a 'RAS' which stood for 'Replenishment at Sea'. Refuelling at sea was something else; imagine refuelling a car whilst driving down a motorway, via a fuel pipe thrown over from a moving petrol tanker in the adjacent lane. Well, RASing at sea is just that although of course the surface is far from flat and it continually moves. It's a complex but well-practised exercise that if carried out incorrectly could spell disaster for a ship laden with missiles and ammunition.

As Writers, Waz and I did our best to avoid 'whole-ship' activities such as duty watches, fire exercises, etc. However we couldn't get out of RASing and we both had parts to play. My part was at the very front of the ship, on the fo'c'sle, playing around with ropes (the fo'c'sle, short for forecastle, is the raised upper deck at the very front of the ship – the pointy bit). To be honest I never really knew what I was meant to be doing but I was pretty good at following instructions and the Senior Rate Seamen, Petty Officers and Chief Petty Officers alike, were rather good at shouting instructions.

We were just wrapping up one particular RAS; we'd disconnected from RFA *Bayleaf* and everyone was doing their stuff to finish off. On completion of my own duties I disconnected my safety harness and left the fo'c'sle to return to the mess to shower and change. As I got to the bottom of the ladder there was a pipe on the ship's public address system: "MAN OVERBOARD, MAN OVERBOARD." MOB was often practised but this wasn't a drill – this was the real thing. Within minutes it became apparent that the man overboard was one of our own, a Jack Dusty by the name of Andy Childs. Now Andy wasn't the most popular member of the mess, probably because he was a bit older than the other Able Rates and fairly opinionated (who wasn't?). Anyway, as per the Naval rule-book, sympathy was something to be found only in the dictionary – somewhere between shit and syphilis. However as the minutes progressed and the bridge kept us updated with pipes, some of us did start to worry. Were we going to lose an oppo? A messmate? Before we sailed a few of the older salts had said that we were bound to lose someone on the trip – the law of averages and all that. Much to Andy's relief the good men of the Seamanship branch swung into action and, courtesy of a couple of rescue boats and their much practised skill, he was recovered minutes before he inevitably became the main meal of the day for another creature even bigger than himself. When he eventually got back down the mess there were various quips such as, "At least you've already had your shower, mate," and, "Must be a bit lonely doing Hands to Bathe on your own." Naval humour, eh? But we were all glad he was alive and well. Of course we were.

On the subject of main meals our Petty Officer Caterer, TCP or 'That C**t Pearson' as he was known, one of the least popular guys on board at the best of times, had done a deal in a previous port to purchase a shedload of steak. On its first night on the menu we queued in anticipation of a succulent cut of thick prime meat, topped with peppercorn sauce and accompanied by the best chips the galley team could muster. No problem with the sauce and chips. However the 'steak' on the galley counter looked nothing like steak. Not thick, not succulent and certainly not steak. Considerable debate ensued as to the origin of this particular meat and whilst I lived with the Cooks and Caterers, no one really seemed to know what it was that TCP had purchased. Our best guess was veal and it made many, many appearances on the menu; it tasted shite.

We didn't drink much at sea although we continued to draw the maximum 75 cans per day. We were building up a significant stash and had hundreds of cans safely stowed under the seats in the mess square and elsewhere. One evening one of the lads got a bit pissed and went wandering down the main passageway bollock naked, gobbing off at anyone who passed comment. Result? The Jossman and his Leading Reg raided the mess and our collection of beer and porn were all removed. I never found out what happened to the beer, recycled probably, but the porn ended up down the Chiefs' mess where the Jossman lived. The Chiefs had a book that you had to sign if you wanted to borrow their porn as they had the best stash. We often had to borrow back our own videos. Double standards? Probably, but no one cared, we knew and accepted the rules of the game.

Whilst at sea I continued to write to the three women in my life – Yvonne, Julie and my mother. I also sent postcards to everyone when in a foreign port, including to my younger cousin Kent who lived in Luton. I wasn't sure what was going to happen with Julie when I returned to the UK. I really liked her of course but her insistence on no sex before marriage didn't appeal to a young sailor with a penchant for sex and a desire to avoid marriage for as long as possible. Time would tell.

The few days before our arrival in Mombasa were particularly uncomfortable as the seas were exceptionally heavy; the ship, her men and her contents were thrown all over the place 24/7. What with a full-on Captain's Rounds with every inch of the ship scrubbed to perfection, we couldn't wait to get alongside.

On 23 August we arrived in Mombasa for what most of us expected would be the highlight of the entire deployment. Mombers was a city much talked about when I was in basic training and absolutely one of the top places that I wanted to visit. I'd heard so many dits spun by older salts that I couldn't wait to get alongside. The city was apparently teeming with bars and women and the 'Sunshine Club' was right up there among the top bars and clubs revered by matelots and ex-matelots worldwide – a real den of iniquity that I and the rest of the lads couldn't wait to experience.

We went through the usual routine prior to the visit: ship's visit memorandum, money-changing, official correspondence, etc; I think some of the other branches did a bit of work too. I remember the Jimmy's spiel the previous evening when he reminded us to practise safe sex (gotta love the Navy's pragmatic and realistic approach). I think he was trying to suggest there may not have been too many virgins hanging around in Mombasa's bars and clubs; apparently around 6,000 American sailors from the US Sixth Fleet had been in a week or so before and it was likely that some of the women, particularly those down from Nairobi for commercial purposes, may have been loosened up somewhat (or infected… I can't recall his precise words).

Entering Mombasa via Procedure Alpha was a great experience. We lined the deck in Number One uniforms; as the ship slowly navigated her way to our berth my excitement and anticipation of an imminent run ashore in a country not visited before grew by the minute; everyone felt it but particularly us younger lads on our first deployment. Procedure Alpha was all well and good but we couldn't wait to get alongside, get ashore and get on it.

Walking across the gangway on the first night of any foreign run is something special; surrounded by mates, hot sun beating down, pockets full of beer tokens and the prospect of a great night ahead; it's difficult to describe the anticipation especially given what we'd been told about Mombers. Whatever else we would encounter, beer and women would definitely not be in short supply in this particular port.

On our first evening ashore we stopped at the first bar we came across and sat outside with a load of lads off the *Exeter*; there must have been around a hundred of us sat at tables stretching from one end of the pavement outside the bar to the other end. Within minutes a group of local girls joined us at our table. Yep, this sure wasn't like Djibouti. Mombers had a completely different feel to it; whereas Djibouti felt like the Foreign Legion outpost that it was, this place felt more like a holiday destination, chilled and relaxed. After a couple of beers and a bit of chat one of the girls and I decided to get to know each other a little better. I looked up to make sure everybody was busy drinking and chatting to each other which of course they were, however, the minute the girl and I stood up there was a round of applause with shouts of, "Rocky's first!" and, "Told you you'd like 'em!" The boys were right – the girls here were so much more attractive than their counterparts in Djibouti.

Having got my end away I rejoined the lads outside the bar; whilst some had moved on most were still there (to be fair, I hadn't been long). The girl in question wanted to spend the rest of the evening with me, which it turned out was the routine in Mombers, but I wanted to get on it with the lads and get on it we did. We toured a few bars and, quite unexpectedly, not, we ended up in the Sunshine Club. The Sunshine Club wasn't that big – lots of tables and chairs, a dance floor, the bar opposite the entrance and toilets outside at the back.

Again, within minutes of entering the bar a bunch of girls joined us. I've got to be honest, I've never seen so many attractive black girls in one place. For what it's worth they were more brown than black and a lot less black than their Djiboutian counterparts; a lot curvier too. As the night progressed lads would disappear, some for a period of time and others not to be seen again until the following morning. One special feature of the Sunshine Club, amongst its other attractions, is that the toilets are the only toilets in the world, or at least to my knowledge, where you can have a piss whilst someone else holds your dick; boy they think of everything in that place.

Mombasa was a great place to wander around during the day. Whilst very much an African city, in common with most ports around the world it had a cosmopolitan feel and the locals in particular, all of whom spoke excellent English, were exceptionally friendly. We did the usual wandering around visiting shops, markets and bars. We'd take in the tourist sites including the famous elephant tusks straddling Moi Avenue and of course Fort Jesus. The city was fairly grimy and in the evenings there was something of a sleazy undercurrent to the place but we all loved it and it was everything that I had expected – there was a real buzz to the place.

Public health was something of an issue and something that we'd been alerted to prior to our visit. There were numerous signs warning of diarrhoea but, rather more importantly but not advertised, HIV/AIDS had just put down its marker in East Africa although little was known about the disease at the time; that said, a few of the older lads who had experienced Mombasa's girls in the past pledged to avoid any sexual contact this time around. The younger single guys didn't care – we were here to enjoy ourselves. Single? Yes, I considered myself to be single. I hadn't known Julie for long and we'd never had sex so I certainly didn't consider myself to be in a relationship. I would cross that bridge when we returned to the UK.

Half of the lads took their Station Leave in the first week whilst I was part of the second batch that would take leave during the second half of our stay. A few of the lads from 3EZ were staying at the Shelly Beach Hotel so the rest of us decided to book into the same place for when our Station Leave commenced. In the meantime we would join up with the guys during the day and also in the evenings but we didn't want to miss out on the Sunshine Club, given it was our favourite bar. There were lots of other bars in Mombers of course and we experienced as many as we could but the Sunshine Club, or Sunshine Bar depending on your preference, acted like a magnet.

One of my mates fell in love with one of the local girls and pretty gorgeous she was too; I'll 'forget' his name for a while so let's call him Micky (not his real name). One night a group of us were sat around a large table with a group of girls, with Madonna's recently released 'Into the Groove' playing loudly in the background (this became something of a theme tune for our visit and every time I hear it to this day I am reminded of the Sunshine Club). Micky was up at the bar getting a round in when I started chatting to 'his' girl. "Oh, Micky he love me," she says, "and I love him but he doesn't want to pay and I have rent and food to buy." Not wishing to see such a beautiful damsel in distress I helped her out; we were gone before Micky got back with the drinks. This time around I was gone for much longer than on the first evening, and for very good reason; I caught up with the rest of the lads at another club later in the evening. Micky's girl wanted to stay with me but you don't buy a kebab and remain in the kebab shop after you've eaten it, do you?

One of the Petty Officers' messes, housing a number of POs, was situated directly opposite the Ship's Office (so only a few feet from our office door). On a number of occasions I would see the same POs with the same girls every single day; essentially they had 'bought' the services and company of the same girl for the duration of the visit. Some of these POs were even single.

One evening at the Shelly Beach Hotel, before my own stay, Stevie and I got chatting to three English girls; all sported the ubiquitous permed, bleached blonde hair so much loved in the 1980s. The girls were on holiday and all staying in the same apartment. We got chatting and after a few drinks one of the girls offered to show me their apartment. I have no particular memory of the apartment itself despite being in it for half an hour or so. When we got back down to the bar her mates gave us knowing looks and one offered Stevie a tour of the same apartment. People are so friendly when they're on holiday.

On another evening three of us decided to go back to one local girl's room together. We let the elder of the three, married, go first. Fuck me, he was at it for ages. The other guy, name conveniently forgotten for the moment, was up second and he was itching to get going. The two of us were sat on chairs behind a makeshift curtain and occasionally we would move it slightly with our feet to see if our messmate had finished but he was going at it for England. Getting pissed off, the other chap decided to get his kit off and join in; I 'joined' in for a minute or two but there wasn't much room as the boys took one end each so I went back to my seat behind the curtain to wait my turn. Ten out of ten for my mates' stamina – they were getting their money's worth. Me? I fell asleep and when I awoke I was in the apartment alone in complete darkness. After temporarily shitting myself I got out as fast as I could and rejoined the lads in the bar where we'd been earlier (I had to navigate a few dark alleys to get there). The fuckers took the piss out of me something chronic but hey-ho, these things happen. The reason for me not revealing certain names is that we had a code: 'what happens on deployment stays on deployment' (I've part complied – events remembered but names 'forgotten').

One afternoon after playing football we went back to the ship to get showered and changed before going out on the piss. It was so hot I couldn't wear underpants or jeans so I put on a pair of loose trousers. The heat was always a bit of a problem for me and one of the reasons why I would never take up an invitation to play golf, although to be honest I couldn't see the point of that game, irrespective of the weather. Obviously it was hot playing football but I normally played in goal and 90 minutes playing football would always be preferable to playing several hours of golf with the old guys. We had a cricket team on board too but that was for the fat lads who were no good at rugby or football.

So no pants but some loose slacks meant I was sitting comfortably in the Sunshine Club. We were sat around our usual table just inside the entrance to the right when it was my turn to get the wets in. I walked to the bar and ordered half a dozen beers for the lads and three more for some local girls who had joined us. One of the girls offered to give me a hand which seemed quite decent of her. As I was waiting for the barman to do his stuff, the girl, 'Bunny' I think we nicknamed her, started fondling me at the bar. I thought she was going to get my cock out there and then and, unsurprisingly, I had a raging hard-on. She picked up the beers for her and her mates and walked back to the table. By the time I paid the barman and arranged the rest of the beers on the tray Bunny was already back at the table sitting down. As I started to walk across the bar towards the table the lads yelled at me and started laughing, pointing to my crotch area. I only still had a fucking hard-on but, holding a tray with two hands and halfway back to the table, there was fuck all I could do about it. The lack of pants and the loose slacks did little to hide my embarrassment. Anyway, Bunny and I got more closely acquainted later on that evening so all's well that ends well.

Whilst HIV/AIDS was a relative newcomer to East Africa and therefore not recognised as a potential problem, the sex trade was certainly not new and many working girls carried health cards to indicate when they'd last been checked out. On one occasion a couple of the lads and I were in town sat on a public bench and an older girl, probably in her late 20s or early 30s, approached us with an eager look on her face. "Go on then," I said, "show us your card." She was keen for the three of us to go back with her and we all had an hour or so to kill before meeting up with the other lads so we all thought 'might as well'. We weren't really that bothered about her card but she wasn't as attractive as the other girls that we'd encountered so we thought we'd check it out seeing as she produced it. She'd certainly been checked out all right although this was 1985 and her last check was in 1975. We went to a bar instead.

12. STATION LEAVE

My turn for Station Leave came and I headed over to the Shelly Beach Hotel where I'd booked a twin room with Gerry for a few days. The hotel was fab and our room opened out onto the beach and the Indian Ocean. There were local guys armed with baseball bats patrolling the beach but we didn't for one minute feel threatened or uneasy. There were quite a few other lads booked in, from both our own ship and also the *Exeter*. There was a large bar with a dance-floor and there was organised entertainment every evening so we were happy; we were more than happy in fact. We had no idea how we'd keep ourselves busy with no work for seven days.

Gerry and I had arranged to spend a night in Nairobi which confused the fuck out of the other lads. "What d'ya wanna go up there for?" one asked. "All the girls have come down here for a fortnight and it's fucking cold and dangerous up there." But it was all arranged, Gerry's idea I think, although that was in a few days' time.

We visited other hotels in addition to the Shelly Beach, notably the Nyali Beach, the Bamburi Beach and the Mombasa Beach. We'd visit them in the afternoons and muck about with a ball in their pools, with beer of course; in fact you were allowed to take bottles of beer into the pools – very civilised and it would have been rude not to. But there was something about the Shelly Beach Hotel and 3EZ had kinda adopted it as our own; quite a few of my messmates were staying with us including Jack, Waz, Soapy, Stevie, Scouse, Tommo, Aids and a few others.

The live entertainment in the evenings was fun and a tad different to say Butlin's or Pontins back home. The African-themed music and dancing was thoroughly entertaining and the musicians and dancers were only too happy for us to get involved; 3EZ's more outgoing members needed little encouragement at the best of times to perform and they got up and joined in. I stayed sat at the table; I was more than comfortable; live entertainment, great atmosphere and a plentiful supply of beer were all that I needed. Well not quite, more females would have helped. But there were few women, other than holidaymaking couples. There were a couple of Dutch girls who were man-free and I'm pretty sure that's the way they stayed, despite some exceptional effort on our part to alter things.

Gerry and I befriended a local guy called Onkwani who used to wander up and down the beach. He didn't have anything to sell and he may have been a mass-murderer for all we knew, or even cared. But he was a nice chap with the fantastic smile that most Kenyan men seemed to possess and the three of us got on very well. We would sit underneath a palm tree on the beach outside our room looking out to the blue waters of the Indian Ocean only a few yards away. The patrolling hotel guards would warn us not to allow Onkwani or anyone else into our room and not wishing to upset any man in possession of a baseball bat, albeit a happy and smiling one, we duly complied. Onkwani taught us a number of Swahili words and phrases and seemed genuinely happy that we were interested in learning as much as we could about his language and his culture. The only words that have remained with me are 'jambo' and 'kwaheri', hello and goodbye, not that they've come in useful anywhere else in the world.

It was one heck of a novelty, and a very pleasant one at that, being ashore on the piss knowing that you could get up at whatever time you wanted to the following morning and go straight down to the restaurant, bar or pool rather than go to work. Yep, Station Leave got our vote – top marks to whoever came up with that one.

The day came for our overnight trip to Nairobi, Kenya's capital city. Clearly a great idea although everyone else disagreed; most had planned to take in a safari during their Station Leave which in their view at least was a far better use of time. Gerry and I decided to take East Africa's equivalent of the 'Orient Express', an overnight 15-hour train journey from the coast to the capital. We were advised that '15 hours' could easily turn into 24 hours, or more, given the system was noted for many things but not its punctuality.

Mombasa's railway station wasn't exactly King's Cross or Waterloo. The whole place was rickety, antiquated and dilapidated; but we wouldn't have had it any other way. We bought our tickets which included dinner and breakfast and we waited on the platform to watch the world go by. This place was busy. Like everywhere else in Mombasa the railway station was a hive of human activity and Gerry and I weren't short of guys coming up to us in an attempt to sell us some tat or, just simply, to have a chat. In common with our shipmates all the guys we spoke to thought we were mad going to Nairobi, warning us of the dangers compared to Mombasa. One fella advised us to remove our watches before we reached our destination; in his words "they'll have your wrists as well as your watches". Apparently the knives in Nairobi are pretty sharp and so too are their owners.

Once on board the train Gerry and I located our first-class compartment; first-class might sound a bit posh but essentially it gave us a compartment for two whereas second-class had four bunks and third-class, according to our new found friends on the platform, probably guaranteed at least a robbery, an assault or both. The train was late leaving but Gerry and I didn't care, we were on holiday, we were in no rush.

Dinner was fantastic, the whole experience somewhat akin to a scene in one of those BBC period dramas. The cups, saucers, plates and the like were straight out of 'Upstairs Downstairs'. The food, all three courses, was excellent; the best food I've tasted on a train, before or since. Given the formality of the experience it felt like the British Empire had returned and we loved it.

Whilst our private compartment was adequate and fit for purpose, and the dining carriage quite wonderful, the toilets were, shall we say, less so. I say toilet but by toilet I mean a hole in the floor; all those squats in Naval gyms would come in handy after all. Whatever you dispossessed yourself of in that toilet, it ended up on the railtrack below, no exceptions.

Gerry and I retired to our sleeping compartment after a few Tusker beers; you couldn't see anything out of the window once darkness had set in and the bulk of the daylight journey would be tomorrow. We both slept well, no surprise given our normal sleeping arrangements on board a Royal Navy warship, and breakfast the following morning turned out to be just as sublime as dinner the evening before.

As the journey continued Gerry and I chatted and drank tea as we looked out of the window. In the early morning sun the view was quite breathtaking, consisting as it did of a vast African savannah, the Rift Valley as I recall. As we passed through villages children would come out and wave frantically at the train, beaming as they did so. Between villages and human habitation the antelopes, zebras, giraffes and other animals made for a spectacular scene; unlike the children they preferred not to wave but they were no less beautiful for it. The train journey was everything that we had expected and, given the service and comfort, it was relatively inexpensive.

As the train arrived in Nairobi, trundling slowly through the slums on the outskirts towards the high-rise buildings in the centre, Gerry and I removed our watches and secured them in our holdalls. Nairobi's railway station was similar to Mombasa's: underinvested, noisy and quite chaotic. The first thing that hit us was the change in temperature – so much cooler than Mombasa with its heat and humidity. Our first job once we'd checked into the hotel would be to swap shorts for jeans.

We'd booked a room in the Hilton prior to leaving Mombasa and the hotel turned out to be a great choice. A 17-storey concrete cylinder rising gloriously from the ground, the hotel was situated in what turned out to be the centre of Nairobi's business and shopping district. Whilst our room on the 14th floor didn't boast the sea views of our room at the Shelly Beach Hotel, it did afford panoramic views of Kenya's intriguing capital city.

Whilst Gerry was having a shower I decided to ring home, completely oblivious to the fact I was adding over a hundred quid to my room bill. But I checked in with Mum and Julie and both were in good spirits. Duty done, freshened up and shorts swapped for jeans, Gerry and I went exploring. We were conscious of all the advice we had received so we didn't venture too far from the city centre.

We wandered around visiting shops, museums and markets. Nairobi was exceptionally busy but despite the noise and congested streets we lapped up its atmosphere and vibrancy. Whilst the capital couldn't boast the natural beauty of coastal Mombasa it did contain some pretty impressive buildings. Oh, and there were statues and plaques, lots of them, mainly honouring Jomo Kenyatta, Kenya's first President who died seven years earlier.

We took a trip up the Kenyatta International Conference Centre, a building whose primary purpose appeared to be an effort to mirror the Hilton in appearance with its striking cylindrical tower whilst beating it in height (size mattered it seemed). It contained nearly 30 floors and had a revolving restaurant at the top offering unbeatable views of the city. When we reached the summit we were informed that all tables were booked but at least we experienced the view, albeit only for a couple of minutes as opposed to the hour or so that we had hoped for.

In the evening we focused on the city's bars where we got into conversation with a number of locals and, in the hotel bar itself, a group of Westerners. To a man and a woman none could fathom why we had left Mombasa with its hot weather and glorious beaches but we wanted to see the capital, it was as simple as that. There was an apparent dearth of available women but we did get chatting to two in particular who seemed very interested in us; unfortunately, not for the first or last time in our lives that interest turned out to be restricted to our wallets and willingness to buy drinks.

The following day we decided to go to the cinema. No idea why. We settled into our seats, having chosen a film whose advertising suggested that it contained lots of blood and gore. Just before the film was due to commence music started playing and the other dozen or so inhabitants of the cinema stood up. Gerry and I continued to chat until some fella wearing a uniform and wielding a baseball bat motioned us, quite aggressively, to stand up. It's difficult to question a baseball bat, especially when it's waving at your face, so we complied and stood up. Turned out it was the national anthem. The Kenyan people were clearly a patriotic bunch as, like Mombasa, there were pictures of the President, Daniel Arap Moi, almost everywhere. Not just in public buildings such as the cinema and museums but in just about every shop and bar that we visited. Anyway, turned out the film was in Swahili; we got bored and left.

When we checked out of the hotel we were asked to show identification; as Gerry hadn't brought his passport with him he showed his Royal Navy ID card, as he'd done the day before. For some reason he was given a discount, around 25%, a military discount we assumed; needless to say I proffered my own ID card for which I received the same discount. Royal Navy ID cards might not have been worth much in Soho's Raymond RevueBar but they were worth something here.

So with Nairobi ticked off our list we left the hotel and caught a cab to the railway station. It had been a fairly uneventful visit but we enjoyed wandering around unfamiliar places and Nairobi was interesting, even though it was a bit of a concrete jungle with more than its fair share of noise and pollution. Despite all the doom-laden predictions, or maybe because of them, we'd avoided any drama; whilst not as friendly as the people on the coast and in many cases somewhat suspicious of our presence, the people were friendly enough. We'd enjoyed the visit but we were looking forward to getting back to the familiarity of Mombasa and our drinking mates.

The return journey mirrored, unsurprisingly, the journey up: dinner, bed, breakfast, fabulous views and shitting in a hole in the floor. We got back to the ship, swapped stories with the lads and went out on the piss. Oh Sunshine Club, we'd missed you!

As we left harbour a few days later the ship's PA system played 'Jambo Bwana', a local pop song that we all had become familiar with during our visit; whilst we didn't know what the words meant we all knew the words and sang along (well, the first few words at least: *Jambo, Jambo bwana, Habari gani, Mzuri sana...*). Mombasa had been a tremendous visit, enjoyed by all.

After a few days it became apparent that Micky had picked up a dose. It's hard to keep these things secret on a ship, especially down the mess where the Medical Assistant lived. Not that I'm saying our Scablifter outed Micky but we all knew he'd picked up a dose and he wasn't happy. "For fuck sake," he would frequently remark, "I only shagged one bird, I get a dose, and he escapes having fucked a different bird every night," (pointing at a fellow messmate). True, Micky had only fucked one girl, probably on every one of the 17 nights of our stay, and our mate had fucked a different girl every night.

"But we all fucked her too, Micky," wasn't the answer that Micky wanted; he got a dose, the rest of us escaped. Micky got some cream from the Scablifter which in conjunction with a few hot showers soon cured him.

13. CROSSING THE LINE

So it was back to sea for around three weeks prior to our next visit to Dubai and boy we needed three weeks to recover from Mombers, a visit that would live forever in all our memories. I say 'recover' but while we were at sea we had an inter-mess 'Superstars' competition where teams of six from all messes competed against each other via 10 different gym tasks. Aids, Jack, Waz, Dave, Scouse and I represented 3EZ and we came 7th out of 10 teams; we were happy with that.

A couple of days later we were in Defence Watches around the Strait of Hormuz; whilst we were all thoroughly enjoying the deployment the serious stuff was never far away as the Iranians continued to fling missiles around the Strait and the wider Gulf of Oman. A visit to the upper deck one morning put everything into perspective – the sight of several abandoned, burned-out oil tankers surrounded by beautiful blue sea was one heck of a sight.

After a couple of weeks at sea patrolling the area around the Strait of Hormuz the Captain announced that we would be having a 'banyan'. Essentially a banyan is a beach BBQ with lots of beer and lots of food. A bit like your garden BBQ except we'd leave our home floating out at sea whilst the ship's helicopter and small boats would transport us to a remote beach to enjoy our shenanigans.

The banyan was great – copious amounts of beer and food and a pleasant opportunity to get off the ship and onto a beach for a few hours. Most of the lads from the mess were there and the Cooks did us proud with the scran. As ever the weather was red hot but I covered up my shiny Irish skin with heavy duty sunscreen and came back even paler than when I'd left, complete with a bright red nose.

Next stop was Dubai which involved another transit of the Strait of Hormuz. Defence Watches ensued just in case the Iranians tried any funny stuff; they would occasionally send out small boats to come up and have a look at us but they knew to keep their distance; our guns were bigger than theirs (or at least HMS *Exeter*'s was as we were limited to rather large missiles).

Dubai turned out, as expected, to be very similar to Bahrain with its fantastic buildings and opulent surroundings. The Gulf States are incredibly clean, tidy and well-organised and given their law and order regimes, some might say barbaric regimes, we always felt 100% safe. We'd wander around as per taking in the sights and sounds of yet another foreign country and most of us bought gold from the souks; I bought Julie a rather expensive gold 'rope' bracelet, even though I was unsure if I wanted to continue the relationship when I returned home; but that dilemma didn't need to concern me out here.

Beer was in short supply and women in even shorter supply. The Western hotels did of course sell beer and with an average pint at £4 we immediately took to Thatcher's Bar in one hotel that had a long happy 'hour' every afternoon selling pints at £2 – happy indeed. I felt quite at home supping pints in a bar adorned with Whitbread memorabilia – reminiscent of the Eight Bells in Peterborough.

I decided that I wanted to grow a beard so it seemed like a good idea to give it a go in the hottest part of the world that I'd ever visited. I duly submitted my written request form to the Captain to 'discontinue shaving'; there are various conditions attached to this including not being allowed on any formal parade during the early days of bumfluff but none affected me.

I was particularly jealous one day when Aids, Paul and a guy off the *Exeter* went to the Dubai Sailing Club courtesy of an invitation from Sheikh Mohammed. We had no idea how they managed that one but when they returned to the ship in the back of a pristine BMW 7 Series they all looked particularly chuffed with themselves.

So it was back to sea for a couple of weeks prior to a visit to the Seychelles. We transited the Strait of Hormuz successfully and carried on with our patrol in the Gulf of Oman. The heat got the better of me and despite slowly turning into George Michael with the beard, in my view at least, I submitted a written request form to 'continue shaving'. The beard was pretty pathetic to be honest and the short but growing hairs had become a major source of irritation in the heat. I'd given it a go and vowed never to bother again.

The next week or so at sea would be really important from a personal point of view as I was due to sit my Leading Writer's Professional Qualifying Examination on 17 October, the day after our arrival in the Seychelles. In between working and shore leave I'd continued with my studies and had made good progress, completing the study guides in mid-September; if I passed the examination I would be promoted to LWTR although it would take a few weeks to find out the result and another few weeks for the glorious 'B13' to arrive (the formal notice to the Captain to consider advancement).

The day before our arrival in the Seychelles we held the Royal Navy's traditional 'Crossing the Line' ceremony for all those who crossed the equator for the first time in their careers. General Grant played the part of King Neptune, a role for which he was eminently suited. This wasn't actually the first time that we had crossed the line but on previous occasions rough seas and operational commitments had prevented the ceremony from being held.

The equatorial virgins among us stood on the flight deck surrounded by our shipmates whilst King Neptune set up his 'court'. The traditional ceremony followed with charges read out and each equatorial virgin dunked head-first into a large pool of water. On completion all ex-virgins were issued with personalised certificates containing a written proclamation signed by Neptune Rex with the words:

"A Proclamation – To all whom it may concern – Whereas by Our Imperial Condescension We give this as a Royal Patent under Our Sign Manual to certify that "WTR H O'ROURKE has this day visited Our Royal Domains and has received the ancient requisite initiation and form necessary to become one of Our Loyal Subjects. Should the above mentioned person fall overboard, having become one of Our Loyal Subjects, we recommend all Sharks, Dolphins, Whales, Eels, etc. under our command to abstain from eating, playing with or otherwise maltreating him. And we further direct all Sailors, Soldiers, Marines, Globetrotters, etc who have not crossed Our Royal Domains to treat him with that respect due to one who has visited Us. Given at our Court on the Equator, in Longitude 55/30 this 15th day of October 1985."

Our arrival into Victoria on Mahé, the largest of Seychelles' 100+ islands, was somewhat different to previous visits as we were 'anchored off' rather than berthed alongside in port. Furthermore we were instructed to wear uniform on shore leave which is never the choice of sailors. Anyway, usual routine of money-changing and official mail sorted, we got ashore as fast as we could. This promised to be a tad different from say Djibouti or Karachi – people paid a lot of money to visit this place and we'd just been deposited here free-of-charge by our employer.

There was a real feeling of calm and tranquillity about Mahé and we all wandered around the capital Victoria acclimatising ourselves to our new surroundings. The food in particular was tremendous – a real fusion of African, French, Indian and Chinese (with a bit of British thrown in here and there). Staples as you would expect included fish and curry but cooked in a way that I had not experienced before; there are some things we have the French to thank for after all. My first meal was 'Spicy Shark' washed down with refreshing coconut water – quite sublime. In the evening we trawled around a few bars on the hunt for local women – there had to be some somewhere surely? But the bars were populated by couples, honeymooning couples, with few local females anywhere to be found. Worse still the bars closed at midnight so it was back to the ship for all of us, no exceptions.

Day Two was the day of my examination for Leading Writer so rather than a morning in the office I was cooped up in an officer's cabin answering a multitude of written questions about pay accounting, personnel records, classified correspondence, cash records, service writing, legal stuff and the like. The exam went as well as it could have and I was confident that my preparation over several months would pay off. I wouldn't get the result for a few weeks but no matter, I had other things to do today.

After my exam I got ashore with the lads and as we were now allowed to wear civvies we were all in high spirits. Most of us headed for the glorious white sandy beaches which even according to the old salts among us were probably the best beaches that any had experienced. Lying on a sun lounger admiring the palm trees and bright turquoise sea whilst drinking cold beer brought it all home to me – this is why I joined the Royal Navy. I could have carried on with my 'A' Levels and gone to uni or I could have stayed in Peterborough and got an office job with Thomas Cook or Pearl Assurance; but I joined the Royal Navy and here was I on one of the world's most glorious islands drinking beer with my mates.

In the evening Bill, Aids, Waz, Larry, Gerry and I toured around a few different bars on the hunt for single women (actually the 'single' bit wasn't particularly relevant as 'available' was the key). But we failed. Maybe we'd visited the wrong bars? But everyone we bumped into told the same story: friendly bars, cold beer, lots of couples and zero available women. The six of us ended up in a disco, got completely shit-faced and danced together on a large dance-floor.

Not sure if we were any good but we enjoyed ourselves nonetheless, women or no women.

A few of the lads took advantage of various 'island hopping' trips although I decided to stick to Mahé on the assumption it probably boasted more sandy beaches and well-stocked bars than any other island in the archipelago. I did decide to do something adventurous and with a few of the lads went parascending. Parascending, or parasailing if you prefer, involves being connected to a very large balloon/parachute with a rope attached to a boat which shoots off at a rate of knots and hey presto, you're up in the air. The Seychelles boasts 115 islands and I was suddenly looking down on more than I could count; the view was absolutely stunning, quite breathtaking. The activity only lasted around 20 minutes but it was an exhilarating experience to say the least.

There were loads of activities to busy ourselves with during the day and many of the lads went diving and snorkelling. In a further spirit of adventure I hired a small boat for an hour, along with a few of the other lads (we were all in separate boats). Nothing to do with me of course but the bloody thing malfunctioned and once out into the sea it suddenly locked and would only move in a large circular direction. I waved frantically to the other lads in their boats out in the distance and they all waved back. Once I'd overrun my hour one of the boat's owners came out on his own, thinking of course that I was taking the piss. Once he'd realised what had happened and rescued me it was him and his oppos who took the piss. But it was a good laugh and there was beer to be drunk so no hard feelings.

The ship's football team had a match vs the Barclays Bank Social Club which promised to be good fun, despite the heat. I let in three goals in the first half although I maintain I was the best player on the field (it's a goalkeeping thing... other goalkeepers will understand). We won the second half 1-0 although Aids summed it up perfectly: "We were shite." Well summed up, mate. After the footie we all headed to the beach for a BBQ; the football result and our performance were soon forgotten.

On our penultimate evening I somehow got tasked with 'Shore Patrol'. Together with the Killick Reg we drove around the island keeping an eye on the various bars and, more importantly, the few hundred sailors off not only the *Cherry B* but also HMS *Exeter*. Sporting a thick Naval Provost 'NP' wristband I felt somewhat important although of course I would rather have been in one of those bars with my mates. Not unexpectedly there were no issues or incidents and the night passed off peacefully. It was rather interesting though seeing all of the bars stone-cold sober – all looked completely different without an abundance of alcohol inside me.

Despite the lack of single women we all enjoyed the Seychelles with its spellbinding beaches, exquisite food and friendly hosts; the Seychellois had really made us feel welcome and we were very grateful for their hospitality. So off to sea again and northwards to the Gulf of Oman to check out those pesky Iranians before we headed home.

Our time done and Armilla completed, HMS *Exeter* and ourselves handed over on 7 November to HMS *Newcastle* (*Exeter's* Type 42 equivalent) and HMS *Jupiter* (our Leander equivalent). The usual practice of lining the upper decks and spraying water across the sea at each other with all horns blaring was dutifully observed and we headed up the Red Sea for our trip home.

Work aside we busied ourselves at sea with the usual frolics including horse racing, a sods opera and a huge raffle, all of which took place on the flight deck. The Writers were tasked with managing the financial side of things for the horse racing event and funnily enough we both ended up ahead.

The sods opera and raffle were both held a couple of evenings before a number of the Ship's Company were due to be flown home for 'Advance Leave'. As with the ship's song contest, 3EZ's Chamois Leathers stole the show. The Spanner Wankers won most of the raffle prizes and whilst the Dabbers and Greenies insisted on a conspiracy theory, the rest of us believed such a ruse to be beyond the wit of Stokers.

A couple of days later members of the Advance Leave Party were transferred via our small boats to RFA *Bayleaf* to hitch a lift to Akrotiri in Cyprus for their flight to RAF *Lyneham* back in the UK. Once they'd enjoyed a spot of leave and early Christmas turkey they would return to the ship after our arrival back to look after the old girl while the rest of us enjoyed a few weeks' leave. I certainly didn't volunteer for Advance Leave as I didn't want to miss out on a visit to Alexandria or another visit to Gibraltar and in any case I preferred my Christmas turkey on Christmas Day. However, Aids, Larry, Tommo and Chuck all volunteered for Advance Leave so the mess was shorn of a few characters for the final weeks of the deployment.

Up the Red Sea and the Gulf of Suez, through the Suez Canal, turn left and after a few miles you have Alexandria on the left. Founded by the young Alexander the Great, Alexandria is a Mediterranean port city sitting on Egypt's north coast and in 1985 had a population of around four million. Unsurprisingly when we got ashore it was an absolute hive of activity, one of the busiest port cities that we'd visited if not the busiest. We quickly learnt that whilst this city shared its name with a number of attractive females, none of them lived here. During the day the city teemed with life and the streets were choked with wall-to-wall traffic; the evenings were a tad quieter and the only women in evidence were rather fat belly-dancers. That said, they still managed to extricate bundles of Egyptian pounds from alcohol-fuelled sailors, me included. The later the hour, the thicker the bundles. They may not have been pretty but these girls had a job to do and they did it rather well.

On one evening a few of us set up a tab with a hotel bar and did our utmost to give our hosts a very profitable night. When we got up to leave a few hours later the presented bill appeared to bear no resemblance to the amount that we had drunk; sure, we had drunk a significant amount but the bill would have paid for the hotel's next refurbishment. I asked to see the manager and he came out with a colleague. I politely pointed out that his team were trying to rip us off. His colleague politely removed his gun from its holster. We politely paid and buggered off elsewhere.

The food in Alexandria was particularly enjoyable especially the street food with its plethora of fresh crab and squid, two of my favourite foods. As with our previous visits there appeared to be a distinct correlation between the quality of the food and the vendor. If the vendor was to be found sitting on a rickety stool in a dusty back-street the food was guaranteed to be the best available. My favourite dish was a bowl of spicy balls; I never did learn what animal produced those balls or what part of that animal the balls came from, but they tasted delicious and nothing else mattered.

We visited temples and mosques, admiring all from the outside rather than the inside. Most of the bars were closed during the day so we satisfied ourselves with the city's culture. Alexandria, like most port cities, is a wonderful fusion of different influences evidenced in its architecture, its food and its people. Cosmopolitan yes but not as cosmopolitan or grand as this city once was.

The highlight of the visit was always going to be the trip to the Pyramids; it's just one of those things you've got to do when in Egypt. After an uncomfortable four-hour bus ride south and east to Cairo we were desperate for some beer and pitched up at a bar close to the Pyramids. A swarm of local men descended upon us; why is it always men and never women (apart from Mombers of course)? One asked, "You want girl?"

To which I replied, "I'd love one, what's she like?" He showed me a picture of an ugly woman who turned out to be his wife so I politely declined.

"You want young girl?" he asked.

To which of course I replied, "Yes please," as if he were asking if I wanted a bag of crisps with my beer. He showed me another picture, this time of a much younger girl, his daughter.

On the grounds of decency and legality I politely declined but undeterred the salesman came back with, "You want boy?" The answer to that was obvious and I carried on with my drinking.

I did, however, cave in to one guy and swapped some folding stuff for a ride on his camel. The ride was fairly bumpy but that was nothing compared to the smell; whilst camels absolutely stink this one had nothing on its owner, the smelliest human being I had ever encountered. I got off after a few minutes and went back to my beer.

The Pyramids themselves and the Great Sphinx of Giza made for some great photo opportunities but I for one was underwhelmed. Call me a heathen but the Pyramids reminded me of Stonehenge; they just didn't do it for me.

Whilst we enjoyed Alexandria it was a fairly uneventful visit although it was good of course to visit Cairo and the Pyramids, underwhelming or not. We sailed west for the final visit prior to our return home, Gibraltar once again.

We were glad to see the rock still there and looked forward to a taste of home, having been away from the UK for nearly six months. On the evening of our first day I bowed to peer pressure and agreed to complete the 'Fleet Top of the Rock Road Race' the following afternoon. Apparently it was only a short distance from the bottom to the top so I trained by bar-hopping 'til 0300.

The following day Gerry and I set off with a couple of hundred other fit young lads to run up the rock. It wouldn't take long and if we put on a bit of a sprint we'd be able to get out on the beer a bit quicker. Run? After a couple of hundred yards it became apparent that it was challenging enough to actually walk. Around halfway up I coughed up a load of blood and cursed myself for agreeing to such a foolhardy exercise. 32.42 minutes after starting off I crossed the finishing line and was duly presented with my certificate for coming 150th. I say a couple of hundred started the race but for all I knew there may only have been 151 as I could only see one other guy behind me.

On the plus side we received a letter whilst alongside with the PQE results for Leading Writer; high up a long list with a pass mark indicating far too much wasted effort on my part I got the news I wanted: I'd passed and due to the pleasant effect of supply and demand I would shortly be advanced to Leading Writer, subject to the Captain's approval of course.

After a couple of nights in Gib with the obligatory bar visits we set off for home. It had been a truly wonderful deployment, my very first, but to a man we all looked forward to getting home. In the words of one of my messmates… "You can't beat a bit of blue vein."

After such a significant deployment Procedure Alpha was a given; the wives, girlfriends and others who had travelled miles to welcome us home wanted to see us in our finery up on the upper deck as the ship came alongside. Me? Nah, none of that bollocks. I did get into my Number Ones but on the correct assumption that no one would notice my absence I locked the Ship's Office door and cracked on with the mail that had just arrived. My mum and youngest sister were somewhere on that jetty and so too was my girlfriend. I had to get to my girlfriend before my mother. Sons of Irish mothers will understand.

When I crossed the gangway Julie was standing a few yards from Mum and my eight-year-old sister Tess. They all remarked that they hadn't spotted me on the upper deck but that wasn't my fault of course, given a couple of hundred young matelots in Square Rig all look the same from a distance. We gave our loved ones a tour of the ship and introduced them to our messes and our mates. Everyone expressed surprise at the basic surroundings and lack of space but that was something that we all had ceased to notice a long time ago. Mum asked how I coped with the noise and the smell to which I replied, "What noise and smell?" I'd come a long way since my first couple of weeks on board.

A couple of hours later I was walking up Plymouth's Union Street with Mum, Tess and Julie. Actually I was walking behind with Tess whilst my mum and Julie walked together a few yards ahead. Once we arrived in our chosen restaurant it became obvious that Julie's mood had changed and it wasn't until the following morning that I managed to find out why. The night before whilst walking to the restaurant Julie had said to Mum, "Hugh's really good with writing letters and sending postcards, isn't he?"

Mum agreed and responded, "He's great; he writes to me, you and Yvonne and he sends postcards to all of us and also to his little cousin Kent in Luton."

When Julie asked mum who this Yvonne was my mum replied, "Oh I'm sorry, I really shouldn't have said that, it's not what you think, they're just friends, oh I'm really sorry, it really isn't what you think." Irish mothers, eh? This wouldn't be the last time that my mother would upset one of my girlfriends with some deliberately chosen words.

14. GUZZ, LONDON AND AMSTERS

We had a few days' leave but returned to the ship after a long weekend as longer Christmas leave was only a couple of weeks away. It was back to Guzz routine but this time we were men of the world – we had dits to spin and dits we spun. Our favourite haunts had survived and it wasn't long before Boobs, the Two Trees, the PR and other watering holes benefited from our presence and more importantly our beer tokens.

Aids and I were out one evening and unusually for me I hadn't done my usual Cinderella trick of wandering off around midnight. Aids and I were walking through the dockyard back to the ship in the early hours when we spotted a ladder on a small building site. "Come on, mate, we can find a use for that," I said to him.

"What the fuck will a Writer and a Caterer find a use for with a ladder?" he unhelpfully replied. Well we came across a fence so the ladder helped us over it and into an area we hadn't been to before. Turned out we were now in the Submarine Refit Complex and as it appeared rather boring we exited on the other side, helped by our new ladder. Amazingly no one noticed our ladder as we clambered up the gangway as the QM and his buddy were deep in conversation. We collected our station cards from the box, said goodnight to the QM and left the ladder on the deck by the hatch.

For the next few days we spotted our ladder being used by the Dabbers whilst they were painting the upper deck. We thought nothing more of it until a week or so later when the MOD Police decided to question us. Now whilst coppers aren't known or recruited for their intellect, the MOD version is a breed apart. Most MOD coppers are ex-squaddies who can't bear life without a uniform so on discharge sign up to guard a gate and carry out the odd investigation into heinous crimes such as missing ladders. Aids and I were both questioned but I'd genned up beforehand, courtesy of Queen's Regulations for the Royal Navy where theft is defined as taking something from someone else with the intention of permanently depriving that person of his or her property. We had no intention of depriving the ladder's owner of his or her property, not on a permanent basis at least. So despite the best efforts of the MOD's very own Plod, Aids and I escaped with our clean criminal records intact.

Of far more importance than a dockyard ladder, my B13 Advancement Order had arrived and with the approval of Lieutenant Whalley, my Supply Officer, I was up before the Captain, Commander Phillips, on 20 December. Duly advanced and backdated to the date of my exam, it was off to the Stores Office to collect my new badges. Going from an 'Able Rate' to 'Leading Rate' is a significant milestone in a young sailor's life as it denotes the first rank of substance (equivalent to a Corporal in the Army and RAF). I was now the youngest Leading Rate on board and wore my badges with pride. Next stop Petty Officer Writer unless I achieved a commission beforehand, something Lt Whalley had floated to me and something that I was definitely interested in.

Christmas leave came and went and for me it was great to get back to the Eight Bells. Having joined up only three years ago as a spotty virgin who had never been abroad I now had tales to tell and a badge of rank to boast of. Not all of the spots had disappeared, however.

Back on board the ship geared up for sea once again; sea trials and exercises before a flag-waving port visit to our very own capital city – London. The more experienced salts often talked of English visits with Liverpool, Newcastle and Hull the three favourites. Hull? The boys were adamant Hull had the best ratio of women to men in the UK and with no Google or Wikipedia in those days who was I or anyone else to argue? As for Liverpool, in Scouse's words: "Scouse girls are really friendly, a great fuck, but don't let them open their mouths unless you're putting something in." I really wanted to visit Liverpool, Newcastle and Hull but Liverpool most of all.

We sailed up the Thames on a cold morning in January, lining the upper deck in our finest. People welcomed us on both sides and from all vantage points, including Tower Bridge as we sailed underneath. Someone shouted up to one of the girls, "Get yer tits out!" for which he was given a severe dressing-down off the Joss who happened to be standing immediately above close to the bridge. I cannot say who uttered those dreadful non-PC words although it may have been a newly promoted Leading Writer.

We berthed alongside HMS *Belfast*, a somewhat older vessel than the *Cherry B*. No money-changing here and no mail on arrival as our Lynx helicopter had brought that on board the day before but I couldn't get ashore as quickly as I would have liked as I'd been volunteered to do some PR stuff in the Wardroom. I shook a few hands and explained my role to a few posh types and as I was about to leave I spotted a handful of invitations on the Wardroom table for a nightclub down the King's Road in Chelsea (none of these were to be found elsewhere on the ship so clearly only commissioned officers were welcome). Once ashore Aids and I headed for the King's Road with a couple of free passes to a posh club in my pocket, trouser pockets rather than jeans as we'd decided to posh up for the occasion.

We checked out a few pubs and after a few beers Aids said, "Come on, Rocky, let's find some posh birds." Not one to disagree with one of my bezzy oppos we headed for the club and the invitations did their trick – no queuing and no entrance fee. The place was so posh it didn't serve pints and half-pints cost as much as two pints elsewhere in the country.

"Mate, this is a bit different to Boobs and the Sunshine Club," I said to Aids but he didn't hear me as he was 100% focused on the eye candy. Wow, this was some club; it was absolutely packed and it became clear very quickly that whilst the girls were somewhat different to the regulars in Boobs they were actually all after the same thing. We quickly got into conversation with a couple of girls and explained how the two of us effectively ran the ship. We had similar conversations with a few others until we landed and those immortal words were uttered: "Would you like to come back to our place?"

'Our place' turned out to be a very small one-bedroom flat with two single beds, one in each corner. Undeterred we got down to it although in complete darkness and conscious of not making too much noise. Around half an hour later I asked Aids if he wanted to swap but his partner had fallen asleep and after I'd taken the piss I realised that so had mine. The next morning I got up before Aids and as I went to the toilet I noticed his partner in the kitchen, clad only in a thong and a short top. Fucking wow, she was so much better-looking than her mate and so much better-looking than the night before (now that made a pleasant change). My partner was still asleep and so was Aids so I helped with the tea and toast-making which took around 20 minutes. I'd never before had sex with someone whilst they were leant over a kitchen top eating toast but with the right girl I can't recommend it enough.

The next morning it was announced that all shore leave was cancelled as some plonker had nicked the ship's bell off the *Belfast.* We all found it rather funny at first but after an hour or so it became apparent that the Jimmy was serious and none of us were going ashore. Following the application of significant peer pressure the miscreants returned the bell and shore leave was reinstated. That evening Aids and I headed back down the King's Road, paid the exorbitant entry fee and scoured the club for the girls. 'Our' girls were nowhere to be seen and we couldn't remember where they lived. We never saw them again.

After a few more nights on the sauce in a multitude of central London pubs and clubs we set sail once again and headed home to Guzz. Everyone had thoroughly enjoyed London, none more so than Aids and I who recounted our first night to the other lads with relish.

Julie was still on the scene but when I decided the time was right to do the decent thing she asked if I'd take her to Peterborough and I relented as that was far easier than finishing with her and I was a coward. I suppose I thought she'd give in and have sex and maybe we'd have a longer and who knows, maybe even a permanent relationship. It wasn't right that only one person in the relationship was having sex even though only one person wanted to.

Taking a girlfriend to meet your mother is always a challenge, even if she's met her before. Irish mothers in particular hold the view that NO girl is good enough for any of her sons. That said it must have been the same with English mothers as the best way I have of explaining my mother's love for her sons is to compare her attitude to that of Gertrude Morel in DH Lawrence's brilliant novel *Sons and Lovers*; essentially no women could love her sons as much as she did so they simply weren't good enough. Mrs Morel once said to herself of one of her son's lovers "she is one of those who will want to suck a man's soul out till he has none of his own life" and I'm pretty sure Mum felt the same about Julie. But I wasn't so sure; thus far Julie didn't want to suck anything.

On one occasion Julie and I were alone upstairs in one of the bedrooms and after a Herculean effort on my part I managed, with Julie's agreement of course, to remove her top and also her bra. This was a humongous achievement on my part but one half does not a naked lady make. Julie kept saying, "Not now," and, "Not yet," so after exercising my tongue I gave up and decided that I needed to end the relationship as we clearly wanted different things. Actually I had no idea what Julie really wanted apart from, I think, marriage; I on the other hand wanted to live the life of a young sailor and any relationship that didn't include sex wasn't a relationship that I wanted. As for telling Julie, I'd do that another day.

Back down to Guzz and after exercises in the South West Approaches we were afforded some 'R&R' via a few days in Amsterdam, or Amsters as it is affectionately known by all matelots. I'd never been to Amsterdam but it was one of those most talked about runs ashore in the Royal Navy; a great port city that had more than enough attractions to keep 220 young lads occupied for a few days.

I put my name down for the visit to Amsterdam's famous Heineken Brewery (not the brewery of today which is located on the outskirts of the city but the original brewery in the city itself which is now used as a visitor centre).

Once alongside in Amsters we opened the Ship's Office for routine business plus the usual queries with money-changing whilst the Seamen on the upper deck did their stuff in safely securing the ship. Then it was off for a shower followed by a quick change into civvies. Nowadays lots of young men visit Amsterdam with their mates but how many get the opportunity to visit with over 200 mates with transport, bed and board all paid? OK, we had to work a few hours every morning but that was a small price to pay.

I remember much about my first visit to Amsterdam, particularly evening meals in a number of different restaurants. The Dutch are known for many things although not their cuisine, unless you like chips and mayonnaise with everything. That said, Amsterdam even in those days had a fantastic array of restaurants offering cuisine from all over Europe and beyond.

But the one thing above all else that I looked forward to seeing was Amsterdam's famous red-light district and its hundreds of 'windows'. The Dutch are a very liberal and tolerant race and rather than prohibit everything that some may consider distasteful, the

Dutch prefer to allow it, manage it and tax it. The red-light district is centred around Amsterdam's many canals and includes sex shops, sex museums, peep shows, strip clubs, theatres and of course those rather wonderful windows.

Wandering up and down alongside the city's canals was a tremendous experience for a young lad. Sure I'd watched a lot of porn movies and read a lot of porn mags (did I say 'read'?) but seeing so many beautiful scantily-clad women in the flesh was something else. I can honestly say that I never went with a prostitute in Amsterdam but I can't honestly say that I wasn't tempted – I did my fair share of window shopping. Mind you, there were a number of 'mornings after' when I couldn't remember the last few hours of the previous evening so I'm not backing my memory with any money or sworn affidavits.

On our second day we had the visit to the world-famous Heineken brewery. We were instructed to wear rig and further instructed, in no uncertain terms, not to go drinking in the city afterwards; we were to return to the ship and get changed into civvies before carrying on with our drinking. 'Normal' visitors to the brewery were afforded a couple of glasses of Heineken in the visitors' bar after the guided tour but we were allocated one hour during which we were allowed as many beers as we could drink. Amsterdam's Heineken isn't to be confused with the weak, watery stuff on sale in the UK in those days, the session beer brewed by our very own Whitbread under licence. No, this was the proper stuff – 5% 'premium strength' beer.

The tour was of particular interest to someone like me who had lived in a pub since the age of ten; like most of my oppos I had never visited a brewery, let alone one as famous as this one. I grew up in a Whitbread pub and my rite of passage into the world of drinking was via Heineken lager, albeit the 3.4% variety sold in Whitbread's vast estate of pubs. Once the tour was complete we all made our way to the bar and took full advantage of the free beer. Young British males, particularly in the 1980s, did not drink beer in moderation; no, we focused on quantity rather than quality because our culture and our weak beers encouraged that. At first it was a bit odd to be drinking out of half-pint glasses and with 'head' that seemed a bit extreme (beer aficionados will appreciate the importance of good head in terms of keeping the bad gas out (oxygen) and the good gas in (CO_2)). However, we didn't undergo a sudden and dramatic conversion to continental drinking habits; no, we drank this stuff as if it were pints of the piss variety that we had become accustomed to at home.

Upon leaving the brewery, completely bladdered and contrary to orders, we decided to visit a bar or two prior to returning to the ship to get changed and return ashore. I say one or two but it turned out to be five or six. Not untypically for me, then or now, I became detached from my oppos and started wandering the streets looking for food and a taxi back to the ship. I wandered down an alleyway and was confronted by three rather large dark-skinned fellas. Within seconds I was on the floor with an empty wallet thrown back at me. Luckily for me I wasn't seriously assaulted, apart from a few kicks to my sides; my assailants went easy on me, clearly satisfied with the contents of my hitherto fat wallet.

A bit disorientated and still pissed I wandered around a bit more, unable to purchase any food or hail a taxi given my now poverty-stricken status. Taking what I believed to be a short cut down another alleyway I was confronted by another three dark-skinned fellas, not quite as large but just as menacing as the last lot (they clearly hunted in threes). Not sure why I resisted more on this occasion given I had nothing worth nicking but after a minute or so of futile defence I was on the floor; one of the guys nabbed my wallet and started waving it around, shouting in a language I didn't understand (it didn't sound Dutch but linguistics isn't my thing). I started laughing, shouting, "Your brothers beat you to it, you wankers," which I think they understood. Two of the guys started kicking me, everywhere except my face which I protected by curling up into a ball, pushing my head in towards the wall with my hands held tightly around it.

I eventually got back to the ship courtesy of a concerned taxi driver who accepted my promise of payment on arrival. When I walked up the gangway, or rather hobbled up as I was in considerable pain, the Quartermaster enquired, "Good run ashore, Rocky?" knowing full well from my dishevelled appearance that I'd been in the wars.

"Better than it looks, mate," I replied, adding, "just gonna nip down the mess to get some ickies to pay the taxi driver."

The taxi driver paid, I returned up the gangway; by this time the QM was a little more sympathetic, saying, "You'd better see if there's a Scablifter on board, you don't look too good." Ignoring his well-intentioned advice I returned to the mess, got changed into my civvies and returned ashore although the remainder of that particular evening remains a blur in my memory.

The rest of the visit passed off peacefully although I couldn't play football the day after my mugging as I was not in a good way; a shame as it was a match against a decent local side and one that I had looked forward to. However, my bruises and battered ego didn't prevent me from getting ashore with the lads and enjoying Amsterdam's hospitality. Live sex shows, peep shows and the sex museum all saw some of my money. One live sex show was particularly interesting; a group of us were sat towards the front having a few beers, ogling a beautiful dark-skinned girl who was sat alone at the next table. We were trying to work out if she was with anyone else and enquired a couple of times if she wanted a drink, which she politely declined. A few minutes later one of the bouncers, a big bald chap, walked up to her and they started chatting; a couple of minutes later they both headed towards the stage. Unbeknown to us they were part of the entertainment and the big bald guy proceeded to give the rather gorgeous girl one hell of a pounding, which she seemed to rather enjoy. We were all rather jealous of course but we'd paid our dues so we concentrated on the entertainment and showed our appreciation.

Sex and beer aside we continued to explore and wander around the city centre; we visited museums, hired bikes, cycled around canals, ate in restaurants and generally lapped up Amsterdam's wonderful hospitality. The Dutch can come across as a tad brusque, especially in speech, but they are a wonderful people whose liberal and tolerant attitudes endeared them to this young sailor and every other sailor for that matter.

My final foreign run ashore on the *Cherry B* completed and thoroughly enjoyed, we returned to the UK. My bruises healed and my wallet was replenished so no harm done.

The ship was due to enter a lengthy period of maintenance and the majority of the Ship's Company, myself included, would soon leave with only a skeleton crew left behind for the duration of the refit. In the remaining couple of months of the commission we spent most of our time exercising off the north east of Scotland or alongside in Rosyth. We did get quite a bit of time ashore and we availed ourselves of the delights of Inverkeithing, Dunfermline and Edinburgh. Inverkeithing was a quiet night out, pubs only, whereas Dunfers and Edinburgh were 'out out'. Dunfers was our favourite; whilst not on a par with the vibrant city of Edinburgh it was closer and had all that we wanted – bars, clubs and girls. For some reason the girls in Dunfermline appeared an awful lot more 'friendly' than the girls in Dumbarton across to the west although that might have been down to the fact I was now more experienced and a lot more confident than in my days back in HMS Neptune.

For the first time ever and possibly the last I was complimented on my 'dancing' by a rather attractive girl in a Dunfermline night-club; I was actually moving my arms above my head in an effort to remain standing as I was pissed and everything around me appeared to be spinning; as Erasure were playing and my movement was anything but conventional I suspect I resembled a gay lad just enjoying himself (so gay the girl in question only wanted to 'admire' my dancing, nothing else).

I decided to use the time alongside to restart driving lessons and signed up to a local school. My instructor Beryl was a wonderful old girl who was certainly closer to 80 than 60 although she could have been the proud owner of a card from the Queen; her car was a sporty little black number and a joy to drive. Unlike my instructor in Dumbarton she never distracted me with comments such as, "Wow, would you look at her," and I grew in confidence. However, I was nowhere near ready for my test after an 18-month driving absence but I vowed to buy a car and apply for an immediate test during my forthcoming leave in Peterborough.

Having previously received a Draft Order for HMS Raleigh, I received a revised order to join the Britannia Royal Naval College (BRNC) in Dartmouth. My previous order related to a Writer's draft whereas the system had now caught up and my draft to Dartmouth was as a Leading Writer. I would leave the ship in early April and after four weeks' leave would join BRNC in early May. Dartmouth sounded like it would be very different to a 'normal' shore barracks and certainly much different to returning to HMS Raleigh, albeit as Ship's Company rather than as a trainee.

After several discussions on the matter my Supply Officer Lieutenant Whalley decided to request that the Captain raise 'CW Papers'. CW stands for 'Commissioning Warrant' and is the first step on the journey from a Rating to a commissioned officer. I appeared before Captain Phillips on 27 March; he gave his approval and papers were raised. The Correspondence Officer Sub Lieutenant Bennett had to pen a few words, Lieutenant Whalley a lot more and the Captain a few more. The report made good reading with the Captain summarising thus: "Leading Writer O'Rourke is a pleasant quick witted young man who is well informed and a good conversationalist. He shows much potential and I consider him a sound candidate for promotion." It wasn't all about pubs, clubs, girls and football.

April arrived and the time came for me and many others to leave the ship. We had a few runs ashore beforehand, quite a few in fact, and we all took leave of each other in the full expectation that we would all bump into each other in the future, either on board another ship or, quite probably, in a bar in Guzz, Pompey or further afield.

I headed home to Peterborough and signed up once again for driving lessons. Unfortunately my plea for an early driving test due to an impending sea draft (I lied) worked rather too well – it was confirmed for one week later. On the day of my test I couldn't control my nerves and my left leg in particular wouldn't stop shaking. I failed.

The day after failing my test I applied for another one, using my military status as a reason to jump the queue. I was told that I would have to wait a minimum of four weeks between tests as that was the law; I emphasised on my application that I was only home on leave for another four weeks and hey presto, another date arrived for exactly four weeks after my previous test.

After looking and nearly buying a Jaguar, and then a Capri, sense prevailed and I bought a Nissan Cherry. Not any old Nissan Cherry. This was a 1.3 SGL Nissan Cherry with stripes down the side and wipers on the front headlights. My old fella kept telling me that my first car should be an older car as I couldn't afford fully comp insurance and I was bound to bang it but what did he know?

I decided to bin my driving instructor and use my own car for both lessons and my next test. Mum took me out for loads of lessons but our similar personalities resulted in much conflict. One 'lesson' involved a 79-mile drive to Norwich with my brother and three sisters in the back. My brother lost no opportunity to wind me up and as per I took the bait; my mum told me to focus on the road and ignore my brother, an irritating sod at the best of times. My mum and I had an argument whilst stationary at a roundabout which resulted in her grabbing hold of my hair, violently pulling my head from side to side. A bit reminiscent of the time she tried to teach me how to play the accordion prior to joining the Royal Navy; that ended in violence too.

My test arrived and Mum dropped me off at the Test Centre after a few hours driving around Peterborough. The examiner got in the car and in a broad Irish accent asked, "Howya young fella?" As I drove off he asked what I did for a living and after explaining that I was in the Royal Navy he informed me that he had been in the Royal Air Force. So an Irishman and an ex-serviceman – this could be my lucky day. As I approached one roundabout and dithered, not knowing whether to stop or carry on, he said helpfully, "No need to stop, carry on through slowly whilst keeping an eye on the right." We enjoyed a bit of banter about Service life, chatted about Ireland and all the time he gently coached me through the test. I passed.

Mum was waiting for me at the Test Centre – she was overjoyed that I'd passed. Whilst Mum could be very difficult she genuinely cared for her children and our success; she certainly did her best to encourage us in all that we did although all three of my sisters focused more on her difficulties than her good points, something that would manifest itself more and more in later life (you only get one mum). I dropped Mum back to the Bells and told her I wanted to go out for a spin on my own and headed off to the 'Parkways', Peterborough's very own racetrack, otherwise known as the city's ring road system. This system was built in anticipation of a significant increase in Peterborough's population which hadn't quite materialised (it certainly would many years later) so the road itself was perfect for a new driver – great surface, light traffic and easy to get up past 100mph. My go-faster stripes certainly worked.

15. A STRAWBERRY BLONDE

So after only a few days as a qualified driver I made the 280-mile trip down to Dartmouth in Devon's South Hams. To be fair I'd had a lot of practice driving my new car which at only 18 months old was in very good nick. Most of the journey consisted of motorways, particularly a long stretch of the M5, although the roads from the A38 in Devon to Dartmouth itself were narrow, bendy and often unmarked (nothing's changed). I arrived at the gates of the Britannia Royal Naval College in one piece and proceeded to Beatty Block, my living quarters for the foreseeable.

Beatty was actually three blocks and as I wasn't a Senior Rating or a Wren, my block was found by a process of elimination. My mess was a two-man mess that connected with a four-man mess and the 'other' man was sat on his bed. Lloyd Hewitt, 'H' to his mates, introduced himself as a fellow Leading Writer although he worked in the Captain's Office and I would be working in the Pay Office. He suggested the pub which seemed as good a place as any for me to kick-start my Dartmouth adventure. We walked down to a cracking little boozer called the Market House and as I supped my first pint and chatted to H I knew that I would enjoy my year or so in this rather quaint little Devon town.

Britannia Royal Naval College is the new-entry training establishment for wannabe commissioned officers – the posh equivalent of HMS Raleigh if you like. The buildings are grand indeed and a hell of a lot grander than their predecessors, two wooden hulks moored on the river where officers trained prior to BRNC opening in

1905. Sitting on a hill overlooking the picturesque town of Dartmouth and looking out to where the River Dart meets the English Channel, there are few better located training establishments anywhere in the world.

Whilst BRNC is famous for its stunning frontage, comprised as it is of Portland stone, red brick, Cornish slate, Torquay limestone and Cornish granite, there are a few fairly bog-standard buildings situated immediately behind the main building. One of these is 'D Block' and that rather functional building housed the Pay Office, responsible for all pay, cash and allowances pertaining to Service personnel, both new-entry officers and the Ship's Company. The Ship's Company was very small, consisting primarily of a Royal Marine band and a few matelots such as myself.

The morning after a few beers with H in the Market House saw my introduction to the Pay Office. My immediate boss was a POWTR by the name of Trev Jones and his boss, and ultimately my boss too, was the Supply Officer (Pay) Lieutenant Neil Russell, an ex-Writer and a Pompey football fan so clearly salt of the earth. My job was to manage a section that comprised a couple of hundred pay accounts, all belonging to new-entry officers, by their nature a tad more complicated than 'ordinary' pay accounts but I won't bore you with the details.

In terms of duties I was assigned to the swimming pool as a lifeguard and that duty would occupy me one or two evenings a week. Yep, I thought someone was having a laugh at my expense too but no, someone was serious. I had no intention of allowing that one to rest.

A stroll around BRNC and its grounds revealed in addition to the swimming pool a decent gymnasium, five tennis courts immediately outside my office and the Britannia Beagles, a pack of hunting dogs. Members of the Ship's Company could use the pool, gym and courts but the beagles were there for other people's 'pleasure'.

Over the following days and weeks I settled into my new life. BRNC was my third shore establishment since passing out from Writer school; I felt somewhat lucky to have served on a helicopter base, a submarine base and now a college of international renown, all in such a short space of time; variety is indeed the spice of life. Oh, and there were pubs aplenty in Dartmouth. And girls it would seem.

Dartmouth boasted 14 pubs in 'the town' all of which were within a short walk of each other. There was also the Lord Nelson at the top of the hill in the town's only housing estate and whilst that might be a bit out on a limb, experience taught me that these pubs often bore the most fruit. Only two pubs opened past 2300, the Floating Bridge and the Country House, both of which opened until 0100. The college employed two 'outside' companies, RCO to do the cleaning and Compass Catering to do the catering. Both of these companies employed lots of young women, many of whom lived in the town. Apparently the Floaters and the Country House were the places to meet these lovely women, after 2300 of course.

When I said I lived in a two-man mess I wasn't being entirely accurate. It turned out to be a two-man, one-woman and one-dog mess. H had recently split up with his wife and whilst she continued to live in their Naval married quarter, H had moved back on board, with his Labrador dog and also Rose, his Wren girlfriend. One evening when I returned from an evening in Cornwall visiting Julie I was getting undressed as quietly as possible, assuming H was asleep in the other bed, when a girl's voice piped up, "Hi Hugh, you OK?" H was elsewhere that night but Rose was in his bed... alone.

As I turned to Rose, completely naked, I replied, "Yeah, you?" As I looked at Rose, a pretty little thing, I became aware that someone began standing to attention so I got into bed as quickly as possible. On another occasion I was standing bollocky buff at the sink one morning having a shave when the shower curtain next to me moved and out walked Rose. This wasn't your usual Naval barracks.

The constituents of the Royal Marine band in Dartmouth had some job. Actually most of them had three jobs. Their 'day job' consisted of prancing around on BRNC's parade ground until midday, their 'second' jobs consisted of whatever they wanted in the afternoons and on many evenings they were back in uniform for their 'third' jobs performing at various functions for which they were handsomely rewarded. One of the most junior Bandies drove a top-of-the-range BMW; the annual insurance must have cost him more than his Royal Marine basic salary.

Fed up with me moaning about being a lifeguard, it was suggested that I become a 'Duty Driver'. I didn't moan for the sake of it but saving someone's life in a pool of water? Come on, I was hardly a round peg in a round hole for that particular duty. To become Duty Driver I had to acquire an additional driving licence, the coveted 'Admiralty Driving Permit'. The day arrived for my driving test, for which no lessons were apparently required, and I took a drive around the college accompanied by a very genial Petty Officer. The test lasted five or ten minutes. I passed and was subsequently furnished with an ADP. Job done.

Once or twice a week and on some weekends I would carry out the role of Duty Driver. There were two parts to this duty and I was always accompanied by another Junior Rating, of Able or Leading Rate, never a Bandie of course as they had better things to do maximising their various income streams. The first part of the duty included frequent drives around the college grounds and perimeter to check that all was OK, including a spin up to Norton Heliport to check that no one had broken into the hangar.

The second part of the duty, unofficial of course, involved giving lifts to local girls so that they could get from the pubs back up the hill to their homes in Townstal. We never charged for this service but it was always much appreciated. If anyone ever asked why the black Mini Metro with an RN registration plate was seen in Townstal the answer was always the same: "Just checking the married quarters, Chief."

The Pay Office turned out to be a great place to work and in addition to the SO (Pay) and POWTR, both top blokes, I got on very well with Juicy Lucy (Wren Writer), Sharon (Leading Wren Writer) and Bungy Williamson, a bespectacled, ginger-haired Leading Writer from Norwich. Lucy was a great laugh but out of bounds as she was seeing Trev, a WAFU based at the college. Sharon was married and lived in Plymouth so unlike Lucy I never saw her ashore. But Sharon did introduce me to tennis and very good she was too, standing still delivering shots all over the court that had me running around like a lunatic. I never won a match but Sharon had great legs and always wore short skirts so I felt like a winner… every time.

Bungy and I came up with the idea of moving out into a flat. It wasn't that we didn't like living on board but Bungy wanted more freedom and I wanted somewhere for Julie to stay overnight, not that I ever discussed this with her of course. We came across a small flat owned by a builder called Jim Atkins; it was part of a large house but Jim owned the whole building which he was converting into flats. When we viewed the flat we asked where the second bedroom would be. Initially Jim looked a bit confused but replied, "Rest assured, boys, there'll be two bedrooms by the time I'm done." Given he was some way through his conversion we had no idea where he would put a second bedroom but as I had a girlfriend and Bungy didn't, that was gonna be Bungy's problem, not mine.

When we moved into the flat the second bedroom had indeed materialised. It could have doubled as a broom cupboard had it been big enough. "That's yours, mate," I said to Bungy and proceeded to unpack my stuff in the larger bedroom. Now Bungy was a great chap and we got on well but he turned into something else after work – a Punk. Remember Viv from the Young Ones? That was Bungy, although not as house-trained. That said we had a lot in common and we got on great.

Bungy did possess some strange habits. I'd often get back to the flat and find a kitchen chair in the bath where he'd eaten some scran whilst having a bath (the chair doubled as a tray). Not that Bungy ever cooked; left to his own devices he would have lived on Coca-Cola and crisps. I taught him to cook Irish stew once. Now I'd never cooked Irish stew before but I'd watched my parents do it, from afar, so how difficult could it be? The key as I explained to Bungy was to let the stew cook for hours on end; my old fella would cook his over several days. It was a Sunday morning when I cooked the stew so off we went to the pub with the meat and veg bubbling away for Ireland; I told Bungy that when we got back three or four hours later the stew would be perfect. When we got back seven or eight hours later the stew was burnt to a crisp and the pot was of no future use to man or beast.

I'd suggested to Julie that she spend a night at the flat in Dartmouth, not to have sex of course, just to go out for the evening and for her to stay over. She promised that she would but she was clearly reluctant. I didn't mind driving over to Cornwall to meet her once or twice a week but on a couple of occasions I did have car trouble; it was scraped by another car as I was stationary on a Cornish country lane after picking Julie up from babysitting and on another occasion I got caught up in a flood when returning to Dartmouth and had to be rescued by a Land Rover. Both events cost me a lot of money, given I was only insured 'third party, fire and theft'.

One evening ashore I was leaving the Country House with Bungy before closing time, no idea why so early, when a girl who was sat beside the entrance with her mate said, "Hey, you gonna buy me a drink?" She was fairly good looking with a couple of great assets so it appeared rude not to comply. An hour or so later we were in her bed where I stayed until the following morning.

Now whilst I had no intention of seeing this girl again I was consumed by guilt. I arranged to meet Julie in Plymouth and after a couple of drinks we were sat in my car in a car park in the city centre.

I'd been putting off the inevitable but I had to do it. I didn't really feel like I'd cheated on Julie whilst on board the *Cherry B* as our relationship had barely begun when I deployed to the Middle East. But now it seemed much more like a girlfriend/boyfriend thing and I had to tell her. I had no intention of finishing with her but assumed it would finish once I'd spilled the beans. There were loads of tears and amazingly Julie said that she understood and that it was her fault for not sleeping with me. Of course it was my entire fault but at least she understood. We agreed to carry on seeing each other although clearly that was the wrong decision for both of us.

It wasn't easy in the mid-80s trying to save a relationship without the benefits of mobile phones, WhatsApp, Messenger, email, etc. The only way I could contact Julie was by phoning her landline at home. The next time I spoke to her she broke down in tears and her father came on the phone and said, "Leave her alone, it's finished."

I replied, "Not until I hear it from her."

To which her father replied, "You'll never hear from her again." I wrote a few letters to Julie and rang a couple more times but received no response.

A few weeks later Lt Russell asked me into his office for a chat. Julie's old fella had only written to the fucking Captain. For fuck's sake, that's all I needed. Neil Russell was a top bloke and he'd been where I'd been – a young, confused lad who wanted the best of both worlds. The boss convinced me to leave it be and move on and, despite not being one to easily take advice, I took his.

So single once again, I thought I'd make the most of it. I was on a night out in Plymouth with a mate off the *Cherry B* when I asked a girl to dance. She was called Julia (typical) and was visiting a mate in Plymouth. She was a mental nurse, that is what psychiatric nurses were called in those days, and she was from Pirbright in Surrey. Over the next few weeks I got to know Julia very well although she never visited Dartmouth or stayed at my shagpad; well, pad, without the shag. We met up in Plymouth a couple of times and during a week's leave I spent most of it in Pirbright with Julia. To say Julia was a goer is an understatement. I'd only had a couple of girlfriends, one of whom was a sex-free zone so this was really good. Julia and I would go out most evenings with her flinging her little Mini around the streets of Pirbright, Aldershot and Guildford. She loved sex, had a great personality and was a mental nurse in more ways than one. We agreed to see each other as often as possible and she promised to come down and stay in Dartmouth as soon as she could get leave.

On the following Monday the college's 'security state' went up a notch to 'Bikini Black Alpha'. That meant security on the main gate had to be beefed up and the various side gates, locked but unsupervised in our normal state, had to be manned. It made sense to utilise the Bandies as they were Royal Marines first and Bandsmen second and they'd all received far more military training that the likes of me and the rest of the Ship's Company. But oh no, they had their various jobs and significant incomes to consider. So while the Bandies pissed off at midday the rest of the Ship's Company, those of us with proper jobs, had to man the gates. Bugger our real jobs, we could catch up later.

I was tasked with 'guarding' a small gate at one end of the base that was used by civilians coming to work early in the morning – cleaners, stewards and the like. The gate was normally locked but it was easy to bypass, as was the gate down by the Floating Bridge pub which afforded easy access to Beatty for civilian girlfriends (I was yet to take advantage of this facility). I had a gun, with no ammo, and was wearing one of those camouflage 'can't see me' suits. I clearly had better things to do especially at the ungodly hour of 6am but at least there was a stream of girls to chat to, albeit briefly, as they made their way to work. One such girl, a cute blonde, took my eye so I spent a bit more time searching her handbag than others. She was very uncomfortable and kept saying, "Can you hurry up please…? I've got work to go to." Her discomfort was obvious and as she may have been an IRA operative I carried on with my diligent search. I picked up some sanitary towels whilst searching her bag and she went bright red; she wasn't trying to hide her IRA credentials after all, it was just the wrong time of the month.

Bungy and I decided to give the Lord Nelson a try up in the Townstal housing area at the top of the hill; it was a bit of a hike but by now we'd tried and tested all of Dartmouth's other pubs including the Floaters, the Country House, Victoria, Seale Arms, Market House, Ship & Dock, Seven Stars, Royal Castle, Mayflower, Dartmouth Arms, Cherub, George & Dragon, Windjammer and Trafalgar. I did like Dartmouth.

As we ordered our first pint I noticed the cute blonde at the bar so I attempted to spark up a conversation with her. She wasn't too keen and the girl with her, who turned out to be her older sister, kept giving me the evils. We all left at the same time, coincidentally of course, to catch a bus down to the town. Turned out the cute teenager was called Belinda and her sister was called Karen. We got on to the subject of hair; Belinda was pissed off because a hairdresser had cocked up her hair and the 'blonde' was now more white than blonde. I asked what her natural colour was, as you do, and she responded, "Strawberry blonde." Now I knew what strawberries were and I also knew what a blonde was but 'strawberry blonde'? I hadn't a fucking clue. I asked Bungy but he was more clueless than I. Given the absence of Google, I remained clueless for some time.

At the weekend Bungy and I were upstairs in the Country House, after 2300 of course, enjoying the disco. Actually we were enjoying the beer and the eye candy as neither of us knew how to dance and neither of us had any intention of embarrassing ourselves. But hey presto, there was Belinda and Karen standing by the cigarette machine. I plucked up the courage to ask Belinda to dance and amazingly she agreed. Whilst strutting my stuff she did remark, politely, on my lack of ability. I was shit and I knew I was but hey, she was cute and I was single. My corniest line of the night was, "I do love your pink skirt and shoes."

"Actually they're cerise," was the response. Again, if only Google had existed in those days. I had no idea what cerise meant but a short skirt and stilettos on a pretty teenager did it for me.

Belinda and I agreed to see each other again but I had a dilemma as Julia was meant to be coming down the following weekend. I didn't want another Julie situation so I phoned Julia to tell her I didn't want to see her again. If only they had emails and texting in those days, it would have been so much easier.

16. BOY RACERS

Belinda and I started to see more and more of each other, so much more in fact I finally learnt what strawberry blonde meant. Belinda was only 17 and her sister Karen, only slightly older than me, played chaperone on the first few occasions. As things developed I started to spend more time with Belinda in her flat and I spent more nights there than I did in my own flat which was costing me considerable rent (and of course its primary purpose as a shagpad had rarely been utilised). However, Bungy had got himself a girlfriend and amazingly he bagged himself a female version of himself – another Punk. Belinda and Karen had to start work at the college every morning at 0600 so I would give them a lift up, drive back to the flat, get changed, have breakfast and drive back to the college.

My new routine became a bit of a pain so I 'moved' back on board whilst keeping my flat. I became the 'Leading Hand of the Mess', 'LHOM' for short, and I had my own single cabin. This worked well practically as I could drop Belinda and Karen off to work, get my head down for an hour or so, have brekkie in Beatty and then go to work. But I was still paying my half of the flat which no longer served its purpose, from my point of view at least. I had a chat with Bungy and we decided to give notice on the flat and he moved back on board too. It had been good while it lasted but it was an expensive shagpad given no shagging was going on there, Punks aside of course.

I'd learnt from my stew mistake with Bungy so one day I promised Belinda and Karen that I would make a stew for them. They worked 'split shifts' which meant that after their morning shift they would have a few hours off before returning to the college for their evening shift. I'd make the stew and have it ready for them for when they got back in the afternoon. A few hours later, whilst eating my wonderful stew, Karen asked, "What the fuck are these?" I'd put in a shedload of black peppercorns as one of the girls in the office had told me that pepper in stew greatly enhanced the flavour. Problem was, I'd never heard of pepper mills or grinders. How was I to know?

Around this time my grandfather, my mother's father, passed away in Luton. Grandad was a heck of a character, an Irish version of old man Steptoe. He passed away in the building where I was born, St Mary's, a few hundred yards from the mecca of football. I visited Grandad in the chapel of rest and I saw him lying in peace. He'd been ill for a while, all started with a sore toe that he kept poking with a pair of rusty old scissors. Funerals are of course sad affairs but Irish people mitigate the sadness with drink and 'craic'. Grandad was the father of ten and the grandfather of several dozen; Irish aunts, uncles and cousins came from all over the place including from far afield as Puerto Rico. We gave the old fella a great send-off – he would have been very proud.

My mate Jock had now left the Navy as his leg had never healed after the footballing injury that he sustained a couple of years earlier. He was now living with his girlfriend Ann, a girl he met at a party in Alloa that he and I attended a couple of years previously. Jock was working for a finance company in Plymouth so we would meet up every now and then, sometimes just the two of us and sometimes the four of us as the girls got on well. Jock and Ann loved Dartmouth and Belinda and I loved Plymouth so all was good.

Work was pretty routine but enjoyable nonetheless. I was studying for my Petty Officer's exam and I was also attending Maths 'O' Level lessons at HMS Drake in Plymouth as that was the one 'O' Level that I was short of for a commission; once I got that under my belt I would be able to attend a three-day Admiralty Interview Board and if successful attend BRNC as an Officer Under Training rather than a Ship's Company Leading Writer. As part of my ongoing development Lt Russell would include me in weekends on Dartmoor when he had to take his turn in assisting the training staff, something all Staff Officers had to do from time to time.

Weekends on Dartmoor were great fun, from the staff's perspective if not the Officers Under Training. I would drive a long-wheelbase Land Rover and together with Neil Russell there were a couple of other officers and also a Leading Cook. Whilst the Officers Under Training would be under canvas for the weekend, sustained by 24-hour ration packs, we would stay in Ditsworthy Warren House near Sheepstor, owned by the Admiralty and later to become famous as a principal setting in Steven Spielberg's film 'War Horse'. Ditsworthy Warren House was a ramshackle old building that provided basic shelter and was known by many as a 'stone tent'. We had basic bunk beds, better than the OUTs' tents, and our chef cooked up some great rustic meals, far tastier than the OUTs' 24-hour ratpacks.

I wasn't involved in the organisation of the expeds on Dartmoor; all I had to do was tag along, drive the Land Rover and help out as necessary. The Staff Officers would direct the young OUTs, give them tasks to keep themselves occupied, invariably involving getting from A to B carrying heavy rucksacks, with a bit of supervision here and there to see who was doing what. A three-hour walk with rucksacks for the OUTs would only be a matter of minutes for us with the Land Rover so we would often find a pub to enjoy some beer and food.

On one particular exped Lt Russell asked the OUTs, I say 'asked' but you get my drift, to move a large granite boulder. "Right lads, the last group up here moved this here from over there – put it back, will you, and keep yourselves occupied once you've finished – we'll be back in a couple of hours." It was a pretty large boulder but the primary objective of these expeds was to give the lads practical leadership tasks, or PLTs as they were known, supervised of course to identify the leaders, the followers and the shirkers. "Come on," said the boss, "let's go to the pub." I was surprised we weren't going to hang around to supervise but who was I to argue?

A couple of hours later, satisfied by a fantastic lunch courtesy of a moorland pub, we returned to the spot where we had left the OUTs. There were around two dozen of them and they were sweating buckets. "You not moved that little rock?" enquired the boss.

"It won't move, sir, we've tried everything," piped up one little Rupert.

"We've even tried ropes," continued the lad with the Eton accent.

"Fuck," said Lt Russell. "Apologies, boys, wrong rock, that one's been there for a couple of thousand years."

That evening we decided to go to the pub again (there's a pattern developing here). We told the lads that when we got back we would try and get into their tents. If one or more of us succeeded, breakfast the following morning was cancelled. If none of us succeeded our chef would rustle up some bacon butties for the lot of them. Off to the pub we went and unlike the lunch-time session this time we had a bellyful of beer. Apparently the drink-driving rules don't apply to military vehicles on Dartmoor after dark.

We got back to Ditsworthy Warren which was in complete silence – no sound or light from any of the tents. We decided which tents we would infiltrate and I headed off to my target. As I got closer I heard some movement within the tent so I lay down in the undergrowth; the minutes ticked by but I was determined to stick it out so I closed my eyes and kept completely still. Next thing I knew I was tied up outside a tent with half a dozen OUTs standing over me smirking. Apparently I'd fallen asleep and when I started snoring, revealing my location, I was captured and taken hostage. The boys got their bacon butties.

We had a new POWTR in the office as Trev had been promoted and moved on. He was replaced by a northern chap by the name of Trev Dean. I got to know Trev and his wife Anita very well; exceptionally down-to-earth, they were typical northerners and great fun.

In the days of no internet and mobile phones social meetings were always pre-arranged so a couple of times a day I would find myself outside the NAAFI shop at exactly the same time each day. Coincidentally the same time as Belinda had her break from the Junior Gunroom where she worked, adjacent to the NAAFI. No short skirts or stilettos but she still looked cute in her steward's uniform (civilian, not RN).

As Belinda and I became a couple it was time to meet the parents… and the grandparents. Belinda's parents and her mother's parents all lived in Devonport, within spitting distance of the dockyard which of course had now become part of my life. Her old fella Mick was an ex-matelot, from Plymouth we think but no one was sure, and her mother Mary was from Malta. Much of the residential area surrounding the dockyard consisted of flats and maisonettes; Mick and Mary lived in a maisonette in Duke Street and the grandparents lived in a maisonette in nearby Granby Green. Whilst these blocks of maisonettes were rather drab and run-down in appearance, they contained couples and families who took great pride in their homes.

On the first occasion that I met Mick and Mary I was introduced to their budgie. Someone let it out of the cage and the little fucker flew straight at me. Sitting there trying to be polite I could see this fucker coming straight at me. It didn't alter speed or course for a single second and flew straight into my face, clasping on to my nose. I was told later that I even swore 'posh'. I'm far from posh but this was Devonport.

Whilst I was very familiar with Devonport there were a number of pubs where matelots simply didn't go; the pubs that I knew such as the Avondale, the Complex, the Royal Naval Arms and the Chapel were all matelot pubs but there were a whole host of pubs elsewhere in Devonport that I'd never heard of; these were the pubs of the dockyard workers. Mick was a 'Jan Dockie' in matelot parlance, a Devonport dockyard worker (define 'worker'?). The pubs in the neighbourhood around the shopping area of Marlborough Street, close to where Belinda's oldies lived, were much rougher and more rumbustious than those elsewhere in Devonport that I was more accustomed to.

When Mick first introduced me to the likes of the Crown & Column, the Beresford and the Brown Bear he told me to keep schtum about being a matelot. However, my short hair and south-east accent always gave the game away within seconds. Mick would introduce me as Belinda's boyfriend and the response was always, "Matelot, eh?" Matelot pubs or Dockie pubs, I loved them all; it's people who don't frequent pubs who I worry about (what are they hiding?).

I continued to attend HMS Drake every week for Maths 'O' Level lessons but they bored me rigid. I worked every day with numbers and figures and was pretty good at what I did. But I had no interest in algebraic fractions, calculus and trigonometry – what a complete load of irrelevant bollocks. But now I would pop round to see Belinda's parents or grandparents prior to heading back to Dartmouth. Belinda's grandfather was a character and a half. Old man Wins had served in the Navy between 1933 and 1955 and he had also served in the Army. He would tell me stories that would have me curled up with laughter but he would also ask me things that clearly related to a different Navy and he could never get his head around the fact that stuff had changed.

Navy stuff aside, Wins and I would always get on to politics. Margaret Thatcher was Prime Minister at the time and he absolutely detested her. I held a different view to him as far as Maggie was concerned and I wasn't afraid to express it; the old fella wasn't used to being questioned and challenged so those conversations were pretty rum affairs (not the kind of rum he preferred). Whilst we got on well he was a brute of a man and in his living room he was still a Chief Plumber and I was only a Leading Writer. As for Belinda's grandmother Helen, she was a darling. Maltese through and through and never with a piece of make-up or hair dye out of place she took great pride in her appearance. She spoke six or seven languages and had her own stories to tell; mind you, her most repeated comment to me was, "Stop winding him up," referring to the old man of course.

I got to like this part of Devonport, 'proper' Devonport as I described it to my Naval oppos who like me previously were only familiar with the pubs up around St Levan Gate. Whilst it was very different to the Luton council estate where I'd spent the first 11 years of my life, given this was a dockyard area comprised mainly of English folk, the people were cut from the same cloth. When Belinda and I visited I would frequently go out with Mick for some neck oil and on other occasions, daytime, I would play snooker with Belinda's little brother in Pot Black, the local snooker club (he always beat me).

I would visit my own oldies of course in Peterborough. As Bungy was from Norwich I would give him a lift to Peterborough and he would catch a train from there for carrot-crunching country. My mum really liked Bungy... he had an endearing oddness. Prior to one return journey back down to Devon I did the usual car checks in our pub car park: petrol, oil and water – all OK apart from the water which was a bit low so I topped that up.

On the way back down a 'hot hatch' with four black fellas overtook us on the A34 as we headed from Oxford to Newbury (a route I hadn't taken before). I fired up the Cherry and we raced the boys for around 20 miles. It was a mega-hot day and steam started to appear from the front end. Bungy asked if everything was OK and I noticed that the temperature gauge was firmly rooted in the red zone.

"Must be the heat," I replied to Bungy's enquiry. We were Writers not Stokers, engines weren't our thing. Eventually the black fellas turned off and waved goodbye – it had been a friendly race and probably a draw depending on the method of measurement. A few miles later, thankfully after the other car had disappeared, the Cherry broke down.

It transpired that when I'd topped up the water in the Eight Bells car park I'd forgotten to put the cap back on the water reservoir; when the AA man lifted my bonnet on the side of the A34 the cap was upside down next to the reservoir where I'd left it whilst topping up; it had remained in place for the duration of the journey courtesy of the bonnet wedged on top. There was steam and smoke all over the place – turned out my motor was a much hotter hatch than the one driven by the black lads.

The journey back to Dartmouth from Oxfordshire, courtesy of the AA, was energy-sapping to say the least. The AA dropped us off at their Bristol depot for a long wait before another truck took us down the M5 and dropped us off at their Exeter depot for yet another long wait. Whereas our ETA in Dartmouth had originally been around 2000, we arrived back at the college around 0700, just in time for everyone to see us on the AA truck with my beloved Nissan Cherry on the back. A £500 repair to the severely damaged head gasket followed to add to my pain (it would cost me far more in the future as the repair was limited, given I really need a replacement head gasket but that was beyond my budget).

Most journeys back from Peterborough were less eventful. On one occasion Bungy and I stopped off in Bristol and had a beer in what appeared to be a pretty decent pub. I particularly liked the music that was playing on the juke box – a combination of Erasure, Soft Cell, Communards, Bronski Beat, Culture Club and the like. As we sipped our beers and looked around Bungy remarked, "It's all couples in here."

Looking around with a bit more concentration, it dawned on me that there were no mixed-sex couples. "Mate," I replied, "it's a fucking gay bar." We left pronto but I gotta say the customers in that bar appreciated good music.

Talking of music, 'Don't Leave Me This Way' by the Communards became my favourite song and about the only thing that would get me up to dance in either the Floaters or the Country House. I'm not sure if it was my dancing or my yellow woollen top tucked into my black speckled trousers but I'm often reminded by others of those days and my dancing to the Communards. What's not to like?

In amongst my day-to-day work, Belinda, pubs, football and the rest, I'd been studying for my POWTR's exam and in February 1987 it was time to give it a go. Unlike the 'PQE' for Leading Writer this would be a 'PPE', or 'Provisional Professional Examination'. Once passed I would be on the waiting list for promotion but at some point I would need to complete a professional course at HMS Raleigh and also 'POLC', the 'Petty Officers' Leadership Course'. I passed the exam with flying colours, was given an immediate pay rise as I was now a 'Scale A Killick' and could look forward to promotion in a year or two, all being well. However, I was yet to complete 'LRLC', the 'Leading Rates' Leadership Course', and that joyous event was scheduled for the following month.

LRLC took me back to HMS Raleigh and I could look forward to two weeks of something similar to basic training, just with a load of 'PLTs' and other stuff thrown in. Whilst I was reasonably fit from playing football and running, I'd upped the ante for the course as I'd been told the physical demands were greater than basic training.

I completed the course in March and did OK although some of the PLTs weren't exactly up my street – they all involved logs, water, ropes, pulleys and the like which Seamen and Stokers are more familiar with than Writers. My course report did note that I was "of above-average fitness" and that I "led by example in his support and encouragement of those less able". As for the PLTs, my report noted "when in charge of a practical task he gave a positive brief, formulated a plan, but his lack of experience led to a shortfall in leadership, as he lost confidence when the plan failed". The 'plan' was a feed of shit – I had no idea what I was doing but I've been lucky, since then I've never had to transfer half a dozen guys across a river with the assistance of ropes and pulleys so no lasting damage done.

My LRLC report also noted "the written work he produced was interesting and informative but marred by poor handwriting". My response to that when some burly Chief read it back to me was, "No problem... my typing is better than my handwriting and at least I can spell." The CPO was clearly not happy with a poxy Leading Rate giving his own feedback but when the spelling errors were discussed and accepted, albeit begrudgingly, the report was taken away for retyping.

One evening in the 'posh' side of the Royal Castle Hotel, Belinda and I were having a few drinks. We rarely drank in this side, preferring as we did the more down-to-earth 'locals bar' on the other side. I was very happy in my relationship and after some consideration and much beer, I proposed to Belinda. She obviously had had a lot to drink too as she accepted. So that was it, we were engaged. How did that happen?

I received a Draft Order to join HMS *Ark Royal*, one of the Royal Navy's two operational aircraft carriers (the other being HMS *Illustrious* with HMS *Invincible* in refit). Much to my dismay the draft was cancelled a few weeks later as the Leading Writer who I was due to replace applied for an extension which was granted. Having spent 18 months on a Plymouth-based frigate which I absolutely loved, I had stated a preference for a Portsmouth-based aircraft carrier for my next seagoing job as I wanted a bit of variety and carriers had always appealed to me.

My car problems continued and I became conscious that my tyres needed replacing. I thought I'd kill two birds with one stone and pop home to Peterborough for a weekend and get the tyres replaced whilst there. On the way up the M5 in heavy rain, just south of Birmingham, the car in front stopped suddenly and I applied my brakes immediately. However, my tyres were clearly worse than I'd thought as the car didn't stop until I smashed into the back of the car in front. With the M5 at a halt and in the pouring rain I proffered my sincere apologies. The police arrived, statements were taken and insurance details exchanged. The car in front was no longer driveable whereas I was able to continue with my journey. My insurance paid out for the damage to the other car but I had to pay for the damage to mine. What was that my old man said about fully comp insurance when I bought the little darling?

I received a revised Draft Order and got my wish; I was to join the aircraft carrier HMS *Illustrious* on 15 September as a Leading Writer in the Pay Office. My relationship with Belinda couldn't have been better; I loved her to bits so we decided to move together to the Portsmouth area. My POWTR Trev Dean had just been drafted to the Fareham area and had moved into a married quarter with his family; Trev and Anita invited Belinda and I to lodge with them as Belinda could stay with them whilst I was at sea.

We moved to Fareham and we moved in with Trev, Anita and their kids. I had a week off before my new job so I thought I'd pop to the dockyard and show my face on the ship; it'd be nice to see who's who and to introduce myself prior to joining. When I arrived at Pompey dockyard I asked the guy on the gate for the whereabouts of HMS *Illustrious*. "Over there," he replied, "turn right at the end of that big building and you'll see her, can't miss her, unless you're blind." I walked to the end of the big building (they were all big buildings), turned left and yep, there in front of me was the splendid sight of a mighty aircraft carrier; boy I was looking forward to this draft.

Once on board I asked the Quartermaster the location of the Pay Office and he gave me some general directions with a few quips thrown in which I chose to ignore. I arrived at the Pay Office, knocked on the closed door and was greeted with a shout of, "We're closed." I knocked again and a grumpy-looking Chief Writer opened the door and said, "You deaf? What do you want?" I introduced myself as "Leading Writer O'Rourke" and his manner completely changed. "Sorry mate, come in, fancy a brew?" That was it with us Writers; we're a friendly bunch, although we tend to prefer our own.

I had a brew and a great chat with half a dozen or so Writers. After about an hour the Chief said to me, "Anyway Hugh, what are you here for?"

I replied, "Thought I'd pop my head in before I join just to introduce myself."

"Your draft was cancelled ages ago," replied the Chief.

"I'm joining next week, Chief," I replied, adding, "I was meant to join the Ark Royal but that was cancelled."

"What ship to you think you're on, mate?" asked the Chief.

"Illustrious," I replied which met with much laughter from all present.

"You're on *Ark Royal*, you dozy twat, *Lusty*'s further down." Having wasted an hour inadvertently entertaining my fellow Scribes I decided to go straight home and not bother with *Lusty* wherever she was; I had two years to look forward to on her and an introduction a week before wasn't really going to make much difference.

17. LUSTY, LUST AND CRABS

The 15th arrived and I joined the mighty *Illustrious*, a truly fabulous-looking ship. The purists would argue that a CVSA/CVSG isn't actually an 'aircraft carrier' but what else do you call a ship that carries aircraft? That's the problem with purists. "Know all, know nothing," as my mother would say.

Affectionately known throughout the fleet but particularly by her Ship's Company as '*Lusty*', the ship was commanded by Captain A P Woodhead and with fully embarked squadrons was home to around 1,200 men. The ship's 'Carrier Air Group' consisted of 800 Naval Air Squadron, 814 Naval Air Squadron and 849 'A' Flight – choppers and jets basically. The choppers included 9 ASW (Anti-Submarine Warfare) Sea King helicopters and 3 AEW (Airborne Early Warning) Sea Kings (the latter being the ship's 'eyes in the sky'). The Sea Harriers, remarkable jets without which we most certainly would not have been able to liberate the Falklands, were able to take off and land vertically, although to conserve fuel the ship's 'ski jump' was used for take-off purposes. These 'VSTOL' aircraft carried heat-seeking Sidewinder air-to-air missiles so they were certainly a force to be reckoned with.

So with her choppers and jets, 22,000 tonnes, four Rolls-Royce gas turbine engines, a Sea Dart surface-to-air missile system and two Phalanx radar-guided guns (reminiscent of R2-D2, the droid character in Star Wars), *Lusty* was a fine example of military and engineering science blended together to form something quite beautiful.

Of course the ship was nothing without its Supply Department, headed up by Commander J J Brecknell (SO) and his deputy, Lieutenant Commander N P Wright (DSO). Unlike frigates and destroyers with their sole Ship's Office, *Lusty*'s Writer functions were split between the Pay Office, the Captain's Office, the Tech Office and the Wardroom Mess Office, all headed up by Senior Rate Writers. My job was to run a section of the Pay Office, reporting to CPOWTR Darby Allen and in turn to the SO (PAY), Lieutenant R J Holder (Dick Holder). There were some great lads in the office including Billy Bingham, Dave Mullett, Dave Parr (a fellow Luton fan), BJ Waterfield (but didn't get any off his wife apparently) and of course the other lads in the Captain's Office, Tech Office and Wardroom Mess Office (more about them later).

The ship had a shedload of NAAFI personnel to keep us in nutty and a further shedload of Chinese personnel to keep our clothes washed and ironed. There were 11 Chinese in total, headed up by the knighted and legendary Yuen Sir Tsin. We even had a 'Padre', colloquially known as 'The Bish' and he headed up the Ship's Chapel which I was reliably informed had rather a loyal bunch of visitors. The chapel would be like the engine room, somewhere I had no intention of visiting.

Messed in the S&S Junior Rates' mess, consisting entirely once again of Writers, Stores Accountants, Catering Accountants, Cooks and Stewards, I was very happy to discover there were no pits in the mess square. Anyway, I was now a Leading Writer so I secured a very comfortable berth right in the back gulch, away from the noise and merriment of the mess square.

The Navy had recently decided to merge Pay Offices with Regulating Offices to create 'Unit Personnel Offices' (UPOs) so courtesy of a new arch in the Pay Office wall we now had RPOs Steve Rigler and Ray Halford in the office. My desk was actually in the old Regulating Office but like my pit down below in the S&S

mess, I was entirely happy with my new surroundings. The desks themselves were similar to those described in *Cherry B*'s Ship's Office; there were just a lot more of them.

Within weeks the usual routine of being 'alongside' took over – work, football and pubs. Pompey had a wonderful array of watering holes and in addition to our mess 'local' the Three Crowns, situated just outside the dockyard and nicknamed 'The Three Nadgers' for some obscure reason, we had the Ship Anson and the Mary Rose within a short walk and in the city centre, also within walking distance, we had the infamous Mighty Fine, the Mucky Duck (Black Swan) and Joanna's (Jo's). Like Boobs in Plymouth Jo's was known as the 'Royal Navy School of Dancing' and appealed to a very similar clientele (drunken sailors and loose women). There were other pubs and clubs of course but these were our favourites.

I played football for the S&S team and also the ship's team although the latter took itself far too seriously. The S&S took on the Wardroom one afternoon on the all-weather pitch at HMS Temeraire just outside the dockyard. The opposition's striker was a young Sub Lieutenant called Andy Walker who remembered Belinda from Dartmouth (he was rather keen on her). Belinda was watching from the sidelines with a few other WAGS so I was determined to prevent Andy or anyone else from scoring. I threw myself all over the place, bruising and grazing myself numerous times on the hard clay surface, but it was well worth it; Andy had loads of chances but I played the game of my life and was instrumental in our 4-0 victory. Afterwards I asked the love of my life, "Did you see all those saves I made?"

To which she replied, "Sorry, I wasn't really watching, I was talking to the other girls."

Nothing to do with the football of course and Belinda's lack of appreciation but I had a real dilemma. I was about to go to sea again and I wanted to be single. I didn't want a Julie situation again and as my relationship with Belinda was much more of a normal boy/girl relationship, as opposed to a sex-free relationship, I decided to end things. I was mad keen on her but I was only 22 and felt I had a bit more living to do before I tied myself down. Being the coward that I am I wrote to Belinda when we set sail for our first visit and that was that... I was single again.

My first foreign run on *Lusty* was Hamburg and we arrived on 8 October for a six-day visit. It was cold and wet but that mattered not a jot; Hamburg was an absolute favourite among matelots, offering as it did a huge selection of bars and women. Money-changing beforehand was on a different scale to the *Cherry B*, given the Ship's Company was around five or six times greater. 'Balancing' one morning after a busy session, we managed to 'lose' the equivalent of £500. Cue loads of checking, counter-checking and more checking. But we couldn't find it and we couldn't identify who was at fault. We could only assume that someone had swiped a pack of notes when one of the Writers had turned his back; fortunately for me I wasn't on money-changing duties that morning. Whilst no disciplinary action was taken we were all gutted, both from a professional perspective but also from a personal perspective; how could a fellow shipmate steal from us?

Hamburg was a great run and we particularly enjoyed the 'Eros Center', deep inside the Reeperbahn in St Pauli, the city's world-famous red-light district and home to more than one thousand prostitutes (pardon the 'deep inside' pun). The Eros Center was a six-storey brothel and its admirable competitors included 'Hotel Luxor', another fine establishment focused on meeting the very explicit needs of its wide customer base. I can honestly say I was never a paying customer in either the Eros Center or the Luxor but I visited both with oppos and we all enjoyed the banter with their employees. The Reeperbahn contained loads of bars, clubs, discos and street-food and at that moment in time it was my favourite place on Earth.

On the way back to Pompey and after a good night's sleep I got up to go for a shower prior to breakfast; just another routine morning at sea. However, as I entered the mess square in flip-flops and towel, carrying my dhobey bag, I noticed the lads sat around were looking a tad pale; there was also loads of stuff out of place much of which was on the deck. "What the fuck's going on?" I asked.

To which one of the lads replied, "We've just sailed through a fucking hurricane, didn't you notice?" I'd slept like a log, completely oblivious to the ship being tossed and turned by the greatest storm the UK had witnessed in nearly three centuries; the 115mph gales caused utter devastation across the southern half of England leaving 18 people dead, 15 million trees flattened, thousands of homes without power and a certain Michael Fish looking completely out of depth in his chosen profession. Despite a ship capsizing at Dover and a Channel ferry driven ashore at Folkestone, the mighty *Lusty* sailed past the white cliffs with many of her company, me included, tucked up safe and sound in our pits; as for the ashen-faced lads in mess squares around the ship – man up for fuck's sake.

We carried on to Portland for two days' noise ranging before taking up position off RAF Valley in readiness for the start of Exercise Offshore Remount, a fast-paced anti-terrorist exercise. On completion we returned to Pompey before putting to sea again for a fleet trial during which we embarked a number of sons for 'Sons at Sea'.

Further exercises followed including Purple Warrior with 40 Commando RM embarked. The bootnecks and their camp beds were strewn around the ship although we managed to house most of them in the hangar. All messes played host to our Green Beret colleagues and the usual shenanigans followed over tins of beer in the evenings. One of the booties challenged one of our lads to a fag-eating contest which I suppose is one way of emptying dirty ashtrays. As the fag-butts gradually disappeared the bootie got sick into the ashtray which met with a load of cheers from the resident matelots but, not to be outdone, the same bootie picked up the ashtray and drank the entire contents (game set and match to the green corner). There was a serious side to the green embarkation of course and assaults were conducted at Loch Ryan and Arran which included a group of officers and ratings who were given the opportunity to experience life in the field with the Royal Marines (I had better things to do so stayed on board).

Back in Pompey for a period of maintenance it didn't take me too long to enjoy my new single status. I was in the Red Lion in Fareham with a couple of lads from the mess when we bumped into a couple of young Wrens. We went back to their place after a few drinks and as I was clearly on a promise I went upstairs with Philippa whilst her mate Angie went to bed next door. As Philippa and I were in bed my hands started to wander and get a bit sticky; as I was about to up the ante Angie reappeared and got into bed with us. Happy fucking days. I started to finger her too and then the two fucking lads appeared. To cut the story short, I went to bed with two fit girls and woke up with two less fit matelots. What actually woke me was Ben's smelly armpit in which my face was nestled. Ben was a top lad but his hairy armpit, similarities aside, was not what I was hoping to wake up smelling that morning.

I did see quite a bit of Philippa over the following few weeks; she was a Punk and liked to wear lots of chains and black clothes. Whilst the sex was pretty good she had a really smelly pussy which I found somewhat off-putting. I told one of the lads I was going to ditch her to which he replied, "You're a fucking idiot… keep fucking her until you find someone else." I ignored his advice and dumped her next time I saw her. I was a bit surprised by her reaction as she contacted me several times and even wrote to me with various promises; my mind was made up and in any case, if I wanted a girlfriend why would I have split up with Belinda?

A period of Christmas leave followed and on return to the ship I was given some great news. The POWTR in charge of the Captain's Office was about to leave the ship and rather than draft in a replacement it was decided that I would be advanced to 'Local Acting' Petty Officer Writer with a new Leading Writer drafted in to replace me. Essentially I would be an 'acting' POWTR until such time as my B13 arrived to promote me properly; in the meantime I would enjoy the pay, benefits and status of a Petty Officer, not bad for a 22-year-old who had been in the Royal Navy for a little over five years.

So with my new uniforms made by our resident Chinese tailor and the formalities of the Captain's Table over, I took charge of the Captain's Office on 14 January 1988. I say 'took charge' as my title was 'Captain's Office Manager' but my boss, the Captain's Secretary, worked from the same office and sat only a few feet from me. The Captain's Sec, Lieutenant Nick Lewin, was a top bloke and the A/Sec, essentially his assistant, was a Sub Lieutenant known to me from when his days as a POWTR (Frank Prescott). Frank was a complete narcissist but entertaining nonetheless. My first experience of being a Divisional Senior Rating saw me oversee the work of two Writers, Tara Brady and Mitch Mitchell, two of my mates from the S&S mess and two better lads you could not wish to meet. The jump to Petty Officer and overseeing two guys of similar age who had been messmates and drinking partners of mine for the previous few months was of no concern to me; whilst we all enjoyed a beer and our runs ashore rank meant something in the Royal Navy, irrespective of age or time served.

Nick Lewin was so posh he was nicknamed 'Lord Percy' by his fellow officers, after a character in Rowan Atkinson's legendary comedy 'Blackadder'. Frank spent a lot of time out of the office although no one knew where he went or what he did. Nick, Frank and I sat on one side of the office whilst Tara and Mitch sat on the opposite side. Whilst we all faced the bulkheads (walls) rather than each other, the craic was great and barely a minute went by without someone taking the piss out of someone else.

No longer in the S&S Junior Rates' mess I was now resident in 6H

Petty Officers' mess, one of three POs' messes on board and located immediately underneath the UPO, my former office. The mess was a mixture of different trades and branches but included the other two POWTRs on board, Taff Gauntlett and Phil Old. Taff managed the Tech Office and Phil managed the Wardroom Mess Office, located a couple of doors down from the Captain's Office. For me it was a new experience to live and socialise with non-S&S and a very good experience it was too, even if the noisy fuckers would sometimes wake me up in the middle of the night when they had to get up and go on watch.

As a POWTR I was now included on the 'Duty RPO' roster, along with the two RPOs, my fellow POWTRs and also the PO METOC, Tony Fernandez; Tony was also a member of my new mess and a truly fantastic bloke. The Duty RPO was responsible to the Officer of the Day for the welfare and discipline of the Ship's Company and would accompany the OOD on evening rounds. Whilst I rather liked my new status and surroundings it was hard to shake off old habits; on one occasion I was leaving the Junior Rates' heads with a couple of Writers when the Fleet Master At Arms pulled me to one side; he made it clear that I was now a Senior Rate and that I had to use the Senior Rates' toilets; different ranks piss in different pots.

Around the same time the UPO CPOWTR left for HMS *Sirius* on a swap draft with CPOWTR Frank Cooper. It was a shame to see Darbs leave but Frank turned out to be a similar character so all was well; I may no longer have worked in the UPO but the Writer clan was close on board and we were all part of the same team so it mattered who came and went.

Along with the other Senior Rates' messes on board 6H had its own bar with draught beer, spirits and the like. No longer restricted to cans and a daily limit I could drink what I wanted. We had a Mess Committee which comprised several roles including Chairman, Treasurer, Bar Manager and Social Secretary. Nick Wilkin was the

Social Secretary and from the stories that I heard it was a job for which he was eminently suited.

The first 'Mess Social' that I attended was a 'Cheese and Wine' party. Despite hating both cheese and wine the evening took a very pleasant turn when I was introduced to a friend of the wife of one of my new messmates. Jan Bevan was absolutely drop-dead gorgeous; I had no idea why she was interested in me but interested in me she was and we arranged to meet up for a drink a few days later.

Jan and I saw each other a few times and I even met her parents and stayed overnight at her house in Cowplain on the northern edge of Portsmouth. Whilst I was a randy fucker at the best of times I decided to play it slow with Jan and never made a move on her, sexually at least. I was madly in love and then one day whilst lying beside her in a very cold field talking about her horse a few yards away she dropped a bombshell; I was dumped. This was awkward. I had just been dumped but I was in a field in the middle of nowhere and I'd got there courtesy of a lift from my girlfriend, now my ex-girlfriend. Jan dropped me back at the ship and I never saw her again. I was absolutely devastated and in private cried my eyes out; maybe she wanted fucking and thought I was a boring twat? Maybe she'd found a better-looking bloke? Who knows? I certainly didn't.

In addition to being a top Social Secretary Nick was also a bloody good Senior Rating and around this time was promoted to Chief Petty Officer; as a consequence he had to leave the mess. Following nomination and a vote (with only one candidate) I was duly elected to the position of Social Secretary. Not really being sure what to do Nick gave me much advice and lots of guidance. The first Mess Social that I would organise would be during our forthcoming visit to Newcastle and given Nick had organised the last one in that city he helped me with the prep for this one.

In February Captain Woodhead left the ship with command handed over to Captain J J R Tod CBE ("one D as in God" if anyone asked him how to spell his name). A big man with an imposing presence, it became clear early on that Captain Tod was a thoroughly decent senior officer; his deputy, the Executive Officer, was also new but Commander N D V Robertson was not as popular amongst the Ship's Company as his boss.

The day after our new Commanding Officer arrived we embarked FOF3, the Flag Officer Third Flotilla and a Rear Admiral by rank, for exercise ASWEX 1988. We became COMASWSTRIKFOR'S flagship and conducted anti-submarine exercises in filthy weather south-west of the Faeroes (not that the weather affected me of course). We had the usual mix of Defence Watches and Action Stations which saw me in my new role in HQ1 'on comms' – a bit like being 'on the switch' in a cab office.

A weekend visit to Rosyth followed and then the big one, a visit to our birthplace, Newcastle upon Tyne. We berthed at Wallsend where *Lusty* was built; it became apparent very quickly that a strong bond existed between the ship, her company and the good people of the north-east who in 1982 had worked 24/7 to complete the build three months ahead of schedule (*Lusty* was commissioned at sea on her way south to the Falkland Islands).

It was February, we were in the north and it was cold; very, very cold. The economy wasn't very bright at that time and there was huge unemployment in Newcastle and Gateshead, the town on the opposite side of the river. Despite the lack of jobs and the lack of warm weather I was gobsmacked at the number of queues outside bars and clubs; in particularly the hardy women of the north east appeared not to venture out in anything other than very short skirts. Lots of bars, lots of scantily dressed women and lots of beer tokens in our pockets; heaven is often a place on earth. To say we enjoyed the bars and clubs in this incredible city and the surrounding area was an understatement. One particular favourite moored on the River Tyne was the *Tuxedo Princess*, known locally simply as 'The Tux' or

'The Boat'. This wonderful 'establishment' with its revolving dancefloor was known as a rather sophisticated venue and was full of big hair and shoulder pads... and now loads of horny boozed-up matelots, one of whom went arse over tit when putting one foot on the dance-floor whilst keeping the other on the non-revolving adjacent floor. Oh, and he was carrying a tray of drinks at the time...

The Mess Social arrived and all our efforts bore fruit. The invitations that we sent out in advance to various establishments including the local hospitals returned with a number of attractive females attached. Nick did us proud with his usual organisational skills, numerous contacts and local knowledge. Within minutes of the start-time the mess was full; smart Petty Officers in 'mess undress' complete with cummerbunds and lots of young ladies complete with short skirts and stilettos. All drinks were free, paid for out of our retained bar profits.

I was sat in the corner engaged in conversation with messmates and a few local girls. I seemed to be doing particularly well with one very attractive girl and had high hopes for the rest of the night. She had to go to the toilet and when she left her seat another girl, less attractive, sidled up to me and started chatting. "Anyway," she piped up, "how do you guys get on at sea without women... you must wank a lot?" Now matelots never admit to being wankers but this kick-started a conversation about sex, one of my favourite subjects right up there with beer and football.

The WAFUs loved spinning the line, "Do you want to see a Sea Harrier?" and the girls lapped it up with a number leaving the mess for a visit to the ship's hangar.

My new friend asked, "Where do you work... you do planes too?"

"Nah," I replied, "I work in the Captain's Office, a lot smaller than the hangar and I have a key."

So up to the Captain's Office we went but when we arrived the door was open with the Captain's Secretary sat just inside beavering away. I introduced Michelle and explained to the boss that I wanted to show her where I worked. Pleasantries done, Nick stood up and said, "I need to pop out for half an hour or so, PO… see you later." Top fucking man.

Half an hour or so later after fucking Michelle on the desk we heard footsteps coming towards the door. I quickly unlocked the door but as I moved it from left to right to open it I noticed a small puddle of white stuff on the floor, right next to the boss's chair. Luckily I always kept some bog roll on my desk as I had a tendency to frequently blow my nose so I grabbed hold of some and quickly mopped up the offending bodily fluid. As Nick walked into the office I was dropping the toilet roll with its sticky muck into the gash sack, sniffing away pretending to have just wiped my nose (God forbid any of that stuff should come from or go anywhere near my nose). Nick was as polite as ever and Michelle and I returned to the mess. "Bit better than sitting in a Sea Harrier surrounded by dozens of other people, eh?" I said as we walked back down to the mess.

I met up again with Michelle and spent the following night at her house in Hexham, some 25 miles inland. Whilst not the best looking girl in the world Michelle was a goer and a half and she had a clit almost as big as an African girl's (you can have lots of fun with those things). Early the following morning a young lad peered around the door and as I shot up in bed he asked, clearly unimpressed, "Not another one, Mum?"

After a fabulous few days in Newcastle which included a 'Ship Open to Visitors' event where Nick and I invited a couple of girls from the back of the queue to join us on board, we set sail to meet up with the Ark Royal as the two air groups wanted to do battle against each other. As the air groups did battle high up in the skies, all was peaceful in the Captain's Office. Suddenly the Captain's Sec piped up, "I hope the PO Writer cleaned his desk after the other night."

To which Mitch replied, "Why's that, sir?"

"Let's just say he entertained one of his mess guests on it."

A few seconds of silence followed after which Mitch piped up, "He fucked her on your desk, sir, not his." I kept quiet and cracked on with my work whilst the boss went to get a wet cloth.

I mentioned that the Assistant Secretary, Sub Lieutenant Frank Prescott, was a bit of a narcissist (more than a bit). He was a decent enough bloke but he really did hold a very high opinion of himself, more so than the Captain it turned out. I was busy typing his S206, his personal report, which contained a number of different boxes with a number of different marks out of ten. Actually I shouldn't have been typing up an officer's report, most certainly not my boss's deputy's report, but Frank was a lazy sod and delegated the task to me (along with his fellow officers' reports). As he was looking over my shoulder he said, "Make that an eight... and that one too... and make that one a nine."

"Are you allowed to fiddle your own report, sir?" I asked.

To which he replied, "The Captain won't fucking notice." The Captain never noticed and I believe Frank eventually made Commander.

Having been to a number of countries and experienced the delights of Mombasa, I had hitherto escaped without any sexually transmitted diseases. But Newcastle and Michelle changed all that. I got a dose of crabs which was easily sorted with a pot of cream from the Sick Bay but the ribbing from the lads lasted much longer of course. Mitch piped up one day, "What do those crabs actually look like?" so I put my hand down my trousers and retrieved one for him. Tiny little fuckers but he managed to see what it looked like. I flicked it into his orange hair which might not have been the most professional thing to do but he never asked again.

18. THE MEDITERRANEAN
AND A BLUE NOSE

Back in Pompey for some leave I received a letter from Michelle in Hexham. She was pretty pissed off and complained that she'd been "fucked and chucked". I could have replied and explained that she'd given me a leaving present but I thought better of it, didn't reply and never heard from her again. Thankfully there were no mobile phones or social media in those days so it was much easier to ignore someone.

A week or so before a planned deployment to the Mediterranean I managed to catch Luton Town in a cup final at Wembley. We were having an amazing season with three fantastic cup runs. Whilst the FA Cup and the League Cup were the big two the Simod Cup was a bit of a bonus, especially for me as I was still in the UK. So on 27 March I went to Wembley on my own to watch Luton Town, from English football's top division, play lowly Reading, a division below and heading for the one below that. Whilst we hadn't played at Wembley since our FA Cup Final defeat in 1959 we were odds-on to win this one; we turned up so of course we were going to win.

We scored in the first 15 minutes courtesy of the living legend that is Mick Harford and were on our way to victory; it was just a matter of how many we would score. Little old Reading then scored four goals and lifted the trophy in front of over 60,000 fans, mostly Reading supporters. I caught the train back to Pompey and when I finally arrived back on board it was 2225 in the evening. As I got to the bottom of the ladder into the mess the television news was just hitting its sports bulletin with news of the game and the result. I had to endure all of Reading's goals once again but none of the lads in the mess took the piss. None of them. OK, all of them.

We sailed for the Mediterranean in early April. Whilst at sea and when not in Defence Watches or at Action Stations the routine was fairly pleasant. In addition to the ongoing banter of the Captain's Office I would frequently disappear to the UPO for banter with my fellow Writers and also 6H below for tea and banter with my fellow POs. In between all of that myself, Phil Old and the Captain's PO Steward 'H' would spend time on the Admiral's Bridge (in his absence of course) chewing the fat, drinking tea and eating whatever delicacy H had knocked up for the Skipper that day (pâté was one of his favourites and quickly became one of mine). Whilst we would never admit it to the WAFUs it was pretty impressive watching the Sea Harriers in particular take off and land; watching a fast jet land vertically at sea is an awesome sight but not one that we S&S boys would admit to.

We arrived in Palma, the capital of the Spanish island of Majorca, on 12 April for a six-day visit. The weather was perfect, moderately hot but not excessive and with Magaluf literally down the road we all knew this was going to be a fantastic run ashore.

With a few oppos I visited the magnificent Gothic cathedral and wandered around the medieval streets admiring the aristocratic townhouses, bustling public squares and teeming markets. Whilst we all enjoyed wandering around, taking in the sights and sounds, this visit was about bars and clubs. Of course all port cities had bars and clubs but Palma had a real holiday feel to it, hardly surprising given its location on a holiday island.

On the second day I was unable to go ashore as I was duty RPO which involved the usual mix of rounds and wandering around the ship checking that all was OK. It was a pretty quiet night with most of the lads out on the piss so I spent quite a lot of time down the mess with a handful of messmates who were also on duty. On one return to the mess after a wander around the ship I was gobsmacked to see Nigel Mansell, one of the world's greatest racing drivers, sitting in the mess drinking a mug of tea. He'd been a guest at the previous evening's officers' cocktail party on the quarterdeck and one of the PO Stewards had invited him to 6H to see how the 'real Navy' lived. Nigel was an interesting guy to say the least. Arrogant, yes, but not in an annoying way; the guy was an international sports star so he was permitted a dose of arrogance. He signed our visitors' book before departing and his signature said everything you needed to know about him: flamboyant, a bit in your face and impossible to ignore. It helped that it was at the top of a new page and every visitor to the mess after that, including royalty and government ministers, remarked upon the flamboyant signature asking, "Who's that?"

Every night ashore was superb and we all got completely wankered. The bars and clubs were chockers with gorgeous, tanned, scantily-dressed young women but the beer won. Until the last night.

I went ashore with an oppo on the final evening absolutely knackered from the exertions of the previous nights. It was gonna be a quiet one 'to get rid of our remaining ickies'. Sitting in a bar slightly off the beaten track a couple of girls next to Tom and I started chatting to us. No one was trying to pull – everyone was chilled. To be honest I just wanted to get rid of my ickies, have a few beers and get back on board before 0300 as leave was always curtailed on the final evening of a port visit to ensure everyone got back on board well before sailing (Junior Rates' leave expired at 0100 and Senior Rates' leave at 0300). One of the girls, Jocelyn, was outstandingly gorgeous, 'essence' in our parlance, and she and I really hit it off. So without trying and relatively sober I trapped a gorgeous girl and at her request went back to her apartment around midnight (maybe there's a lesson there?).

Joss was a travel rep and was working the season in Magaluf. I couldn't get over how gorgeous she was and even more I had no idea what she saw in me; I was punching way above my weight but so what? I intended to enjoy the next couple of hours before I returned to the ship. We had amazing sex and I had a fantastic sleep, so fantastic I didn't wake up until around 0700. I absolutely shat myself, exchanged addresses with Joss and took a taxi back to the ship. Luckily I arrived back on board before the ship sailed and amazingly I wasn't trooped. It was hugely embarrassing to be the only member of the Ship's Company to be adrift but the Fleet Master At Arms took pity on me for some reason and after some straightforward advice I was allowed to continue and get ready for work. That was one in the bank for the FMAA and if cats have nine lives sailors have far fewer so I needed to ensure that this was a one-off. It wouldn't be.

We sailed from Majorca and met up with other RN ships heading for the Persian Gulf before breaking off to exercise with the new Italian carrier, the *Giuseppe Garibaldi*. The ship hosted a load of Italian VIPs, some of whom visited 6H mess; VIPs would always visit the Wardroom, the Fleet and Chief Petty Officers' mess and one Petty Officers' mess, normally 6H as we were the biggest of the three (and of course the best). There wasn't too much conversation given we had no Italian speakers and they only had a couple who spoke English but we enjoyed their visit and they enjoyed our hospitality.

On 24 April the mighty Luton Town met Arsenal in the League Cup Final at Wembley (back in the day when this trophy meant something). I asked the Captain a week or so before if I could fly home but he politely declined my request. I had a match ticket which I'd bought as soon as they went on sale but I had to give it to my brother; I was a member of the club so along with season ticket holders I was guaranteed a ticket. I was gutted that I couldn't attend the biggest match in my lifetime but that was life in a blue suit – duty came first.

This was our first appearance in a League Cup Final and Arsenal, appearing in their fourth final, were holders having beaten Liverpool the previous year to lift the trophy. I had no way of keeping up with the match and whilst Arsenal were hot favourites having beaten league champions Everton home and away in the semi-final, I had a feeling that we could upset the odds. It was a Sunday at sea and I spent the afternoon down the mess chatting with the lads. Frustrated with not knowing how the lads were doing at Wembley I decided to go for a shit and a shower.

I'd been away from the mess for quite a bit, both the shit and the shower taking longer than I'd anticipated. When I left the heads, in flip-flops and towel, I was about to take the first step down the ladder to the mess when one of the Dabbers walking by said, "Luton are on the radio." By fuck, it was on BFBS Radio, the forces' radio station which was being piped throughout the ship right at that very moment. I quickly realised the game was into its last ten minutes and Arsenal were 2-1 ahead and coasting to yet another trophy. Not only that but they were awarded a fucking penalty and we only had our reserve goalkeeper in goal; 3-1 down with nine minutes to go and that would be it, game over.

The legend that is Andy Dibble saved Nigel Winterburn's penalty, a minute or so later Danny Wilson equalised for the Town and in the last minute Brian Stein scored the winner. In flip-flops and with a towel around my waist I was dancing in the flat above the mess, absolutely overjoyed. Luton Town, little old Luton Town, had won a major trophy – absolutely incredible.

Having given birth to kittens during those ten minutes above the mess I was desperate to get down below and tell the lads. "Fucking hell, Luton won, we won the League Cup, we fucking stuffed Arsenal!" I bellowed as I got down the mess.

"We know," said Taff, "we listened to it while you were in the heads."

"We only scored the winner a few minutes ago, mate… I caught the last ten minutes on BFBS," I replied.

"Daft twat," said Taff. "BFBS announced when you left the mess that the game had ended, Luton had won and that they would replay the last ten minutes after the news… you were listening to a recording." I had no idea that every fucker on that ship except me knew the bloody result; I had no idea that it was announced whilst I was scrubbing my balls in the shower. Anyway, it's worth repeating, we stuffed Arsenal and lifted the trophy in front of nearly 96,000 supporters – our very first piece of silverware in our 103-year history. My most memorable Sunday at sea without a shadow of a doubt.

Whilst we'd been alongside in Palma we'd received a letter addressed to the Captain from three British girls who worked at our embassy in Rome, inviting three officers to join them for an evening in Italy's capital. For some reason I forgot to pass the letter on to the relevant officer and said to the lads in the office, "Fancy an overnight trip to Rome, boys?" to which of course the answer was a big fat 'yes'. I asked the boss if the three of us could have a couple of days' leave, something unheard of unless it was official Station Leave or an organised ship's visit.

Nick Lewin being the top guy he was, agreed – I even told him about the letter. "Go for it, PO Writer," he said, "just look after the boys." Fuck, that was some challenge. Maybe he was taking the piss?

Whilst at sea we did the usual stuff to keep ourselves occupied and amused. We played volleyball in the lift well and bucketball and 'It's a Knockout' on the flight deck. It's a Knockout included 'flipper football' which utilised balls made of masking tape whilst participants wore flippers on their feet. In the Petty Officers' mess we had horse racing and frog racing, both involving shedloads of beer, lots of betting and a distinct lack of horses and frogs. Horse racing involved magnetic 'horses' on the metal deckhead and frog racing involved wooden 'frogs' which were manoeuvred from one end of the mess to the other via long pieces of rope. Frog racing involved great skill and wrist dexterity with non-riders betting on the outcome of each race. All profits were split between the mess fund and the ship's charity.

Less fun than flipper football and frog racing was many, many hours typing up a dissertation for a university degree. Not for me. Nope, a favour for my brother who was in the last year of his architecture degree course. I'd offered to type up the dissertation as he couldn't type and in those days word processors were a rarity. But I had a word processor and I had time on my hands, in the evenings at least. As I would find out later in life, typing academic dissertations is a ball-ache, even when they're based on a subject of the typist's choosing. But this one wasn't. This one was about churches in Chicago. How the hell one could produce 12,000 words on bloody churches is a bit of a mystery but Patrick managed it and I typed it. Boiling my head would have been more fun.

We arrived in Naples in late April, sailing in to the port with Mount Vesuvius serving as a stunning backdrop. Unusually for Naples the weather was cold and wet but that was of no consequence to the Ship's Company; Palma had been great but Naples offered something different and, as they say, variety is the spice of life. Trips were organised to neighbouring Pompei, the ancient city ruined by Vesuvius's eruption in 79AD, the most infamous of its 50+ eruptions, and also the neighbouring island of Capri. Given the lads in the Captain's Office and I were off on a jolly to Rome, Pompei and Capri were visits we would have to forego.

On the first night ashore I handed out dozens of Mess Social invitations to a load of Filipino girls in a bar close to the docks. "Mate, they're all whores," one of the lads remarked.

"So what?" I responded. "Let's hope they all turn up." Whilst I'd organised the Mess Social in my role as Social Secretary I would miss the do itself as I'd be in Rome with Mitch and Tara. That first night was a helluva night – Naples is one fantastic, vibrant and friendly city but nonetheless we all followed the advice of the old salts: "If you shake hands with a Neapolitan make sure you count your fingers afterwards."

The lads and I took the train up from Naples to Rome and sat outside a bar, as arranged with the girls. They were attending a Sting concert in the city's Stadio Flaminio; despite Sting sharing his birthplace with *Lusty* the lads and I all agreed he was a prick and preferred waiting in the bar to actually seeing him perform. After an hour or so, three good-looking English girls approached us and one said, "Hi, Hugh I presume?"

"Wow, well-spotted," said I. "How did you know it was us?" I didn't really think it was a stupid question as there were thousands of people out on the streets and in the bars but apparently three English lads drinking pints of lager stood out like sore thumbs against the thousands of handsome tanned Italians, most of whom were drinking coffee out of cups that resembled thimbles.

The girls took us around numerous bars and the lads agreed that it was clear the three girls were all up for it. We had a great night and eventually got back to their pad behind steel security gates in the embassy compound. We ended up in their living room, making polite conversation, waiting until we paired off for the inevitable shagging sesh. But only one girl was interested and it wasn't the one that I was trying to make a move on. So one of the lads had a great night whilst the other two, of which I was one, made small talk into the early hours before falling asleep.

Without giving away too much detail the shagger felt terrible about it as he had a girlfriend/wife at home and he'd never before bagged off out of watch. Anyway, the girls had work to do and we had a load of sightseeing to fit in before our return to Naples. They say Rome wasn't built in a day and we could see why. There was so much to see and clearly we couldn't fit in everything but we did catch the Spanish Steps, the Trevi Fountain, the Colosseum and the breathtaking Pantheon. After a pretty hectic morning and afternoon we headed off to the Vatican City, something a good Catholic boy like me simply couldn't miss.

Having been brought up with images of the Vatican and St Peter's Basilica from my days as a loyal and devout altar-boy, I knew fully what to expect. A bit like the Pyramids – an iconic, glorious masterpiece standing alone in wondrous grandeur some distance from man and all the crap that he built. Our arrival was more disappointing than my arrival at the Pyramids in 1985 whilst serving on board the *Cherry B*. We got off the packed noisy bus and found ourselves stood a few feet from some columns. We had no idea where we were going but walked through the columns and there it was, there we were. We were in St Peter's Square and there it was to the right, the Basilica itself. The place was teeming; I couldn't get over how close it was to the rest of Rome, part of Rome, assuming as I had that it was some distance away standing in splendid isolation away from the noise and smell of the city.

Not me of course, unsuccessful as I'd been, but one of the lads was still feeling pangs of guilt from the night before and he wanted to confess. So in we went and into one of the confessional boxes for one of our party. I turned to the other and said, "You gotta admire his style; bags off out of watch, feels guilty as fuck and confesses in St Peter's – if you're gonna do it you might as well do it in style."

Rome was fabulous and it was a great shame we didn't have longer. Whilst not in as good repair as St Peter's or the Pantheon, the latter being around 2,000 years old, the Colosseum did it for me and really fired up the imagination; I closed my eyes and tried to imagine what it was like to sit there in ancient Rome with around 70,000 others watching gladiators do their stuff in the biggest amphitheatre ever built. Rome is a breathtaking, exhausting, noisy, incredible city and I vowed to return again one day to do it justice but not just yet; Naples was next, then Gibraltar.

On our return to Naples I asked one of the lads down the mess how the social went. "Fucking ace," he replied, "fucking loads of Filipino girls turned up… enough for two each." So whilst I'd been busting a gut trying to get into an English girl's knickers in Rome, unsuccessfully of course, my mess down in Naples was overflowing with Filipino fanny that I myself had invited. A bit like my trip to Nairobi with Gerry in 1985 when that city's girls had all decamped to Mombasa for the week. Oh well, sightseeing is more important than shagging… according to some at least.

On our final evening in Naples Tony Fernandez, Mitch and I went out for a few wets. We were a bit of a strange threesome but that was the thing with the Navy – it threw different people together. Tony and I got on very well and so did Mitch and I, although Tony and Mitch wouldn't have mixed too much beforehand given they were in different branches, in different messes and of different ranks.

Being the last night prior to sailing, leave expired early; Junior Rates had to be back on board by 0100 and Senior Rates by 0300. The three of us were in a bar around midnight when Mitch reminded us he had to get back to the ship before 0100. The sensible course of action would be for us all to walk back to the ship but oh no, we had the best part of three hours' drinking left. "You'll be fine, mate," I said to Mitch. "Tony and I are on the Duty RPO roster, you'll have no bother getting back on board with us." Being a Junior Rate Mitch had to leave his station card in a box before leaving the ship whereas Tony and I as Senior Rates had pegboards. Mitch hadn't submitted his station card as he'd lost it a day or so before so at least the box would be empty after 0100 and no one would realise he wasn't back on board; Tony and I would square it with the Duty RPO when we got back on board when of course it would become obvious that Mitch was late.

So we drank for another couple of hours and got back on board just before 0300. The Duty RPO was Steve Rigler, a 'proper' RPO and didn't he fucking know it. To make matters worse there was one single station card in the Junior Rates' box – Mitch's. Fuck knows what it was doing in there; maybe he'd forgotten to pick it up the day before and the Quartermaster had just left it there knowing he was on board. Anyway, tonight we had a fucking welcoming party at the top of the gangway waiting for us.

Having been adrift in Palma I wasn't going to get away with it again. Mitch got trooped for being adrift whilst Tony and I got trooped for 'aiding and abetting'. Stood outside the Fleet Master At Arms' office a couple of days later waiting for Captain's Table must have looked pretty odd to some, including as it did not just two Petty Officers lined up with the other miscreants but two Petty Officers from the Duty RPOs' roster. Deputising for the Captain, the Executive Officer awarded Mitch three days' Number 9 punishment but Tony and I couldn't be punished with 9s, given we were Senior Rates, so we were awarded three days' stoppage of pay. I always loved that word – 'awarded'. After a discussion with the Writer who looked after the POs' pay our penalty was mitigated somewhat by the fine being spread over three monthly paydays, contrary to the Commander's instruction to deduct over one payday. Perks of being a Writer...

May began with Exercise Dragon Hammer in company with the US carrier USS *Eisenhower*, supported by a number of British, Turkish and Italian ships and submarines. A cornerstone of the exercise was an amphibious landing on Sardinia supported by our air group. We had an exchange of personnel with the *Eisenhower* and I was lucky enough to be one of those winched across to the American ship. The tour of the ship was revealing – it was absolutely immense. *Ike* had around 5,000 men and was in essence a floating town. The Yanks' equivalent of our RPOs toured the ship armed with baseball bats (I wanted one) and the fast food joints were open 24/7. There was no beer on board, American ships being 'dry', but at least we enjoyed a decent burger.

We popped into Gibraltar for a couple of days on the way home and I declined the opportunity of running up that rock thing – been there, done that, got the t-shirt (literally). Gibraltar hadn't changed since my last visit which was of course welcome so I revisited my old haunts, a few like the London Bar several times.

Back in Pompey for a few days we hosted Staff College Sea Days with the Flag Officer First Flotilla embarked; we spent the latter part of May and early June alongside in Pompey before sailing for Rosyth to be the main attraction of their Navy Days weekend. After Rosyth and the inevitable visits to the pubs and clubs of Fife and across the water in Edinburgh, we headed north to take the lead in a JMC exercise. Whilst at sea we held another 'It's a Knock-Out' event and also a tug-of-war competition, organised by Clubz, our Chief PTI famous for his hair transplant that, let's say, was less than successful (but no one was allowed to mention it). On completion we returned home for some maintenance and three weeks of welcome summer leave.

Summer leave was pretty non-eventful and I spent most of it working behind the bar in the Eight Bells. No football given the footie season had ended and no women; the Eight Bells was a blokey pub and the women that we attracted were generally in a different age group to me. I played pool for the pub team which was always a good laugh, especially the away matches in pubs elsewhere in the city. I visited relatives in Luton so I kept myself busy but I was keen to get back to the ship.

We sailed in mid-August for a 'shake-down' exercise to test our newly modified gearbox and returned to Pompey on completion to star once again in Navy Days, albeit this time our own (we were the base for flying displays). Navy Days is a great way of showing the ship off to the public but to be honest it bored most of us, unless we got an opportunity to chat with unattached single girls of course.

Off to sea again for a major NATO exercise, Exercise Teamwork, the Admiral and his staff embarked so his bridge was out of bounds to Phil, H and I for our regular tea-breaks (a tad inconsiderate on the Admiral's part). We sailed around the west of Ireland to the south-east of Iceland and then across the Arctic Circle, close to the stunningly beautiful snow-capped Norwegian coast. This excursion saw me and others awarded personalised 'Blue Nose' certificates which stated: "All Sailors, wherever and whoever Ye may be, GREETINGS, know all Ye by these presents that Hugh O'Rourke did appear in the NORTHERNMOST REACHES of my Realm, in HMS Illustrious bound for the Dark and Frosty wastes of the Land of the Midnight Sun and did with our Royal Consent enter this Dread Region by crossing the Arctic Circle by virtue of I, NEPTUNUS REX, Ruler of the raging Main do hereby declare him to be a loyal and trusty salt-lined and brine-encrusted BLUENOSE and do call upon all ICEBERGS, SEA LIONS, NARWHALS, POLAR BEARS, WHALES, MERMAIDENS and other CREATURES of the Frigid North to show him due Deference and respect. Disobey under pain OF OUR ROYAL DISPLEASURE". The certificate was signed by Neptunus Rex and Aurora Borealis, Queen of His Majesty's Pallid Polar Regions. Luckily for me and the rest of the boys there was no being tipped headfirst into a pool of water for this particular certificate.

On our way home we were called to assist the oil rig Ocean Odyssey which had suffered a major fire; we sent four Sea Kings plus medical teams to assist with transferring survivors and to treat the injured. One young man, Timothy Williams, was killed in this horrific incident but it could have been so much worse; just over two months earlier the Piper Alpha disaster killed 167 offshore workers. The Ocean Odyssey came within a hair's breadth of being blown to pieces.

The ship was gearing up for another deployment, this time west to the United States and the Caribbean. Before that I took a group of lads from the mess and a couple of wives up to the Eight Bells for a

'Sporting Weekend' that included pool, crib, darts, dominoes and on the Sunday morning a five-a-side football match. We all wore mess undress which impressed my old fella and his regulars; a photographer from the local paper took a picture of the whole group including Petty Officers and Eight Bells regulars, with me handing over a ship's crest to the old fella. The photo and a story were published in the next edition of the Peterborough Evening Telegraph which was great PR for the pub. As for the results of the sporting fixtures, no one can remember who won, the pub or the ship, given a huge amount of beer was consumed on the Saturday night.

19. FLORIDA AND SOUTH CAROLINA

A couple of weeks before we sailed Martin and Anne invited me around for tea and the inevitable pub crawl around Plymouth's Stoke Village (it isn't actually a village but the locals like to pretend it is). They were a bit more precise than usual with the details which I considered a bit odd as they were normally very chilled and laid-back. When I arrived at their flat my ex-girlfriend Belinda was there. I'd been set up.

I hadn't seen Belinda for the best part of a year. Martin and Anne had remained friends with Belinda; Martin was always keen to be 'friends' with my girlfriends, particularly after he married Anne, but that's a story for another day. We ate, we went out for a few beers and when we returned to Martin and Anne's flat they had an early night, for a reason of course, to leave Belinda and I alone. Belinda and I chatted for a bit, not for long, and then had fantastic 'make-up' sex on Martin and Anne's sofa. That was it... we were back together.

So all change on the personal front and change also in the Captain's Office. Lieutenant Edwards replaced Nick Lewin, Sub Lieutenant Mellor replaced Frank Prescott, Writer Johnson (Johnno) replaced Mitch and Writer Shore (Arty) replaced Tara. My new Writers were good lads but initial impressions were that they would be somewhat 'quieter' than their predecessors and as for the officers, I wasn't impressed. Nick Lewin was one of life's top blokes and Frank Prescott might have been a dick but he was an entertaining dick; they would be sorely missed. I knew nothing of my new boss, the Captain's Secretary, but his assistant Barry Mellor was known to me from training in HMS Pembroke.

Store Ship and other deployment preps completed, we set sail on 3 October for the Western Atlantic. We were accompanied by the destroyer HMS *Newcastle*, the nuclear submarine HMS *Sceptre* and our support ship RFA *Olmeda*; our journey involved several crew exchanges between ships and submarine but having been on several subs during my time at HMS Neptune I decided to let others visit our unwashed brethren.

On the way across the pond we amused ourselves with a Sods Opera which saw Taff, myself and one other PO play three members of an IRA terrorist cell who had been shot dead in Gibraltar earlier that year. I happened to have a t-shirt with "IRELAND – 20 YEARS OF RESISTANCE" emblazoned across the top above a photo of British soldiers with "TROOPS OUT MOVEMENT" underneath. How on earth I got away with that one nobody knows. But we had a great Sods Opera which as always was thoroughly enjoyable.

On our way across the ocean we shifted our clocks back five times to be in sync with the Americans for our arrival in Mayport on 18 October, a visit we all were looking forward to, especially those of us who had never previously visited the States. Mind you, those who had visited Mayport before informed us that it wasn't much different to Pompey or Plymouth.

The new members of the Captain's Office proved, as expected, to be a lot quieter than the guys who had left and there was a lot less banter than had previously been the case; Barry Mellor liked to talk but only about himself and engaging the boss in any sort of banter was virtually impossible. I started to spend more time in the UPO and down the POs' mess, preferring to catch up on work in the evenings. In a rare moment of humour the Captain's Sec drew a picture of me on a brown gash-sack and put it on my chair as I was spending more and more time out of the office when not busy. The office just wasn't the same and there was far more banter to be had with the Writers in the UPO and the POs down the mess.

We arrived in Mayport on Florida's north-eastern coast in mid-October via Procedure Alpha although I managed to swerve that particular task as the Captain's official correspondence wasn't going to open and process itself. 800 and 849 disembarked to the nearby American base at Cecil Fields for 'continuation training', whatever that was, whilst the rest of us got out on the piss as soon as possible.

Whilst a fairly brief visit of only a few days Mayport did offer us our first taste of American hospitality. The massive US Naval base had fantastic facilities including its own beaches and the nearby city of Jacksonville, known as 'Jax' to the locals, was full of bars and entertainment. Now that I was no longer single, women were off the agenda but I made full use of the bars and beaches, although drinking was far more preferable to sunbathing (Irish genes… what more can I say?).

After our drinking session in Mayport we sailed for the deep blue waters off Andros Island in the Bahamas for torpedo trials although of far more interest to me was the banyan; ferried in via our ship's boats for beer and a BBQ we all enjoyed the crystal clear warm water, soft golden sands and swaying palm trees. To think, we got paid to do this stuff.

Some of the lads were flown off by helicopter to visit Nassau but I didn't make the list which was a shame, especially as the lucky buggers who went thoroughly enjoyed themselves and didn't stop banging on about it on their return.

Back at sea and in between the usual exercises with our American friends we kept ourselves busy with various activities on the flight deck including a 'Village Fete' which raised over a thousand pounds for Children in Need's Great Ormond Street Hospital appeal, horse racing involving all messes and deck hockey, always one of my favourite activities at sea. Hands to Bathe was as enjoyable as ever although a visit by a family of sharks brought that particular activity to a premature end.

From Andros we sailed north to Charleston with a new Admiral embarked (Rear Admiral Grose). On the way I decided to submit 18 months' notice to leave the Service, given I was now engaged and didn't want to combine marriage, children and a life spent intermittently at sea. Everyone said I was mad considering my age and how quickly I had advanced to Senior Rating; most reckoned that I would withdraw my notice at some point. Giving notice resulted in the cancellation of my 'CW Papers'; I had no idea what I would be doing a couple of years from now but clearly being a commissioned officer was no longer on the agenda (to be honest, it never really appealed to me).

Once again swerving Procedure Alpha we arrived in Charleston, South Carolina; whilst somewhat chillier than the warmer regions that we'd left behind I for one was quite grateful although a number of the sun gods on board wouldn't stop dripping. A few of us went to see an American football match which despite all the razzmatazz just didn't do it for me. Lots of showmanship but a bollocks sport and certainly not football (how do they get away with calling it that?).

Charleston, named after our very own King Charles II, is a particularly charming city with its narrow cobbled streets, horse-drawn carriages and multitude of pre-Civil War buildings. Rich in history, much of it tumultuous, the city contains an eclectic mix of people, architecture, music and cuisine. With its colourful buildings, plethora of churches, parks and beaches, Charleston really does have a lot to offer.

There were lots of bars of course with my favourite being Tommy Condon's, a 'traditional' Irish bar. Not Irish traditional you understand, American/Irish traditional. Tommy's sold the usual piss American beer but the food was good and the craic even better. Drinking and sightseeing aside, we did squeeze in two football matches against local teams, one of which we won and the other we lost, the latter being no fault of our goalkeeper (defeats never were).

We left Charleston in early November to exercise with the Yanks; Fleetex 1988 was a particularly big exercise although I didn't get too involved, the Captain's Office didn't run itself of course (contrary to popular opinion). Much of this exercise was spent in the waters off the Caribbean island of Puerto Rico; a real shame we didn't visit the island as I had several first-cousins living in Ponce courtesy of one of my many Irish aunts who had married a wonderful Puerto Rican many years previously.

Whilst we didn't visit Puerto Rico we did enjoy a banyan just to the east in Virgin Gorda, part of the British Virgin Islands. Whilst all banyans were pretty much the same with their mix of food, beer, sunbathing and sport, it was impossible not to enjoy them; I'm pretty sure we would have voted to have one every week given the chance.

Next stop was the planned highlight of the deployment, a ten-day visit to Fort Lauderdale on Florida's south-eastern coast which would include five days' Station Leave. We entered via Procedure Alpha once again although this time I had to play my part and line the upper deck with several hundred other sailors (the locals always loved this stuff).

For some unknown and clearly stupid reason I agreed to join Taff and a few of the lads for a round of golf on the first day (it's a Petty Officer thing). The prospect of playing golf in the Florida sun held absolutely no attraction for me but I thought I'd give it a go. Several hours in the sweltering heat doing the same thing over and over again nailed it for me; golf is not a sport and it is something I vowed would never again interrupt my life.

Fort Lauderdale is a truly fantastic run ashore awash as it is with bars, hotels, nightclubs, gorgeous women and seven miles of sandy beaches. Every night was spent in bars admiring stunning women and the golden beaches only yards away. American beer was not so stunning however; the Yanks were not known for their beer in 1988 although to be fair they've got a lot better in recent years (by copying British IPAs and reinventing them as APAs).

One evening a bunch of us went out in rig, a condition of a free invite to one of the city's nightclubs. One of my messmates John and I spotted a couple of fat birds on their own in the middle of the club, clearly desperate to bag a matelot. Not that I had any intention of trapping, given I was now engaged and my relationship with Belinda was a hell of a lot different to my relationship with Julie back in 1985 when I was out in the Gulf (who knew that copious amounts of sex helped a relationship?).

John and I walked slowly across to the fat birds with at least a dozen or so of our messmates watching on, plus many locals and tourists. As we approached the wide units it seemed that everyone in the club was looking at us. Two good-looking Petty Officers from the Royal Navy were about to make their day. "Hey, fancy a dance?" I asked the fattest of the two (there wasn't much in it – *Lusty* had less girth than these two).

"Nah, you're OK," she replied. Clearly a bit hard of hearing, I asked the same question again to which she replied, "You fucking deaf?" Our walk back to our mates was a long one indeed and if everyone wasn't watching us before, they sure were now.

Undeterred, John and I got chatting to two rather prettier ladies than those who had embarrassed us earlier. Although not one to bullshit about what I did in the Navy, I decided to play along with John's suggestion that we make out we're Harrier pilots. After a bit of chat one of the girls asked, "So you fly those jets on your deck, do you... how many have you got?"

"Ten," I replied.

"So why do you need so many pilots?" came her reply.

"Ah, there are only 20 of us, two for each Sea Harrier."

"That's funny," she said, "we've met at least a hundred pilots since you arrived." Busted, we decided to drink with our mates… less embarrassing.

Nick and I decided to hire a car for our five days' Station Leave with a plan to drive around Florida, staying in different motels en route which we'd check into as and when required. We hired a white convertible sports car, the absolute dog's bollocks. Nick and I both loved driving, especially this beauty in the Florida sun, so we decided to split the driving 50/50. Unlike Station Leave in Mombasa back in 1985 most of the lads ventured beyond the port city which served as our temporary home. Most went to Orlando to stay in hotels, especially the married guys whose wives had flown over, whilst some headed south to Florida Keys.

Nick and I drove to Miami, some 30 miles south of Fort Lauderdale. The skyline on entry to Miami is breathtaking and on its own worth the quick visit; it reminded me of Dubai but our drive over a bridge towards the skyscrapers gave it much more theatre. We didn't stay overnight but we did have a look around the beach area and a couple of neighbourhoods on the outskirts. We then headed west across the Everglades with its stunning and unparalleled landscape, stopping to admire a few crocs on the way.

We headed north after an overnight stop and enjoyed a cracking couple of days in the Tampa Bay area. We had a great night out in Clearwater, dressed in suits and ties (Nick's idea – the Yanks love suited and booted Brits). We ate in a fantastic restaurant overlooking Clearwater's incredible white sandy beach, both choosing the swordfish steak which proved to be truly sublime. We went on to a disco where a whole baseball team pitched up in a limo but they failed to cramp our style. Nick being single and in any case much smoother than I trapped a rather 'fine lady' in his words (Nick never struggled to pull).

We visited Busch Gardens (an African-themed animal park) and somehow ended up in the Budweiser hospitality suite. Nick bumped into an old friend called Rachel from Brighton and her mate Liz – that guy knew everybody. After Busch we went for a high-speed late night drive around the Tampa Bay area, eventually parking up back at the motel so that we could go clubbing.

Tampa and Clearwater ticked off our list, we then headed north east to Orlando. We did all the usual tourist stuff in Orlando visiting Epcot Center, Disney World and SeaWorld. Of the three attractions SeaWorld proved to be my favourite; whilst it was a wonderful experience feeding and petting the dolphins in particular I couldn't help but think the dolphins we encountered in the Mediterranean must have been far happier, given their swimming pool was a tad larger than this one. We bumped into quite a few messmates whilst strolling around the various parks, including Phil Old and his girlfriend.

We did fall foul of the local police a couple of times, once for littering and on another occasion for an illegal turn; we somehow picked up the slow coast road on the way back to Lauderdale doing around 30mph; we were trying to get back to the highway when I made an illegal right turn. When stopped the female cop asked us to open the boot and after drawing her gun she had a quick search. We played the ignorant Brits; "Sorry, Officer," I said meekly, adding, "your roads are so big and wide, we're not used to them." Allowing us to carry on with our journey she pointed us in the direction of Boca Raton, advising us to lock our doors and keep our windows closed whilst driving through as we would be approached by innocent-looking bystanders if we slowed down and these guys were apparently anything but innocent. As I drove down a hill towards a set of traffic lights I noticed a few guys on either side of the road loitering so I slowed down to a crawl in the hope the lights would change before I needed to stop; as we approached the lights several big black guys started to move towards the car from either side but luckily the lights changed just in time and I floored it.

On another occasion we nearly got mowed down by a massive truck; I was driving but managed to escape at high speed onto a garage forecourt, nearly knocking a couple of Hells Angels off their bikes in the process.

As expected Station Leave turned out to be everything we'd hoped for and we managed to tick everything off our list. We'd enjoyed a very full five days although being single Nick managed to pack in a bit more than I, especially in the evenings. The man was truly a legend – incredibly comfortable chatting up women, especially the gorgeous variety.

Our time in Florida done, we sailed for home on 1 December. We had the small matter of the ship's raffle with an incredible amount of prizes, a shiny BMW worth £20k being the top prize. The day before the draw there was a dummy run to make sure that the drum that housed the tickets worked OK. I was informed that one of my tickets came out first. On the day of the draw itself none of my tickets came out, despite the fact I'd bought more than most. C'est la vie.

After a relatively uneventful but pleasant journey across the pond we arrived back in Pompey on 15 December, having covered 23,916 miles during our deployment. I'd played golf, met Mickey Mouse, seen a few crocodiles, petted a few dolphins, got turned down by a couple of munters and generally had a great time; like all Naval deployments, Westlant 88 would live long in the memory.

20. RANK HAS ITS PRIVILEGES

Back in England I spent Christmas with Belinda in our new rented flat in Plymouth – she moved whilst I was on deployment without telling me! Whilst I loved the Royal Navy I had no regrets about deciding to marry and leave; Belinda was a fabulous girlfriend and I had no doubt she would also be a fabulous wife and mother in due course.

We sailed again on 23 January, up to Rosyth prior to another JMC in those familiar waters to the north-west of Scotland. Most of the next few weeks involved NATO exercises but we managed a few days in Amsterdam for a bit of R&R. Usual stuff in Amsters with lots of beer, restaurants, live shows and a couple of football matches (again, one we won and one we lost).

We returned to Pompey for the Ship's Company Dance on 23 February in Southsea's Sandringham Hotel; not only did we all have a great evening but as a member of the organising committee I was thoroughly relieved that everything went to plan – our efforts paid off in full. On the following day we held a 'Families Day' but we couldn't put to sea for the air display due to the inclement weather. My mum and sister Tess came down for the event and even though we remained alongside in the dockyard they seemed to enjoy their day on board an aircraft carrier.

I started to attend Portsmouth football matches with Taff. Whilst not a Pompey fan (that would come many years later) I absolutely loved Fratton Park and of course I loved football. Having visited more football stadia than I can recall, I can think of none better than

Fratton Park for atmosphere; the ramshackle old stadium and the incredibly noisy fans produce something very special indeed. Portsmouth is the most densely populated city in the United Kingdom, the only one situated on an island, and many of the city's residents literally live on top of each other. Combine this with incredible loyalty courtesy of the city's links to the Royal Navy, plus a lack of ethnic diversity (in those days at least), and you have an atmosphere that's almost a bit Neanderthal if that isn't too harsh. I never saw kids wearing Liverpool, Arsenal or Man Utd shirts around the streets of Fratton, Eastney and Milton – they wore the blue of Pompey. I visited entirely as a neutral although a deep affection would take hold many years later. But Luton Town has always been and will always be my number one – you only have one birthplace.

My weekends were now spent travelling to and from Plymouth; my single days were over. Not that that bothered me; Belinda was a wonderful girlfriend, I was getting loads of sex and of course I was a tad familiar with Plymouth's pubs and clubs which Belinda and I frequented on a fairly regular basis. I would normally share a car with a shipmate making the same journey at weekends which halved costs. The highlight of the trip was always the food shack just off the old A30 near Exeter Airport – the best bacon rolls in Devon, certainly after midnight.

Although the ship's commission was drawing to a close there was no let-up in the day-job and we had yet another exercise planned prior to some R&R in Hamburg. In March we endured the pleasantries of Exercise North Star in Norwegian waters, ensuring the pesky Russians didn't breach our defences and wreak havoc on the UK (for exercise purposes at least).

I had been looking forward to our Hamburg visit for a very special reason – a trip to Berlin to visit the city, the Berlin Wall and the Brandenburg Gate. It was planned to take a party of 25 members of the Ship's Company on a three-day visit to Berlin; this visit, hosted by the British Army, would include 13 officers and 12 ratings. The visit was massively over-subscribed so names went into a hat and luckily mine came out. This would be a very special visit – West meets East and all that.

In early 1989 Berlin was a divided city in a divided land. Germany was split in two and Berlin lay inside the communist-ruled East Germany. The city itself was bisected by the infamous wall, erected in August 1961 to prevent the East German population slipping over to the West; one side was controlled by the West and the other by the East. The wall was a concrete representation of the Cold War, dividing both a city and a continent.

However, it transpired that no host unit could be obtained for the visit so it was cancelled and the Ship's Company was so informed on Daily Orders on 2 March; this stated "no host unit means no staff clearance and no military train". A signal despatched from the ship on 1 March to the British Naval Attaché in Bonn stated that "notwithstanding cancellation of military train, remain very keen to achieve visit if at all possible".

A signal was received from the BNA in Bonn on 2 March, addressed rather strangely to 'REV PUDNER', the ship's Padre. The signal informed the Bish that a visit had now been arranged for 15 people and requested the ship's "revised list of 15 names ASAP for staff clearance". The ship replied to this signal on 3 March, by signal, with a list of 15 officers' names, including all of the officers on the visit originally planned for 25 with the exception of one who was unable to obtain security clearance from the Director of Naval Security and stated that the ship was "most grateful for all efforts to re-establish this visit on our behalf". This signal also requested that 15 seats be made available on a Berlin military train.

It was quite clear that this visit was the original visit re-established. The details of this visit were not promulgated to the Ship's Company and I only learnt of its existence by chance, during a conversation in my mess involving a PO Radio Supervisor who worked in the ship's Communications Centre (which handled all incoming and outgoing signals). I was disappointed to say the least that all ratings had been scrubbed from this visit. There is a saying in the Royal Navy, 'RHIP', which means 'rank has its privileges'. That may be so, but this was taking the piss. I spoke to the Padre who informed me that he'd had no involvement in organising the second visit and he presumed that he had been mentioned personally because of his long-standing friendship with the BNA in Bonn.

A dog with a bone, I carried on with my 'investigation'. I was pissed off and whilst not one for dripping, this was a matter of principle. I spoke to my Divisional Officer, the Captain's Secretary, and he spoke to the ship's officer who was in charge of the organisation for the Berlin visit; the latter stated that there was no apparent reason why ratings could not attend the second visit but he had been told by the Commander, the ship's Executive Officer and second-in-command, to make preparations for officers only.

If you're really pissed off with something in the Royal Navy and you wish to take a formal stance, there are two available options. If it's a specific matter, you can state a 'complaint', but if it's more general you can make a 'representation'. I decided to state a formal complaint.

I submitted my written request form to state a complaint to my Divisional Officer who, unable to satisfy it, passed it to my Deputy Head of Department, the Deputy Supply Officer. He too, after an informal discussion with me, was unable to satisfy my complaint so he passed it to my Head of Department, the ship's Supply Officer and a Commander in rank (Commander C A Scott). My HOD and I had an informal discussion in his cabin that lasted approximately half an hour. I stood for the whole of this discussion whilst my HOD sat down and this caused me a lot of unease.

My HOD stated that the second visit had nothing to do with the first visit and that it was not, contrary to my opinion, a re-establishment of the first visit. He further stated that this second visit was organised privately by the Padre as a result of his friendship with the BNA in Bonn and it was therefore not an official visit. I was permitted to air my views but was told by my HOD that I had become "confused" and that I must be "incredibly stupid" if I could not understand the facts as he had given them to me. To say that Commander Scott was both patronising and condescending would be an understatement. My HOD informed me that if I wasn't happy with his explanation then the rules allowed me to take my complaint to a higher authority. I requested, and was granted, some time to consider my decision.

I thought it best first to speak to the Padre in order to confirm the details of the conversation that I had had with him prior to the submission of my complaint. The Bish assured me that he had had no communication with the BNA in Bonn regarding the organisation of this visit and that, as far as he was aware, the current trip to Berlin was not a private visit. He further stated that he was "amazed" when he saw his name at the top of the signal, believing that he was mentioned personally because of his friendship with the attaché and also as a result of the ship's efforts and consequent success in organising a Royal Marine band for the visit (they were going to play a fund-raising concert at the Hamburg English Church).

After my chat with the Bish I informed my Divisional Officer and Head of Department that I wished to take my complaint further as I had not been satisfied with the explanation so far given. Although I had seen my HOD informally, I was required to appear formally at his table to request that my complaint be taken to a higher authority. I appeared at my HOD's table on 6 March, feeling very uneasy and nervous. I was first on but had to wait for some time outside the UPO in the main passageway along with several Junior Rates before I was called in. I had to explain the full facts of my case again, in the presence of my HOD, DHOD, Departmental Co-ordinator,

Divisional Officer and three other officers who were Divisional Officers to the other ratings due to appear after me at the table. Furthermore the UPO Writers were congregated in the other half of the office (through the archway), within earshot and in sight out of the corner of my eye.

My HOD stated that the second visit was separate from the first and was not available to ratings. He asked if I thought I had the right to go on the second visit to Berlin. I replied that I thought I had the right only to be considered along with the other ratings who were on the list of 25 earmarked to go on the original visit. My HOD gave me the option of taking my complaint to a higher authority or letting the matter drop; I told him that I wanted to take it to a higher authority.

On 8 March I appeared at the Executive Officer's table in his cabin (Commander N D V Robertson). This was a formal table in the presence of not only the Commander but also my HOD, my Divisional Officer and the Warrant Officer Master At Arms. As with my HOD's table I found the formality of this table very nerve-wracking. Due to the ship's violent motion I also found it awkward to stand at ease correctly for the duration of the table which lasted about half an hour. The Commander's cabin was situated in 3U, the most aft section of the ship so disproportionately affected by the ship's movement.

The Commander informed me that he had personally taken the decision to send only officers on the second visit and that he had in fact considered including ratings but had decided against it. He informed me that ratings could go to Berlin privately but they would have to pay the full private transport and accommodation costs. Was this an unfair application of 'rank having its privileges'? I certainly thought so. The Commander agreed that it was indeed an official visit and stated that if he had decided to "delegate downwards" it would probably only be to WO/CPO level and he didn't "see any WO/CPO complaining" in front of him. I replied that several Chief

Petty Officers I had spoken to who had heard that I had complained agreed entirely with my views but considered it a "waste of time" in submitting a complaint as they "never got anywhere" and only ended up "reflecting badly" upon the complainant. The Executive Officer replied that my complaint reflected badly upon me.

I asked the Commander if I had the option to take my complaint to the Commanding Officer, the Captain, but he informed me that I had no such option as I did not have the grounds and that all I had was an opinion with which he disagreed and a disappointment with which he sympathised. Although still unhappy I had no further option available and the table was terminated.

This dog still had its bone and no one was going to take it from me. I decided to make a representation which I duly submitted in writing to the Commanding Officer on 10 March (entitled 'The Complaints Procedure in the Royal Navy'). It did not seem right that a complaint about a decision could be 'satisfied' by the very same officer who made the decision that was the subject of the complaint (natural justice?). At least this way I could make the Captain aware of the facts and the shoddy way in which my complaint had been treated. Captain's Standing Orders Article 0117 stated "all requests to state a complaint are, in essence, an appeal against the decision of someone in the command structure. Although it may not be possible to reverse this decision, a great deal of good is always done by the very process of carrying out a thorough investigation".

I received a lot of support from the Ship's Company; one Chief Petty Officer remarked, "It's about time someone took a stand... the whole procedure is a complete feed of shit."

Another said, "The Commander's a c**t, at least the Captain's a good egg."

I outlined my case in detail, including all the facts stated above with a few opinions of my own. I stated that in the Royal Navy it is accepted by all who "sign on the dotted line" that there is no union or federation (as with the police) to whom sailors can refer their complaints. If a rating feels strongly enough about a particular decision then his only option is to submit a request form "in order to state a complaint" and, in making such a complaint, acts virtually on his own. All complaints should, if possible, be satisfied, even if the decision that is the root cause of the complaint cannot be reversed. If complaints are considered not to be investigated thoroughly or dealt with sensitively then faith in the system is lost and a rating's only other option, if he remains so unhappy with the system, is to submit his notice to leave the Service.

I made several suggestions in my representation including the obvious, that complaints should be handled by a senior officer who was not personally involved in the events or decisions that led to the making of a complaint. I stated, "although not wishing to encourage endless 'dripping' in the Service, the complaints procedure must not be so formal and daunting to the would-be complainant that it acts as a deterrent against many genuine complaints being aired and, invariably, being resolved to the good of the man and the Service".

I was not suggesting that individual decisions of the sort that led to my complaint cause people to submit their notice. However, decisions of this nature, taken collectively with other such decisions, do in my opinion lead men to become disillusioned with Service life and opt for a civilian career. Whilst withdrawing my notice was always an option, this was no longer the case; I loved the Royal Navy but this whole episode left a very bad taste in my mouth.

The Captain never responded to my formal representation and that was the end of the matter. I never visited Berlin and the wall, a physical representation of Europe's divide and suffering, a wall that had been in place for 28 years, fell later that year, gloriously consigned to history. I lost my chance to visit the Berlin Wall and that opportunity, so much looked forward to, could never present itself again. The wall may now be a footnote in history but RHIP in the Royal Navy, very much older than the wall, continues its existence with not a crack in sight.

21. GOODBYE

We arrived in Hamburg in mid-March and this was one Procedure Alpha I certainly would love to have avoided but alas... no chance. The long, slow journey down the almost frozen Elbe River from the North Sea to the port of Hamburg was painful – I'd never known it so cold on the upper deck. These visits were normally 'routine' but for some reason we had to enter harbour with the deck fully lined.

More disappointing than the cold was the fateful discovery when we got ashore that the Eros Center had closed! This particular fleshpot had been in existence since 1967 and its demise was sorely felt by the Ship's Company. The Eros Center had served well many thousands of seafarers from across the globe for a couple of decades...the end of an era indeed.

Alternative fleshpots were visited, some familiar and some not so familiar. The cold certainly didn't put us off but it did put a slight dampener on the visit. The ship played one game of football against a local team which we won 2-0; I'd have preferred more action in goal as I was bloody freezing but the boys played well that day, preferring to run around a tad more than usual as to stay motionless for too long would have been far too uncomfortable.

We returned to Pompey for Easter and we passed the ship into dockyard hands for 'Preservation by Operation', a period where the ship would no longer be operational but maintained to a level whereby she could be readily commissioned if for example the Falklands reignited (well, that was the theory). We had a service of thanksgiving in the hangar which was attended by the ship's sponsor, Princess Margaret, the Queen's sister. As part of her ship's tour the old girl, the princess rather than the ship, visited our mess. She came across as pretty ignorant and well up herself, preferring to allow her lady-in-waiting to answer all questions directed to her. When she signed our visitors' book she remarked on the flamboyant signature at the top of a previous page, Nigel Mansell's. Princess Margaret's signature was much less flamboyant than Nigel's, dull and boring in fact, symptomatic of her personality.

Luton Town, winners last year and current holders, once again progressed to the League Cup Final at Wembley Stadium. The match was played a day after Belinda's sister's wedding in Dartmouth; when I got up the next morning I left Belinda in bed and drove to London, forgetting to pay the tab in the B&B (I got some earache for that one). We were leading at half-time courtesy of our legend Mick Harford; however, Nottingham Forest were awarded a penalty in the second half following a ridiculous foul on Steve Hodge by our wonderful but erratic goalkeeper Les Sealey. Les remonstrated for ages with the referee, Roger Milford, the country's top referee at the time. It was clearly a penalty, Nigel Clough scored and Forest went on to win the match 3-1 and lift the trophy.

A few years later I found myself in Roger Milford's office in Bristol. Roger had retired from football and was working as a Regional Manager for a large fruit-machine company. After the meeting we got chatting about the cup final and the penalty award which ultimately led to our defeat. "Dunno why you lot were moaning at me... it was clearly a penalty," he said.

"We weren't moaning at you, Rog," I replied, "we were moaning at Les for such a stupid foul... Hodge was only just inside the area and wasn't even in a goalscoring position... in any case why was he complaining to you?"

Roger replied, "He got up and started shouting at me... I replied,

'What's up, Les? It was a clear penalty, you brought him down.' Les replied, 'I fucking know that but last time I looked you were on the fucking half-way line.' I thought you Luton fans were shouting at me... I thought you were all blind." Les Sealey was a character but so too was Roger Milford.

So my time on *Lusty* was complete. In the past two years the ship steamed over 80,000 miles; every person on board consumed five times his own body weight in spuds and together we consumed over five miles of sausages and over one million eggs; the Sick Bay dispensed 30,000 aspirin plus three miles of bandage and the Sea Harriers flew over 3,000 embarked hours. As for Writers, we'd been far too busy to measure our work but we'd got through an awful lot of paper and ink. The ship's time was done, for now, and so too was mine – I left the old girl on 30 June.

So that was it, goodbye to *Lusty* and hello to my next job; I had been drafted to HMS *Fearless*, a Portsmouth-based amphibious assault ship undergoing refit in Plymouth's Devonport Dockyard. I would see out my last six months or so on the *Fearless* prior to leaving the Service in early 1990. I would live at home with Belinda and work on the ship during the day. My main priority would be to play my part in bringing the ship back into service which would involve working in a portakabin on the jetty until such time as the ship was ready for us to move all functions back on board. The ship and her company would gear up for operational duties whilst I would do the opposite and embark on a period referred to by matelots as 'RDP', short for 'run-down period'. On the personal front my main priority prior to joining the *Fearless* would be a wedding – Belinda and I were going to marry in Plymouth's Registry Office on 6 July.

So after seven years of service my time was coming to an end. In a few weeks I would be a married man and within a year I would be a civilian. The future held many exciting challenges but the past seven years held many wonderful memories, memories that I would treasure for the rest of my life.

As I was due to leave the Service early the following year Captain Tod completed and signed my 'Certificate of Qualifications', effectively a reference for potential civilian employers. His words read thus:

"Petty Officer O'Rourke has had a short but successful career. Joining the Royal Navy in September 1982 as a Junior Writer, he served in four shore establishments in quick succession before joining his first ship in September 1984. In October 1985 O'Rourke was advanced to Acting Leading Writer and in March of the following year his outstanding potential was recognised as the first steps towards him attaining a commission were taken as he became a CW candidate.

"In May 1986 O'Rourke joined BRNC Dartmouth where he served for 16 months before joining HMS Illustrious in September 1987 as a confirmed Leading Writer. In January 1988 he was advanced to Acting Petty Officer Writer as a billet became available; he was qualified and had shown that he possessed the intelligence and ability to succeed even though comparatively young for the position. Advanced to Acting Petty Officer Writer in his own right in August 1988 O'Rourke has done well to get so far in such a short time.

"Throughout his time in the Service O'Rourke has pursued the highest professional standards and displayed exemplary personal conduct. A man of tremendous ability and potential who will undoubtedly be extremely successful in civilian life."

No mention of marching like a fucking giraffe.

22. NAVAL TERMINOLOGY/SLANG

('JACK SPEAK')

Not an exhaustive list but I've listed most of the more common terms in use in the Royal Navy in the 1980s (NB: some terms may not be 'politically correct' and as a result may no longer be in use, but they were in the 1980s!).

Adrift	Late for work or duty
Andrew (The)	The Royal Navy
Arse Bandit	Male homosexual
Babies' heads	Steak & kidney suet pudding
Bag off	Have sex
Bag off out of watch	Cheat on partner
Bag Shanty	Brothel
Banyan	Beach party with lots of beer
Bashing the Bishop	Wanking
Beer tokens	Money
Belay	Stop/cease
Bezzy	Best, as in bezzy oppo (best mate)
Bible Basher	Christian
Big eats	Food, normally a takeaway after beer
Bish (The)	Padre/Chaplain
Black ham	Black female

Blanket Stacker	Stores Accountant
Blue card	Matelot who doesn't form part of the Duty Watch
Blue liners	Cigarettes issued by the Royal Navy
Boats	Submarines
Bootneck/Booty/Bootie	Royal Marine
Bravo Zulu/BZ	Well done
Brown Hatter	Male homosexual
Brown Hatter's handlebars	Long sideburns or long moustache
Brown Hatter's overalls	Pyjamas
Buffer	Chief Bosun's Mate
Buff up	Polish
Bulkhead	Wall
Bunting	Member of the Signals branch
Busted	Disrated (reduced in rank)
Buzz	Rumour
Call the hands	Wake up/get out of bed
Canman	Canteen Manager
Cheesy 'ammy eggy	Toast covered with a mixture of cheese/ham/egg
Chippy	Shipwright
Chockheads	Aircraft Handlers
Chokie/Chogey laundry	Chinese laundry
Civvie/Civvy	Civilian
Civvies	Civilians or civilian clothes worn by matelots
Clanky	Member of the engineering branch
Clubz/Clubs/Clubswinger	PTI – Physical Training Instructor
Colours	Ceremonial hoisting/lowering of the

	White Ensign
Crab/Crabfat	Member of the Royal Air Force
Cross the bar	Die/pass away
Crusher	Member of the Regulating branch
Dabber/Dabtoe	Seaman (member of the Ops branch)
Daily Dits	Daily Orders
Deck	Floor
Deckhead	Ceiling
Deeks/DQs	Royal Naval Detention Quarters
Dhobey/Dhobie	Wash
Dhobey dust	Soap powder
Dipped in	Unexpected gain
Dipped out	Unexpected loss
Dip your wick	Have sex
Dit	A story (usually short and humorous)
Ditch	Dispose of
Divisions	Formal parade
Dockie	Dockyard worker
Dockyard jellyfish	Phlegm
Dockyard pizza	Vomit
Dog's bollocks	Something that's 'great'
Dose	Sexually-transmitted disease
Draft/Draft Order	Movement order
Drip/Dripping	Moan or complain
DTS	Dinner time session (lunchtime drinking)
Essence	Gorgeous (woman)
Exped	Adventurous training
Fanny Rat	Ladies' man (womaniser)

Flash	Start up suddenly (machines or temper)
Flat	Passageway between compartments
Flat top	Aircraft carrier
Flunky	Steward
FRISP	Fucking repulsive ignorant Scottish pig
Full set	Beard & moustache
Galley	Kitchen/Dining area
Gannet	Greedy
Gash	Rubbish
Gash bin	Rubbish bin
Gash hand	Useless person
GI	Gunnery Instructor
Gizzits	Freebies
Gobbler's gulch	Area between stocking top and suspender belt
Goffer	Large wave
Golly	Member of the Electronic Warfare branch
Greenies	Electricians
Grey Funnel Line	The Royal Navy (seagoing)
Gronk	Ugly woman
Gronk board	Mess board with Gronk photos
Grunter	Naval Officer
Gulch	Area of messdeck between bunks
Guzz	Plymouth
Heads	Toilet
Hook	Anchor
Hooky	Leading Hand
Ickies	Foreign currency

Jack	Sailor
Jack Dusty	Stores Accountant
Jackproof	Robust bit of kit/equipment
Jack Speak	Naval parlance
Janner	Someone from the SW (usually Plymouth)
Jenny	Wren
Joss/Jossman	Master At Arms
Jimmy	First Lieutenant/Executive Officer
Jockanese	Scottish lingo
Jolly	Run ashore
Junior Rate/Rating	Leading Hand and below
Killick	Leading Hand
Kit Muster	Kit inspection (formal)
Knuckle Bosun	Matelot who likes to fight
Liberty boat	Small boat to take matelots ashore
Loafing	Lazing around
Lower deck lawyer	Someone always quoting rules & regs
Mailey	Letter (usually from home)
Make & Mend	Afternoon off
Matelot	Sailor
Mess/Messdeck	Living quarters
Mombers	Mombasa, Kenya
Muffdiving	Oral sex performed on a female
Muscle Bosun	Fitness fanatic
Muster	Meet/gather together
NAAFI	Navy, Army and Air Force Institutes
NATO Standard	Tea/Coffee with milk + two sugars
Nines	No.9 punishment (stoppage of leave)

Number One	First Lieutenant or No.1 Chinese laundryman
Nutty	Chocolate/Sweets
Nutty Fiend	Someone who eats a lot of nutty
OD	Unruly sailor
Oggie	Cornish pasty
Oggin	Water (usually the sea)
OOD	Officer of the Day
OOW	Officer of the Watch
Oppo	Friend
Ovies	Overalls
Pig	Naval Officer
Pig's meat	Wrens who only shag officers
Pillow Fluffer	Steward
Pipe	Announcement (main broadcast)
Pipe down	Shut up or go to sleep
Pit	Bed
PJ	Poxy Jock (Scotsman)
Pompey	Portsmouth
Pongo	Soldier
Pot Mess	Stew (usually eaten on exped)
Pusser	Supply Officer (or simply the Royal Navy)
Rabbits	Souvenirs/Presents
RDP	Run down period (last period of current draft)
Reggy/Reggie	Member of the Regulating branch
Rescrub	Do it again (usually messdeck rounds)
RHIP	Rank has its privileges
Rig	Clothing

Ringpiece	Arse
ROMFT	Roll on my fucking time
Roughers	Heavy seas
Rounds	Formal inspection
Royal	Royal Marine
Run ashore	Out on the piss
Sailor's mattress	Wren
Scablifter	Member of the Medical branch
Schoolie	Instructor Officer
Scrambled egg	Gold leaf on a senior officer's cap
Scran	Food
Scribes	Writer (cream of the Royal Navy)
Sea dust	Salt
Secure	Finish work
Senior Rate/Rating	Petty Officer and above
Shake	Wake someone up
Shippers	Shipmate
Shitnit	Be quiet!
Shitnicks	Underpants
Shit on a raft	Kidneys on toast or fried bread
Shiters	Drunk
Shoot through	Fail to turn up or leave early
Shufti	Take a look
Sick on toast	Sandwich spread
Sin Bosun	Padre/Chaplain
Sitrep	Situation Report/Update
Skidmarks	Shit stains on underpants
Sky Pilot	Padre/Chaplain
Slops	Clothing store

Snapper	Male homosexual
Snorkers	Sausages
Sods Opera	Ship's concert
Spanner Wanker	Mechanic (Engine Room)
Sparky	Radio Operator
Split/Split-Arse	Wren (member of the WRNS)
Spondoolies	Money
Sports pages	Letter from a girlfriend
Sprog	Newbie, normally just out of training
Square Rig	Junior Ratings' uniform
Stand Easy	Tea break
Station Card	Junior Ratings' leave card
Steaming Bats	Navy issue non-slip work boots
Stoker	Mechanic (Engine Room)
Stow	Put away tidily
Sun Dodger	Submariner
Swamp	Wet the bed
Swampy	Someone who wets the bed
Sweaty Socks/Sweaties	Jocks (Scots)
TAS Ape	Sonar operator
Thin out	Go home/leave/depart
Tiff	Artificer (engineering technician)
Townie	A shipmate from the same town
Trap	Pull (to pull a woman, for sexual purposes)
Troop	To charge with an offence
Turn in	Go to bed
Turn to	Start work
Uckers	Ludo – Naval version

WAFU	Member of the Fleet Air Arm
Wardroom	Officers' mess
Weigh off	To punish
Wet	An alcoholic beverage
Woolly pully	Naval issue blue woollen pullover
Zeds	Sleep

ABOUT THE AUTHOR

The son of Irish parents, Hugh was brought up on a Luton council estate and moved to Peterborough just before his 11th birthday where he spent his teenage years living and working in the family pub. He joined the Royal Navy as a 17-year-old, rising from Junior Writer to Petty Officer Writer in a little over five years. Leaving the Royal Navy in April 1990, Hugh went into business management; he has spent the past 25 years as a multi-site manager having picked up a number of formal qualifications along the way including an MBA master's degree in business, economics and finance.

Having lived in several different towns and counties since leaving the Royal Navy and now a proud father and grandfather, Hugh is happily settled in Devon where he lives and works.

Oak Road, Luton - where my love of football began - spot the entrance!

The Luton team when I was a boy.

When Luton Town won the cup in 1988...

The Eight Bells, Peterborough.

HMS Raleigh - where it all began.

HMS Raleigh,1982 - Passing Out.

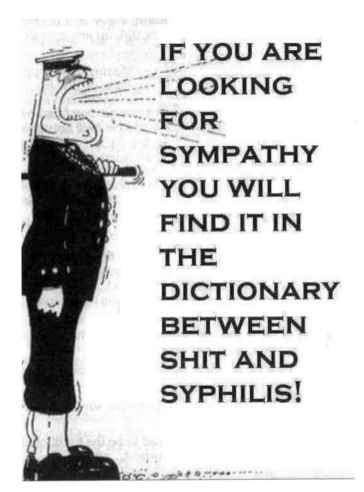

If you're looking for sympathy it's in the dictionary.

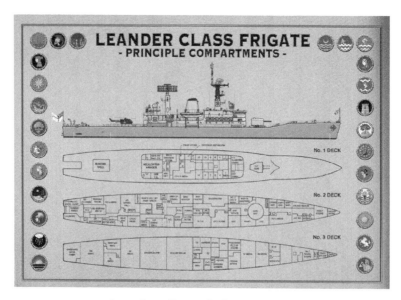

Leanders - Principle Compartments.

Quink Ink - every Writer's best friend.

Captain's Office, HMS Illustrious –
Arty and I doing the important stuff.

Captain's Office, HMS Illustrious –

Tara and I keeping the ship afloat.

Cherry B - Sods Opera - the famous Chamois Leathers.

Cherry B - me sunbathing.

Some of 3 Easy's characters...including Doris.

Mr & Mrs Competition in the Indian Ocean.

Crossing the line...

Lusty off Gibraltar.

It's probably fair to say not many of your mates down the pub can talk about the time they took a dip in the ocean while a marksman scanned the horizon for sharks.

Hands to Bathe... mind the sharks!

Mixing with the 'locals' - Bahrain, 1985.

Portland - my favourite greasy spoon.

Roughers - Arabian Sea – 1985.

GIBRALTAR
DJIBOUTI
BAHRAIN
COLOMBO
KARACHI
MOMBASA
DUBAI
SEYCHELLES
ALEXANDRIA
GIBRALTAR

T-Shirt - Armilla Patrol, 1985.

T-Shirt - Armilla Cruise, 1985.

HMS Charybdis - Alexandria, Egypt.

HMS Charybdis - London.

HMS Illustrious - Autumn Deployment, 1988.

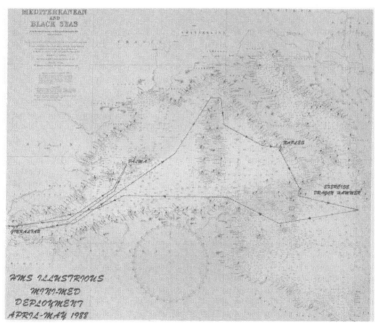

HMS Illustrious - Med Deployment, 1988.

HMS Illustrious Petty Officers vs the Eight Bells, Peterborough.

HMS Illustrious - Fort Lauderdale, 1988.

Lee and I during one of our regular trips around the west of Scotland –
Steve's car and Steve taking the photo.

Printed in Great Britain
by Amazon

57372790R00151